Introduction to Graphic Arts

ROBERT M. SWERDLOW, Ph.D.

Department of Technology and Industrial Education, New York University

 American Technical Society   CHICAGO, IL 60637

Preface

INTRODUCTION TO GRAPHIC ARTS is an overall view of graphic communication from initial idea through final product. The book is divided into 37 concise units.

The opening sections explain the development of graphic arts and methods of printing and communication. The middle sections of the book explain preparation of manuscript, typography, art, and photography. The book then develops each aspect of production: photography, platemaking, printing, papers, inks, binding, and finishing. The last section in the book includes *Careers in the Graphic Arts.*

INTRODUCTION TO GRAPHIC ARTS is a basic introductory book. The book is presented in short, easy-to-grasp units. The units may be studied in any sequence, as each is complete in itself. This book is heavily illustrated, including a section on *Color Printing* in full four-color process. A second color is used throughout the book to emphasize important points and to show key processes.

Objectives are given for each unit, and a *Test Your Knowledge* section in each unit corresponds directly to the objectives. These allow you to check your progress and find your weak areas. Each unit also includes a section called *Terms to Know.* These are the key terms introduced in the unit. All terms are defined in a *glossary* at the end of the book.

The Publishers

Production

Edited and Coordinated by *Patricia L. Reband*
Designed and Produced by *Wm. T. Jaycox Associates*
  Production Coordinator: *Georgia Jaycox*
  Production Artists: *Gayle Henson*
                              Greg Surufka
  Technical Illustrator: *Carl Hudson, Jr.*

Composition work furnished by *Typographic Sales Inc.* using
  Linotron 606. Text is set 11/14 Helvetica; Captions
  10/10 Helvetica Italic.

Printing and Binding by *Kingsport Press,* an Arcata National
Company.
  Printing by Offset Lithograph on 77" presses,
  both two color and four color.

Acknowledgements

The author wishes to express his sincere thanks and appreciation
to the many people who assisted in the preparation of this book.
Special thanks are due to Barbara Lach and Mary Sandy for their
help in typing the vast amount of correspondence that was required; to Tsun Tam and Frank Mondelli for assisting in the preparation of several photographs; and to Russ and David for helping
to keep the pencils sharpened. And, of course, thank you, Judith.

Contents

SECTION 1

INTRODUCTION TO THE GRAPHIC ARTS

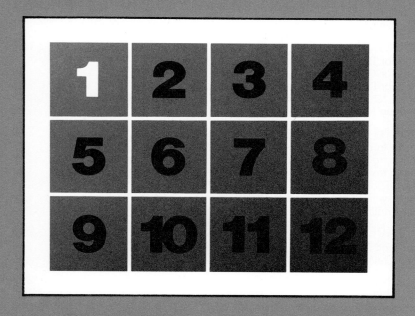

UNIT 1

THE GRAPHIC ARTS INDUSTRY OF TODAY

Objectives

When you have completed this unit, you will be able to:

1. Identify at least ten products produced in their entirety by the graphic arts industry.
2. Identify at least nine products made by other industries with the help of the graphic arts industry.
3. Explain why products are printed.
4. Define the terms *communication* and *graphic communication*.
5. List at least ten business enterprises and/or occupations that are part of the graphic arts industry.
6. Describe the services that are provided by a book publishing company.
7. Describe the size of the graphic arts industry in terms of the value of products and services sold, the number of printing establishments, and the number of persons employed.

Terms to Know

Here are some of the words you will need to understand before reading this unit. If the meaning of a word is not clear to you, look it up in the Glossary in the back of this book.

message	graphic communication	publisher
communication	compositor	artist

ITS PRODUCTS ARE ALL AROUND US

When we think about an industry, we generally think in terms of its major product or products. The steel industry produces steel and the automotive industry, automobiles. But what does the graphic arts industry produce? The answer is *things that are printed* or related to the printing business, such as paper, inks, films or bindings.

Printed products are all around us. Some of these are shown in Figure 1-1. Books and magazines, newspapers and catalogs, maps and charts, posters and brochures, stamps and paper money are some examples of products produced in their entirety by the graphic arts industry.

Printing plays a key role in the generation of products produced by other industries as well. For example, textiles, wallpaper, toothpaste tubes, soft drink cans, candy wrappers, oranges and baseballs all contain printed images. Even the circuits used for electronic devices such as calculators and television sets are printed, Figure 1-2.

The list of products produced in whole or in part by the graphic arts industry is almost endless. Think about it. Printing is all around us.

Figure 1-1. *A sampling of products produced by the graphic arts industry. (Sun Chemical Co.)*

ITS PURPOSE IS TO COMMUNICATE

Most printing is done in order to convey a message from one person or group of

Figure 1-2. *Circuits used in a variety of electronic devices are printed using graphic arts techniques.*

SCOPE OF THE INDUSTRY

This book is a product of the graphic arts industry. Several individuals and business enterprises played an important role in its creation. Together these individuals and enterprises represent the scope of the industry. So let's now take a brief look at how this book was produced.

Introduction to Graphic Arts is a textbook that deals with the organization, tools, materials, and processes of the graphic arts industry. The content, or message, of this book was developed by the author after consultation with the publisher.

The publisher provided design and editorial assistance and managed the production and sale of the book.

Type had to be set by a company that specializes in type composition, Figure 1-3. This company is called the *compositor* or *typesetter*. Illustrations were gathered. Artists created drawings and photographers made photographs.

The assembled type, artwork, and photographs were sent to a printer, who made plates, Figure 1-4, and printed the pages. The printer then sent the pages to a bindery where they were folded, sewn together, trimmed, and encased in a cover, Figure 1-5.

people to another. Newspapers, books, magazines, catalogs, greeting cards, labels, and business forms are all examples of printed products used for this purpose. They all contain messages. When a message is sent by one person and received by another, *communication* takes place.

Printed messages are graphic or visual in form. They are made up of symbols, drawings, and photographs. Communication through the use of printed images is called *graphic communication.* The primary purpose of the graphic arts industry, then, is to produce products that communicate graphically.

Figure 1-3.
The compositor
sets type to form
words, sentences,
and paragraphs.
(Typographic
Sales, Inc.)

Figure 1-4.
Multiple copies of
the assembled type,
artwork, and
photographs are
produced by the
printer.
(R. R. Donnelley
& Sons Co.)

Figure 1-5.
The binder folds,
sews, trims, and
encloses the printed
pages within a cover.
(R. R. Donnelley
& Sons Co.)

The author, editor, publisher, compositor, artist, photographer, printer, and binder all played an important role in the creation of this book. Supplies such as paper and ink products and printing equipment were needed as well. The graphic arts industry encompasses a wide range of occupations, activities, and enterprises.

SIZE OF THE INDUSTRY

The United States has the world's largest graphic arts industry. The value of all products and services sold by the industry in 1977 amounted to 47 billion dollars. Sales are expected to grow to about 60 billion dollars by 1982.

There are over 40,000 commercial printing establishments in the United States. This is the largest number of establishments in any U.S. manufacturing industry. Graphic arts companies are located throughout the country especially in and around areas of high population and industrial development.

Well over one million people were employed by graphic arts firms during 1977. The industry's annual payroll amounted to 14.5 billion dollars. It is anticipated that the work force will expand in the years ahead.

TEST YOUR KNOWLEDGE

1. List ten items produced entirely by the graphic arts industry.
2. Identify nine products that contain printed images and are produced by industries other than the graphic arts industry.
3. Explain the primary reason for producing newspapers, books, magazines, and almost all other printed products.
4. Define the terms *communication* and *graphic communication*.
5. List ten business enterprises and/or occupations that are part of the graphic arts industry.
6. Describe the role of a publishing company in creating, producing, and selling a textbook.
7. Describe the size of the graphic arts industry today. Include information concerning the value of products and services sold, the number of printing establishments and the number of persons employed in the industry.

UNIT 2

A BRIEF LOOK AT WHY AND HOW THE INDUSTRY DEVELOPED

Objectives

When you have completed this unit, you will be able to:
1. Explain why the graphic arts industry developed.
2. Name three important problems that our ancestors had to overcome in order to make maximum use of the graphic communication process.
3. Trace the development and spread of printing throughout the world.
4. Define *movable type.*
5. Describe the contribution of Johann Gutenberg to the development of printing.
6. Trace the development and spread of papermaking throughout the world.
7. Trace the development of inks and inkmaking technology.

Terms to Know

Here are some of the words you will need to understand before reading this unit. If the meaning of a word is not clear to you, look it up in the Glossary in the back of this book.

printing   relief printing

WHY THE GRAPHIC ARTS INDUSTRY DEVELOPED

People have always needed to communicate with other people. By learning to write and communicate graphically, our ancestors overcame a major limitation in spoken communication—the need for direct contact between people.

However, there were important problems to overcome before our ancestors could make maximum use of the graphic communication process. For example, materials for writing and printing had to be invented and developed. Then ways had to be found to reproduce many copies of a message. Because of their need to communicate efficiently, our ancestors learned how to solve each problem. As they did, the graphic arts industry grew.

HOW PRINTING DEVELOPED

Our ancestors developed a variety of techniques for reproducing many copies of a graphic message. *Printing* is the term that describes these techniques.

In its earliest form, printing was done from hand-carved wooden blocks. The complete message was cut in reverse into the block. Then the block was inked and pressed against the material to be printed. This is called *relief printing*. The Japanese used this technique as early as 770 A.D. The Chinese are credited with producing the first printed book, *The Diamond Sutra*, in 868 A.D.

A major limitation of wood block printing is that each new message requires carving a new block of wood, and carving is a slow and tedious process. This limitation was overcome with the invention of *movable type*.

Movable type consists of individual letters of the alphabet that can be assembled to produce a printed message, disassembled and then assembled again to form a new message. Movable type characters made from hardened clay were used in China as early as 1041 A.D. By the middle of the thirteenth century, Koreans were casting type in bronze.

In 1439 Johann Gutenberg became the first European to print from movable type. It is not known whether he invented the process on his own or if he was aware of the developments that had occurred in the Orient. Not only did Gutenberg print from movable type, but, even more important, he developed a practical means of casting type. A por-

Figure 2-1. *A portion of a page from the Gutenberg Bible.*

tion of a page from the famous Gutenberg Bible is pictured in Figure 2-1.

Early printing was done on hand-operated wooden presses, Figure 2-2. The printing of 250 sheets of paper in Gutenberg's time was considered a full day's

Figure 2-2. *An early printing shop. (Eastman Kodak Co.)*

work. By the middle of the seventeenth century, 2000 sheets a day could be printed. Today high-speed presses can print many thousands of sheets in a single hour.

THE SPREAD OF PRINTING. The art of printing spread rapidly throughout Europe soon after Gutenberg began his printing activities. By the end of the fifteenth century, printing was firmly established in England. From England printing moved to the American colonies.

The first printing press in America was set up in the Massachusetts Bay Colony in 1639. Steven Daye, the first American printer, operated this press. His first book, *The Whole Booke of Psalmes* was printed in 1640. Typesetting, printing, and binding of the 1700 copies of this 300-page book took almost a full year to complete.

The most famous American printer was Benjamin Franklin. Franklin established his own printing business in Philadelphia in 1728. His most notable publications included the *Pennsylvania Gazette,* a leading colonial newspaper, and *Poor Richard's Almanack,* issued in 1732.

Developments in the last 100 years have revolutionized the printing industry. Printing has changed from an art to a science, from a craft to a technology. But the development of printing is not over yet. New materials, machines, and methods are constantly being invented in order to satisfy man's need to communicate.

HOW PAPER DEVELOPED

Ts'ai Lun, a Chinese court official, is credited with the invention of paper. He did this nearly 1900 years ago in the year 105 A.D.

Before the invention of paper, people wrote on a variety of materials. For example, animal skins called *parchment* and *vellum* were used by the ancient Greeks. And *papyrus,* a writing surface made by pounding a woven mat of papyrus reed into a thin, hard sheet was used by the ancient Egyptians. The word *paper,* in fact, is derived from the word *papyrus.*

In the tenth century A.D., techniques for making paper by hand were introduced to the Western world. North African Moors discovered papermaking while trading with the East. In conquering Spain, the Moors brought papermaking to the West. See Figure 2-3.

Figure 2-3. *Making paper by hand.*

The first paper mill in America was established in 1690 by William Rittenhouse. It was located near Philadelphia. By the beginning of the nineteenth century, hundreds of paper mills had sprung up throughout the country. However, it was not until the middle of the nineteenth century, when papermaking machines were put into general use, that the urgent demand for inexpensive paper could be met. Today, an average of well over 400 pounds of paper per man, woman, and child is used each year in America.

HOW INK DEVELOPED

Printing ink was also invented in China. Wei Tang is credited with developing an ink for block printing about 400 A.D. He made ink from plant substances mixed with colored earth and soot.

By the time of Gutenberg, inks were being made by mixing varnish with lampblack. The varnish was made by boiling linseed oil. These inks were used, with little modification, until the end of the eighteenth century.

During the nineteenth century, advances were made in the use of driers to speed the drying of ink. Various new pigments for producing colored inks were also developed.

It was in the twentieth century, however, that major developments in ink making came about. Rapid technological advances in printing during the past fifty years brought about changes in the composition and manufacture of printing ink. Today ink manufacturers employ thousands of chemists who are constantly working to improve old inks and develop new ones.

TEST YOUR KNOWLEDGE

1. Briefly explain why the graphic arts industry developed as it did.
2. List three important problems that had to be overcome in order for our ancestors to make maximum use of the graphic communication process.
3. Prepare a chart which highlights the development and spread of printing throughout the world. Include a time line on this chart.
4. Define what is meant by *movable type.*
5. Describe Johann Gutenberg's contribution to the development of printing.
6. Prepare a chart which highlights the development and spread of papermaking throughout the world.
7. Prepare an outline which traces the development of inks and inkmaking technology.

SECTION 2

METHODS OF PRINTING

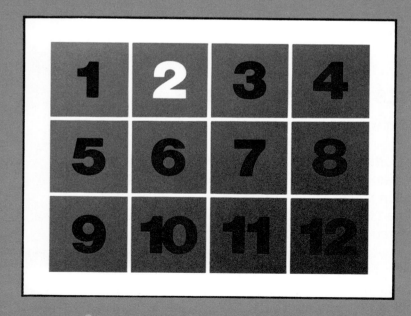

UNIT 3

PRINTING FROM A RAISED SURFACE

Objectives

When you have completed this unit, you will be able to:
1. Define the terms *relief* and *letterpress printing*.
2. Illustrate how relief or letterpress printing is accomplished.
3. List four kinds of type that are used in letterpress printing.
4. Name four kinds of relief plates.
5. Describe the basic steps involved in printing from a raised surface.
6. Explain why the raised image on type and relief plates must be prepared in reverse.

Terms to Know

Here are some of the words you will need to understand before reading this unit. If the meaning of a word is not clear to you, look it up in the Glossary in the back of this book.

relief printing	Linotype	wood cut
letterpress printing	Ludlow	wood engraving
foundry type	linoleum block	photoengraving
monotype		

RELIEF OR LETTERPRESS PRINTING

When ink is applied to a raised surface and paper is pressed against the inked surface, the ink is transferred to the paper, Figure 3-1. *Relief* and *letterpress* are terms that describe printing methods that use this principle. The rubber stamp, Figure 3-2, is a device that prints by the relief or letterpress method. It transfers ink from a raised surface to paper. Typewriter elements, Figure 3-3, also print in this way.

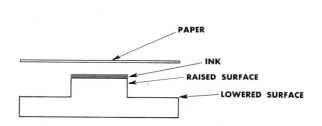

Figure 3-1. Relief or letterpress printing. The lowered surface does not print because it doesn't come in contact with the ink or the paper.

Figure 3-2. Printing with a rubber stamp is a form of relief or letterpress printing.

Figure 3-3. Relief printing elements are used in typewriters. (IBM Office Products Division)

Foundry type, Monotype, Linotype, and Ludlow are used by the letterpress printer to transfer letters and numbers to paper, Figure 3-4. The plates shown in Figure 3-5 can also be used in letterpress printing. Their raised surfaces can print photographs and illustrations as well as letters and numbers.

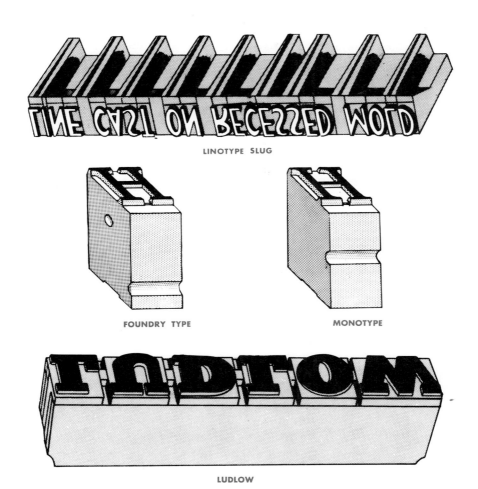

LINOTYPE SLUG

FOUNDRY TYPE

MONOTYPE

LUDLOW

Figure 3-4. *Linotype, Foundry type, Monotype, and Ludlow slugs.*

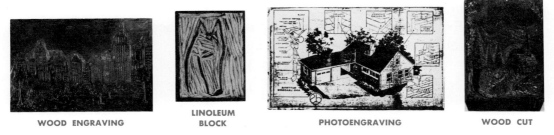

WOOD ENGRAVING

LINOLEUM BLOCK

PHOTOENGRAVING

WOOD CUT

Figure 3-5. *Letterpress plates include linoleum blocks, wood cuts, wood engravings and photoengravings.*

IMAGE REVERSAL. As you can see, the principle of printing from a raised surface is not difficult to understand. There is one problem to consider, how-ever. Look at Figure 3-1 again. Note that the shape of the raised surface that printed the letter *P* on the paper is "wrong reading" or backwards. The raised surface was purposely prepared this way so that it would print a "right reading" image on the paper. See Figure 3-6.

Figure 3-6. The raised surface of a letterpress plate must be prepared in reverse. The symbols or characters on this type of plate are "wrong reading" or a mirror image of what is to be printed. Hold this page up to a mirror to find out what this plate will print.

THEN AND NOW. Relief or letterpress printing is the oldest printing method. It was first used by the Japanese around 770 A.D. They used this method to print multiple copies of a picture from a single wooden plate (woodcut). Today a wide variety of letterpress plates (Unit 22) are used on several types of presses (Unit 27) to print a rich and varied assortment of products including newspapers, books, and magazines.

TEST YOUR KNOWLEDGE

1. Describe what is meant by the terms *relief printing* and *letterpress printing*.
2. Draw a simple illustration showing how relief or letterpress printing is done.
3. List four kinds of type used in letterpress printing.
4. List the names of four types of relief printing plates.
5. List in proper sequence the basic steps involved in printing from a raised surface.
6. Explain why the raised image-producing surface on type and relief plates must be prepared in reverse.

UNIT 4

PRINTING FROM A LOWERED SURFACE

Objectives

When you have completed this unit, you will be able to:
1. Define the terms *gravure* and *intaglio printing*.
2. Illustrate the major differences between relief printing and intaglio printing.
3. Describe the basic steps in printing from a lowered surface.
4. Explain why the lowered image on gravure plates must be prepared in reverse.
5. List six products often printed by the gravure process.

Terms to Know

Here are some of the words you will need to understand before reading this unit. If the meaning of a word is not clear to you, look it up in the Glossary in the back of this book.

gravure printing   intaglio printing

GRAVURE OR INTAGLIO PRINTING

In Unit 3 you learned that relief printing transfers ink from a raised surface to paper. The gravure process is just the opposite. In gravure printing, ink is transferred from a lowered surface to paper. The image area of a gravure plate is cut below or into the surface of the plate, Figure 4-1.

Intaglio (pronounced in-tal-yo) is another name for gravure. Figure 4-2 illustrates the gravure or intaglio process. The entire surface of the plate is inked and then wiped clean. This leaves ink in the lowered areas of the plate. Paper is then pressed against the plate and ink transfers to it.

Paper is flexible. It can bend and stretch to get into the lowered areas of a gravure plate. Figure 4-3 shows how ink is transferred to the paper.

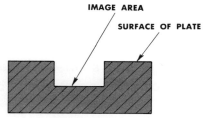

Figure 4-1. *In gravure printing, the image area is cut below the surface of the plate.*

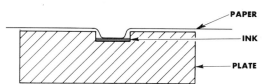

Figure 4-3. *Paper is flexible. It can bend and stretch to get into the lowered areas of a gravure plate. Ink then transfers to the paper.*

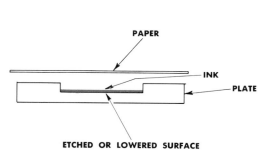

Figure 4-2. *Gravure or intaglio printing. Ink is transferred from the lowered surface of the plate to the paper. The top surface of the plate does not print because the ink has been removed.*

IMAGE REVERSAL. Like the raised image on a relief plate, the lowered image on a gravure plate must also be prepared in reverse. Look at Figure 4-4. Note the shape of the lowered surface that printed the letter *P.* It is "wrong reading" or backwards. The lowered surface was purposely prepared this way so that it would print a "right reading" image on the paper.

THEN AND NOW. Karl Kleitsch is generally credited with inventing the gravure process in 1879. In 1894 he developed a press that could print from etched copper cylinders instead of flat plates. Within twenty years gravure cylinders were being used to print a variety of products including a portion of the *New York Times.*

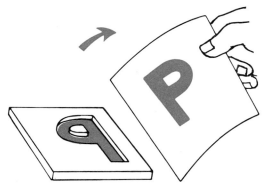

Figure 4-4. *The lowered surface of a gravure plate must be prepared in reverse. The symbols of characters on this plate are "wrong reading" or a mirror image of what is to be printed.*

Today both flat and cylindrical gravure plates (Unit 23) are used on a variety of presses (Unit 28) to print Sunday newspaper supplements, magazines, major mail order catalogs, stamps, and even paper money. Much of our printed fabric is also produced by gravure.

TEST YOUR KNOWLEDGE

1. Describe what is meant by the terms *gravure printing* and *intaglio printing.*
2. Using simple diagrams, illustrate the major differences between relief and intaglio printing.
3. List in proper sequence the basic steps in printing from a lowered surface.
4. Explain why the lowered, image-producing surface on a gravure plate or cylinder must be prepared in reverse.
5. List six categories of products often printed by the gravure process.

UNIT 5

PRINTING FROM A FLAT SURFACE

Objectives

When you have completed this unit, you will be able to:

1. Define *planographic printing.*
2. Illustrate major differences among relief, intaglio, and planographic printing methods.
3. Give a practical example showing how grease and water do not mix.
4. List the basic steps in printing from a flat surface.
5. Identify the grease receptive and water receptive areas on a lithographic plate.
6. Explain why the image on a lithographic plate is transferred to a rubber blanket during the offset process.

Terms to Know

Here are some of the words you will need to understand before reading this unit. If the meaning of a word is not clear to you, look it up in the Glossary in the back of this book.

planographic printing	blanket	impression cylinder
lithography	plate cylinder	dampening system
offset press	blanket cylinder	

PLANOGRAPHIC OR LITHOGRAPHIC PRINTING

You have already learned how printing can be done from a raised surface and from a lowered surface. It is also possible to print from a flat surface. *Planographic* and *lithographic* are both terms that describe methods of printing from a flat surface.

Planographic printing is based on the principle that grease and water do not

Figure 5-1. *Grease and water do not mix. If you have ever tried to wash greasy hands with just water, you know that grease and water do not mix.*

mix, Figure 5-1. The process works this way. First, a greasy image is placed on a flat plate. The image may be drawn directly on the plate with a grease pencil. It may also be placed on the plate photographically instead.

Next, water is applied to the plate. The water will cover the non-image area of the plate. Water will be repelled from the image area because WATER *AND GREASE DO NOT MIX!*

The entire plate is then coated with ink. Ink is a greasy substance and adheres to the greasy image. Ink is repelled from the wet areas of the plate because *WATER* AND GREASE DO NOT MIX!

Paper is then pressed against the surface of the plate and the inked image is transferred to the paper. The process of printing from a flat surface is shown in Figure 5-2.

Planographic or lithographic printing prints from a plane or flat surface, one neither raised nor depressed. The printing image is formed chemically by making some areas of the plate *grease receptive* and *water repellent,* while others remain *water receptive* and *grease repellent.*

21

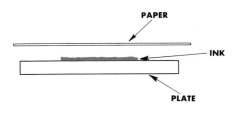

Figure 5-2. *Lithographic printing is done from a flat surface.*

OFFSET PRINTING. Lithographic printing is often called *offset printing.* Unlike plates for letterpress and gravure (which have their printing surfaces shaped to form the desired image), the printing image on a lithographic plate simply rests upon the plate's surface. The image can rapidly wear away when paper rubs against it during the printing process. This is especially true when the plates are used on high-speed printing presses. To minimize wear the image on the plate is first offset (transferred) to a rubber blanket, Figure 5-3A. Note that the right-reading image is reversed on the blanket. Figure 5-3B shows how the paper receives the image from the blanket. The paper does not make contact with the printing plate. The entire offset lithographic process is diagrammed in Figure 5-3C.

THEN AND NOW. Alois Senefelder of Germany discovered the lithographic

Figure 5-3. *Offset printing. (A) The image is first transferred to a rubber blanket. (B) The paper then receives the image from the blanket. (C) Major parts of an offset-lithographic press.*

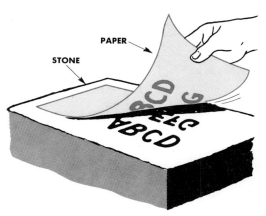

Figure 5-4. *Stone lithography. The process is slow and tedious, but for the artist the results can be quite rewarding.*

printing method in 1796. He printed directly on paper from a grease image applied to a heavy piece of limestone. Stone lithography, Figure 5-4, is slow and tedious.

Today a wide variety of lithographic plates (Unit 24) is used on high-speed offset presses and duplicators (Unit 29) to print more products than any other printing method. A high-speed lithographic press is shown in Figure 5-5.

Figure 5-5. *Today's high-speed lithographic presses can produce many thousands of newspapers per hour. (Rand McNally & Co.)*

TEST YOUR KNOWLEDGE

1. Describe what is meant by the term *planographic printing.*
2. Using simple diagrams, illustrate the major differences among relief, intaglio, and planographic printing methods.
3. Lithographic printing is based on the principle that grease and water do not mix. Figure 5-1 illustrates this principle. Identify at least one other example of grease not mixing with water.
4. List in proper sequence the basic steps in printing from a flat surface.
5. Draw a rectangular box on a sheet of paper. This box will represent an offset plate. Draw a simple picture on the plate. This represents the image. Now identify and label each of the following areas on the plate: grease receptive, water receptive, grease repellent, and water repellent.
6. Explain why the image on a lithographic plate is transferred to a rubber blanket during the offset process.

UNIT 6

PRINTING WITH A STENCIL

Objectives

When you have completed this unit, you will be able to:
1. Define *screen-process printing*.
2. Illustrate major differences among relief, intaglio, planographic and screen-process printing.
3. List the basic steps in printing with a stencil.
4. Describe three techniques for preparing a stencil for screen-process printing.
5. Prepare a hand-cut paper stencil.
6. Describe the function of each of the major parts of a screen-process printing frame.

Terms to Know

Here are some of the words you will need to understand before reading this unit. If the meaning of a word is not clear to you, look it up in the Glossary in the back of this book.

screen-process printing   stencil

SCREEN-PROCESS PRINTING

You now know how printing can be done from a raised surface (Unit 3), a lowered surface (Unit 4), and a flat surface (Unit 5). It is also possible to print by forcing ink through openings or holes in a stencil, Figure 6-1.

One common type of stencil printing is *screen-process printing.* This method is also called *stencil printing, screen printing* and *silk screen printing.*

STENCILS. The stencil controls what is to be printed. Basically a stencil is nothing more than a thin sheet of paper, film, or other nonporous material with lettering or a design cut through. The lettering or design is right reading, not reversed. A type of stencil you are probably already familiar with is shown in Figure 6-2. Stencils for screen-process printing may be hand cut from paper or film, prepared photographically, or painted directly on the screen.

PRINTING SCREENS. A stencil with open areas representing the desired image must be adhered to a screen. A screen is a piece of woven material, such as silk, nylon, dacron or stainless steel mesh, stretched tightly over a

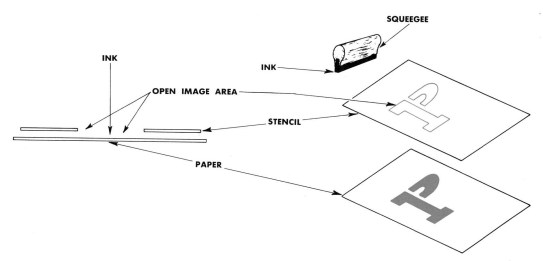

Figure 6-1. Screen-process printing. A squeegee is used to force ink through holes in a stencil onto the paper.

Figure 6-2. *A stencil used for hand letter-ing.*

wooden or metal frame. The frame serves as the printing press in screen-process printing. A simple printing frame is shown in Figure 6-3.

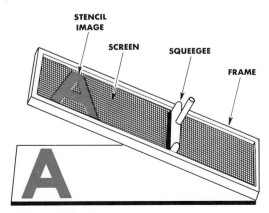

Figure 6-3. *A frame with woven screen material stretched across it serves as the printing press in screen-process printing.*

THE PRINTING PROCESS. Screen-process printing is easy to understand. After paper is placed under the printing screen, ink with a paint-like consistency is applied to the top of the screen. Finally, the ink is spread and forced through stencil openings onto the paper below the screen. This is done by pulling a rubber squeegee over the screen. The screen process of printing is illustrated in Figure 6-4.

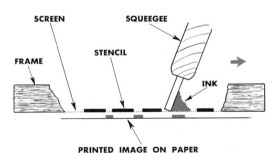

Figure *6-4.* *In screen-process printing, ink is forced through a stencil that has been adhered to a screen. The ink creates a printed image on the paper.*

THEN AND NOW. The idea of applying decorations to objects by stenciling is very old. Evidence shows that stenciling techniques were widely used in China to decorate pottery and other objects. Screen-process printing methods as we know them today were probably first used in Japan hundreds of years ago.

In 1907 the first patent for silk screen printing was issued to Samuel Simon of Manchester, England. Screen-process printing developed rapidly during the early twentieth century. A wide variety of stencil materials has been developed over the years (see Unit 25). Today, just about any surface of any shape or size can be printed using screen-process methods (Unit 30). A modern screen-process printing press that can be used to print on paper or fabric is shown in Figure 6-5.

Figure 6-5. An automatic screen-process printing press. (Advance Process Supply Co.)

TEST YOUR KNOWLEDGE

1. Describe what is meant by *screen-process printing.*
2. Using simple diagrams, illustrate the major differences among relief, intaglio, planographic, and screen-process printing.
3. List in proper order the basic steps in printing with a stencil.
4. List three ways in which stencils for screen-process printing can be made.
5. On a sheet of paper, print your initials approximately one inch high. Widen each of the lines so they are at least ⅛ inch thick. With scissors cut the letters from the sheet of paper. You have just made a hand-cut paper stencil. What means can you devise to keep the interior portion of certain letters, such as the center of the *O,* from falling away from the stencil?
6. Describe briefly the function of each of the screen-process frame parts identified in Figure 6-3. Items to be described are: frame, screen, stencil image, and squeegee.

UNIT 7

OTHER WAYS OF DUPLICATING COPIES

Objectives

When you have completed this unit, you will be able to:
1. Define *spirit duplication.*
2. List the basic steps involved in spirit duplicating.
3. Illustrate how spirit duplication is accomplished.
4. Define *mimeograph duplication.*
5. List the basic steps in mimeograph duplicating.
6. Illustrate how mimeograph duplication is accomplished.
7. Define *electrostatic copying.*
8. List the basic steps involved in the transfer process of electrostatic copying.
9. List the basic steps involved in the direct process of electrostatic copying.

Terms to Know

Here are some of the words you will need to understand before reading this unit. If the meaning of a word is not clear to you, look it up in the Glossary in the back of this book.

spirit duplicating	solvent	electrostatic copying
mimeograph duplicating		stencil

LIMITED-COPY DUPLICATION PROCESSES

The four major methods of printing are relief, intaglio, planographic, and screen-process. These methods have been used for years to produce high quality printed products.

Traditionally, skilled people have been needed to operate the sophisticated machines and perform technical activities associated with each of the printing methods. Recently, however, simplified techniques based on these printing methods have been developed.

Machines and materials for the rapid duplication of graphic information have been improved and refined. Some machines turned out to be so economical and simple to operate that business and industry quickly adopted them for in-house duplicating. The most important of these limited-copy duplicators are the

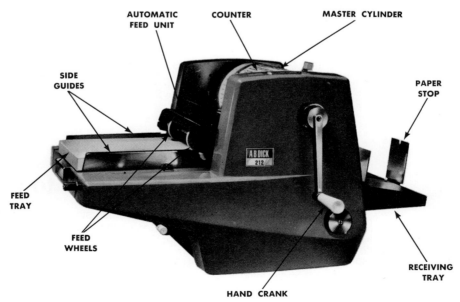

AUTOMATIC FEED UNIT   COUNTER   MASTER CYLINDER
SIDE GUIDES   PAPER STOP
FEED TRAY
FEED WHEELS
RECEIVING TRAY
HAND CRANK

Figure 7-1. *A spirit duplicator with its major parts identified. (A. B. Dick Company)*

spirit duplicator, the mimeograph machine, and the electrostatic copier.

SPIRIT DUPLICATING

Spirit duplicating is a planographic process. Printing is done from a flat sheet of paper called a spirit master. The image area on the master is formed by the addition of an aniline dye. The spirit master containing the aniline-dye image is attached to the master cylinder of a spirit duplicator such as the one shown in Figure 7-1.

To print, a solvent capable of dissolving aniline dye loosens the top surface of

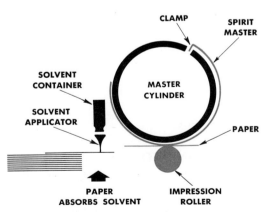

Figure 7-2. The spirit duplicating process. As the moistened paper contacts the spirit master it causes some dye to dissolve. Image transfer occurs as the paper passes between the spirit master and the impression roller.

the dye image. To do this each sheet of paper is moistened with solvent before it contacts the spirit master. As the moistened paper meets the spirit master, some of the dye dissolves and remains on the paper. Spirit duplicating is diagrammed in Figure 7-2.

MIMEOGRAPH DUPLICATING

Mimeograph duplicating is based on the screen process of printing. A stencil controls the placement of ink on the paper.

A mimeograph stencil is a porous, tissue-like material coated with wax on both sides. The wax does not permit ink to pass through the porous base. To form the image area of the stencil you push away the wax coating with a ballpoint pen or stylus or by typing directly on the stencil. This exposes the porous base. Then attach the stencil to the cylinder of a mimeograph duplicator such as the one shown in Figure 7-3.

Fill the stencil cylinder with ink. During printing, this ink passes through holes in the stencil cylinder and onto an absorbent pad located under the stencil. As paper passes between the stencil and impression roller, ink is forced through the stencil openings onto the paper. The

Figure 7-3. *A mimeograph duplicator with its major parts identified. (A. B. Dick Company)*

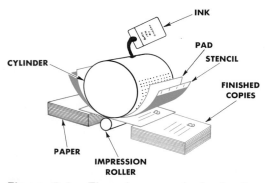

Figure 7-4. *The mimeograph duplicating process. Ink passes through the holes in the cylinder and onto an absorbent pad. Image transfer occurs as the paper passes between the stencil and impression roller. The increased pressure forces ink in the pad through the openings in the stencil.*

mimeograph duplicating process is diagrammed in Figure 7-4.

ELECTROSTATIC COPYING
Specially prepared plates, masters, or stencils are not required for electrostatic copying. Instead, duplicates are produced directly from almost any handwritten, typed or printed original.

Electrostatic copies can be made on plain paper by the *transfer process* or on specially treated paper by the *direct process*. Both of these processes are based on the principle that opposite electrical charges attract, while like charges repel.

TRANSFER PROCESS. A selenium-coated plate or drum is given a positive electrostatic charge, Figure 7-5A. The charge must be given in total darkness because it would be lost if exposed to light.

After it is charged, the plate or drum is

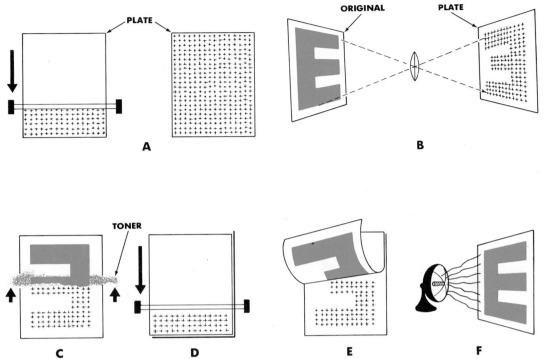

Figure 7-5. *The electrostatic transfer process. (A) The plate is given a positive charge. (B) The charged plate is exposed to the original. Light removes the charge from the non-image areas of the plate. (C) Toner is given a negative charge. It adheres to the positive image areas on the plate. (D) The paper is charged positively. (E) Because opposite charges attract, the toner is transferred to the paper. (F) A heating element is used to fuse the toner to the paper.*

exposed to the original copy through a system of lenses. Light reflecting from the white (non-image) portion of the original strikes areas of the plate or drum causing the charge to be lost in these areas. Because the dark (image) portion of the original reflects little if any light, the selenium plate or drum will retain an electrostatic charge corresponding in shape to the image on the original. Note that the electrostatic plate image is a mirror image of the original and is not yet visible, Figure 7-5B.

A black pigment in the form of a fine powdered toner is now given a negative charge. It is then poured over the sele-nium plate or drum. Because of its negative charge it adheres to the posi-tively charged image. A visible but re-versed image now exists on the plate or drum, Figure 7-5C.

A sheet of paper is next placed over the plate and given a positive charge, Fig-ure 7-5D. Because the positive charge on the paper is stronger than the charge on the plate, the toner transfers to the paper, Figure 7-5E.

The last step in the process is to fuse the image formed by the toner to the paper. A heating element is used to melt the toner and bond it to the paper, Figure 7-5F.

DIRECT PROCESS. The paper used in the direct process must be specially treated with zinc oxide. This makes the paper quite a bit heavier than regular, untreated paper. In the direct process, the electrostatic image is placed directly on the print paper.

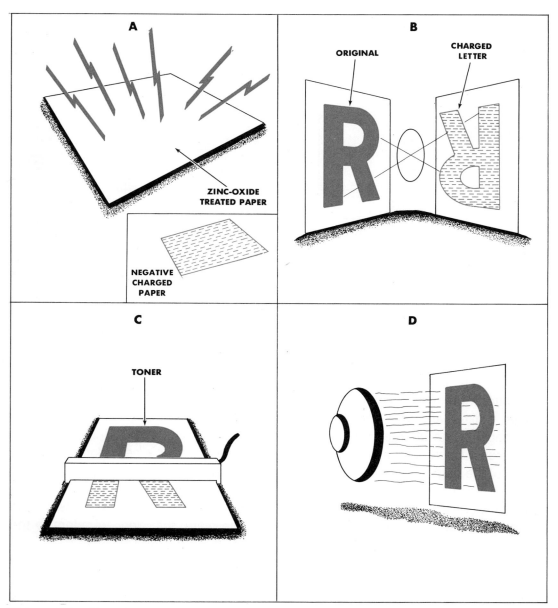

Figure 7-6. *The electrostatic direct process. (A) Zinc-oxide paper is given a negative charge. (B) The charged paper is exposed to the original. Light removes the charge from the non-image areas. (C) Toner is given a positive charge. It adheres to the negative image areas on the zinc-oxide treated paper. (D) Heat is used to fuse the toner to the paper.*

The zinc-oxide treated paper is first given a negative charge, Figure 7-6A. It is then exposed to the original copy through a system of lenses. This causes the negative charge to disappear in the non-image areas. Areas of the coated paper that correspond to the original image remain charged, Figure 7-6B.

A positively charged black toner is then used to make the image visible, Figure 7-6C. As in the transfer process, heat is used to fuse the toner to the zinc-oxide treated paper, Figure 7-6D.

DUPLICATING PROCEDURES

Techniques for preparing masters and stencils are described in Unit 26. Unit 31 contains detailed procedures for using spirit and mimeograph duplicators and electrostatic copying machines.

TEST YOUR KNOWLEDGE

1. Describe the principle of *spirit duplication.*
2. List in proper sequence the basic steps in spirit duplicating.
3. Draw a simple diagram, illustrating the spirit duplication process.
4. Describe the principle of *mimeograph duplication.*
5. List in proper sequence the basic steps involved in mimeograph duplicating.
6. Draw a simple diagram illustrating the mimeograph duplication process.
7. Describe what is meant by the term *electrostatic copying.*
8. List in proper sequence the basic steps in the *transfer process* of electrostatic copying.
9. List in proper sequence the basic steps in the *direct process* of electrostatic copying.

SECTION 3

COMMUNICATING
GRAPHICALLY

UNIT 8

THE COMMUNICATION PROCESS AND A COMMUNICATION MODEL

Objectives

When you have completed this unit you will be able to:

1. List ten techniques our ancestors used to communicate with others.
2. Give three advantages of written communication.
3. Explain the difference between a pictograph and an ideograph.
4. Define *communication* in terms of the elements that comprise it.
5. Describe the relationship among the elements of communication.

Terms to Know

Here are some of the words you will need to understand before reading this unit. If the meaning of a word is not clear to you, look it up in the Glossary in the back of this book.

communication   graphic communication   message

THE DEVELOPMENT OF GRAPHIC COMMUNICATIONS

Even before primitive man developed spoken language, he was able to communicate by grunting, laughing, frowning, screaming, and by using physical force. In these and other ways he made his message clear to others.

As time went on, man developed other ways of communicating. He learned to mark trails with piles of stones or cuts on trees. He discovered how to control fire and use smoke to signal others. He learned to communicate through a spoken language. And then he learned to write.

THE EVOLUTION OF WRITING. Writing made it possible to record information. It also made it possible to send messages over great distances without direct contact. Most important, though, it enabled man to transmit knowledge to future generations.

Pictographs. Evidence of man's early attempts at writing can be found on the walls of caves 30,000 years old. The writing was in the form of pictures painted on cave walls, Figure 8-1. These paintings are called *pictographs.*

Figure 8-1. *Cave drawings provide evidence of man's early attempts at writing. Pictures were used to record the hunt. (Spanish National Tourist Office)*

Ideographs. As man's need to communicate grew, picture writing gave way to idea writing. Pictures began to take on abstract meanings. Instead of representing the objects pictured, the pictures took on new meanings. They began to represent the feeling or idea that each was supposed to suggest. Graphic symbols that represent ideas are called *ideographs,* Figure 8-2.

Hieroglyphics. Hieroglyphics are a form of ideograph. They are highly sophisticated renderings perfected by the Egyptians around 2500 B.C. Each picture represents an idea, not a sound as

生 拿
火 個
。 燈
你 來
去

Figure 8-2. *Graphic symbols that represent ideas are called ideographs.*

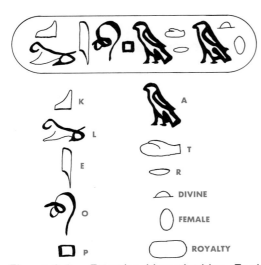

Figure 8-3. *Egyptian hieroglyphics. Each picture represented an idea and not a sound as do modern letters.*

modern letters do. Hieroglyphic writing is shown in Figure 8-3.

Cuneiform Writing. The ancient Assyrians, Chaldeans, and Egyptians used wedge-shaped letters. Originally these letters were cut by chisel into stone.

Later letters were pressed into clay tablets with small brass or copper punches. This form of writing is called *cuneiform*. A cuneiform tablet is shown in Figure 8-4.

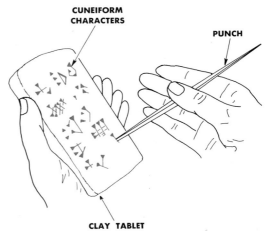

Figure 8-4. *An ancient cuneiform tablet.*

The Alphabet. The alphabet as we know it today is based on an early Phoenician system used around 1500 B.C. The Greeks adopted this system of writing about 1000 B.C. The Roman alphabet, which we use today, is based on the Greek adaptation of the Phoenician alphabet. Figure 8-5 illustrates the evolution of our alphabet.

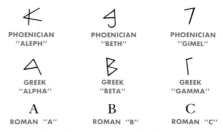

Figure 8-5. *How our alphabet evolved.*

DEVELOPING COMMUNICATIONS TECHNOLOGY. Writing is an essential part of graphic communications. It enabled our ancestors to communicate with others without the need for direct contact. Writing allowed them to record their history, their art, their science, their knowledge and their skills. It allowed our ancestors to communicate with future generations.

To advance the communications process, limitations had to be overcome. Ways had to be found for reproducing several copies of a message without having to rewrite the message each time. Writing and printing materials, such as inks, had to be invented and developed. Refer back to Unit 2 for a brief look at how these things were accomplished.

THE COMMUNICATION PROCESS

One way to understand a complicated machine like an automobile or computer is to look at its parts. Once we understand each part, we can study how they all go together. We can use this same approach to look at a complex event or process. Communication is one such process.

A COMMUNICATION MODEL. *Communication* is the process of conveying a message from one person or group of people to another. Like the automobile, the communication process consists of some basic parts. The drawing presented in Figure 8-6 is an attempt to identify these basic parts and to present them in simple form.

Figure 8-6 presents a *model*. The term *model* as we are using it here means "a simplified representation of the communication process." The model describes the major parts of communication and how they go together.

Source. Someone must initiate the communication process. Whoever initiates the process is called the *source.*

Need. The source initiates the process because there is a *need* to communicate. For example, the need or purpose may be to inform, influence, stimulate, question, or entertain.

Message. A *message* is the product of the communication process. It is the information transmitted from a source to a receiver. The message consists of an organized sequence of symbols and signals, Figure 8-7, designed to convey a desired meaning. When signals or symbols are grouped or arranged to convey desired information (the message), they form a code.

Vehicle. Information in the form of a coded message is transmitted from

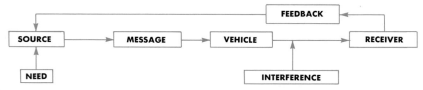

Figure 8-6. *Communication is the process of conveying a message from one person or group of people to another. This model provides a simplified representation of the communication process.*

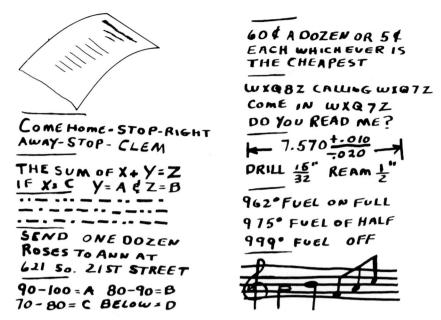

Figure 8-7. *A message is an organized sequence of symbols designed to convey a desired meaning.*

source to receiver by means of a *vehicle.* The vehicle is simply the carrier of the information. It is the link between source and receiver on which or through which a message travels. Examples of vehicles include air, wire, space, paper, tape, etc.

The pairing of a message with an appropriate vehicle results in the formation of a *communications medium.* Some examples of communications media are shown in Figure 8-8.

Receiver. The vehicle carries the source's message to another person or audience. The person or audience receiving the message is called the *receiver.*

Feedback. The way in which the receiver reacts to the message lets the source know whether or not his communication was successful. We call the receiver's reaction *feedback* because it is fed back to the source.

MEDIUM	= MESSAGE COMPONENT	+ VEHICLE COMPONENT
Book	Printed Symbols	Paper
Television	Electrical Signals	Radio Waves
Telephone	Electrical Signals	Wire
Voice	Words	Sound Waves
Recordings	Magnetic Signals	Tape
Data Processing	Holes	Cards

Figure 8-8. *A medium is the result of a message and a vehicle.*

Interference. Negative feedback or total lack of feedback from the receiver could indicate that certain conditions interfered with successful communication. For example, a transistor radio blasting in your ear might interfere with your ability to concentrate and successfully complete your homework. A condition that interferes with communication is called *interference.*

GRAPHIC COMMUNICATIONS

Graphic communications use printed images to convey messages. Newspapers, books, magazines, catalogs, greeting cards, labels, and business forms communicate graphically.

A sender must convert his thoughts and ideas to visual form in order to communicate graphically. Symbols, drawings, and photographs are available for this purpose and are the subject of Unit 9.

TEST YOUR KNOWLEDGE

1. Identify ten techniques used by our ancestors to communicate with others.
2. List three advantages of written communication.
3. Describe the difference between the pictograph and the ideograph form of writing.
4. Define each of the parts or elements of the communication model in Figure 8-6.
5. Explain the relationship among the elements or parts of the communication model in Figure 8-6.

UNIT 9

THE IMPORTANCE OF GRAPHICS IN COMMUNICATION

Objectives

When you have completed this unit, you will be able to:

1. Define *graphic arts.*
2. Describe three techniques used to generate graphic symbols.
3. Define the term *photographic statement.*
4. List three methods of obtaining photographs.
5. Explain the difference between pictorial drawings and technical illustrations.

Terms to Know

Here are some of the words you will need to understand before reading this unit. If the meaning of a word is not clear to you, look it up in the Glossary in the back of this book.

artist   pictorial drawing   technical illustration
graphic communication

COMMUNICATING GRAPHICALLY

When you send a visual message to someone who understands it, you are *communicating graphically.* To do this you must convert your thoughts and ideas to visual form with symbols, photographs, or drawings.

SYMBOLS. Letters of the alphabet and numbers are graphic symbols. Most visual messages are conveyed by generating and then reproducing these symbols in quantity, Figure 9-1.

Symbols used in graphic communication can be handwritten, typed, or composed on special machines. Figure 9-2 shows a composing machine commonly used for this purpose. A variety of techniques and machines for generating graphic symbols are discussed in Section 6.

PHOTOGRAPHS. It is said that one picture is worth a thousand words. This may or may not be true. The actual worth of a photograph, for communication purposes at least, depends on what the photograph has to say.

A good photographic statement is very much like a good spoken or written

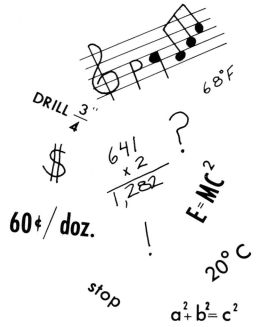

Figure 9-1. *Types of symbols used to communicate graphically.*

statement. They have both subject elements and predicate elements. The *subject* is the main element in the photograph; it is what the photograph is about. The *predicate element* tells us something about the subject; it shows what the subject is doing. What is the subject of Figure 9-3? What is its predicate? The repairman is the subject. The predicate includes the thing he is repairing and the tools he is using.

Figure 9-2. *This photocomposing machine is used to set type at a rapid rate. (Typographic Sales, Inc.)*

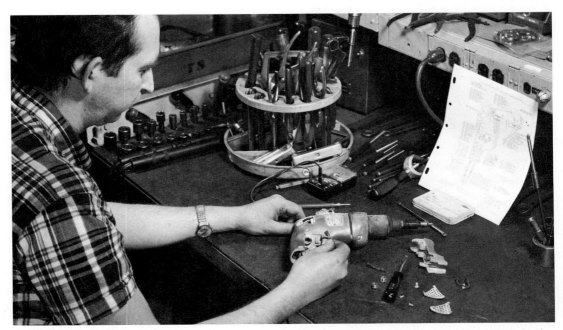

Figure 9-3. *Photographic messages are much like spoken or written ones. What is the subject of this photograph? What is its predicate? (Black & Decker Mfg. Co.)*

Reproducible photographs can be purchased from professional sources. Sometimes they can be obtained at no cost from industrial concerns and advertising agencies. Most often, however, a photograph showing the desired subject and predicate will have to be taken.

A camera, Figure 9-4, plays an important role in graphic communication. Creating, obtaining, and using photographs are discussed in Unit 15.

Figure 9-4. *The single lens reflex camera is often used to create photographs for illustrating printed products. (Vivitar Corp.)*

DRAWINGS. Drawings are pictures created by artists and drafters. Artists working in the field of graphic communications are often called illustrators.

Artists or illustrators generally create their own pictorial drawings. Illustrators may also convert photographs and technical drawings into line illustrations. They can retouch photographs to remove unwanted backgrounds and highlight wanted areas. Retouching is done with an airbrush and compressor, Figure 9-5.

Figure 9-5. *The airbrush and compressor is used by illustrators to retouch photographs. Illustrators may remove unwanted background areas to highlight the subject of the photograph. (Brodhead-Garrett Co.)*

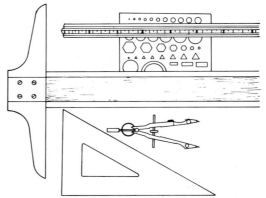

Figure 9-6. *Drawing instruments are used by drafters for technical illustrations.*

Drafters develop technical illustrations usually with drawing instruments, Figure 9-6. Their drawings are often used to show parts and assemblies described in service and operation manuals. An example of a technical illustration is shown in Figure 9-7.

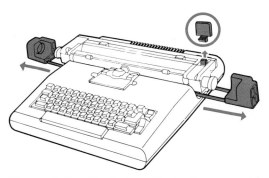

Figure 9-7. *Technical illustrations are often included in service manuals to show parts and assemblies.*
(Olivetti Corp. of America)

Artists and drafters must be able to create drawings that present accurate visual messages. Persons involved in graphic communications must know how to obtain and use illustrations. Creating, obtaining, and using illustrations are discussed in Unit 14.

TEST YOUR KNOWLEDGE

1. Describe what is meant by the term *graphic symbols.*
2. List three techniques that can be used to generate graphic symbols.
3. Describe what is meant by the term *photographic statement.*
4. List three methods of obtaining photographs.
5. Describe the difference between a pictorial drawing and a technical illustration.

UNIT 10
PRINCIPLES OF DESIGN

Objectives

When you have completed this unit, you will be able to:
1. Define *design.*
2. Identify the six principles of design.
3. Explain three factors that influence the size and shape of a printed page.
4. Use the diagonal-line method to reduce and enlarge an illustration.
5. Identify layouts that exhibit formal and informal balance.
6. Locate the true and optical centers of a piece of paper.
7. List twelve techniques for emphasizing a portion of a printed image.
8. Demonstrate how to control eye movement across a printed page.
9. Define *unity.*
10. Give four reasons for including color in a printed product.

Terms to Know

Here are some of the words you will need to understand before reading this unit. If the meaning of a word is not clear to you, look it up in the Glossary in the back of this book.

design	balance	true center
diagonal-line method	optical center	contrast

WHAT IS DESIGN?

A *design* is a plan, a means to an end. When you selected your clothes this morning, you were designing. You made certain choices probably based on how you wanted to look, feel, and act today.

Choices must also be made to select and arrange type and illustrations that make up a printed product. Understanding the principles of good design will help you make intelligent choices.

PRINCIPLES OF DESIGN

Certain principles are basic to understanding graphic design. These include proportion, balance, contrast, rhythm, unity and color. These principles provide guidelines for developing a successful printed product.

PROPORTION. Proportion refers to how parts of a whole relate to one another and to the whole.

Page Proportion. Before a job can be printed, its general size and shape must be decided upon. Usually the product itself will determine this. For example, a business card must be easily carried in a wallet or shirt pocket. A poster must be large enough to be read at a distance.

After approximating, the designer must decide upon a final size and shape for the product. Usually this final decision is based on how a product will look rather than on its use.

Figure 10-1. *Shapes and sizes of several common printed products. (Sun Chemical Co.)*

Generally rectangles are more pleasing to the eye than squares. Square shapes seem dull and unmoving; rectangles seem to convey motion and direction. A good proportion for a rectangular page is approximately two units wide and three units long.

Several common printed products are shown in Figure 10-1. Business cards measure about 2 × 3½ inches. Photographs may measure 4 × 5, 5 × 7, or 8 × 10 inches. And, of course, most business letterheads measure 8½ × 11 inches.

Element Proportion. The size and shape of type and illustrations in a printed product must also be properly proportioned. Again, rectangular elements will usually appear more attractive than square shapes. The size and shape of each element and the surrounding white space must each be considered in relation to all the other elements.

One easy and quick way to reduce or enlarge illustrations or copy is the *diagonal-line method.* It is a valuable aid to making design decisions. This method will be explained in Unit 14.

BALANCE. *Balance* is a visual effect. When type and illustrations are arranged in a pleasing way, a feeling of stability or equilibrium is conveyed. When elements are out of balance, the printed product may look top heavy or too heavy on the right or left.

There are two types of balance: *formal* and *informal.* Figure 10-2 shows a layout that is balanced formally. A center line drawn through this layout would cut each major element in half. Figure 10-3 is an informally balanced layout. Type and illustrations are not placed on a common center line. However, the layout still looks balanced. Elements appear to be in equilibrium.

Figure 10-2. *A formally balanced layout. Elements are visually cut in half by the center line.*

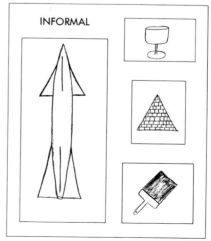

Figure 10-3. *An informally balanced layout. Elements are arranged so that they appear to be in a state of equilibrium.*

Optical and True Centers. Printing located at the vertical center of a piece of paper appears to be too low. Major type or illustration elements should not be placed at the *true center* of a page. Instead they should be raised approximately one-tenth the distance from the true center to the top of the page. This position is known as the *optical center.* It is the part of the page that the eye sees as being the center. Figure 10-4 shows the relationship between optical center and true center.

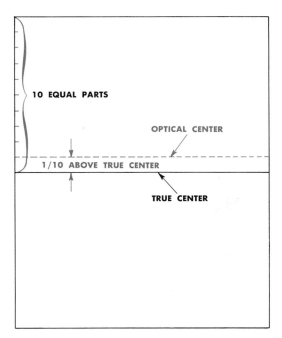

10 EQUAL PARTS

OPTICAL CENTER

1/10 ABOVE TRUE CENTER

TRUE CENTER

Figure 10-4. The relationship between the true center and the optical center of a page.

CONTRAST. Contrast provides emphasis to a word, a series of words, or an illustration. Contrast can also be used to relieve monotony in a printed message. Several ways of providing contrast are shown in Figure 10-5.

Change the size of the type.
Use CAPITAL letters.
Use SMALL CAPITAL letters.
Use *italic* type.
Add a different type face.
Underline one or more words.
Use symbols ◗ to direct the eye.
Alter type position.
Box the word.
Emphasize by adding color
Use reverse type.
Add screen tints.

Figure 10-5. Contrast is used to provide emphasis and relieve monotony in a printed message. (Type set by Typographic Sales, Inc.)

RHYTHM. Eye movement across a printed page may be slow or swift, left or right, upward or downward, flowing or jerky. We call this motion *rhythm.*

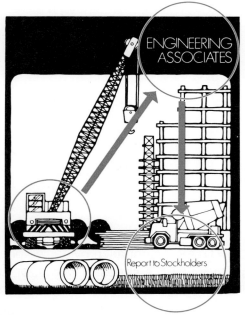

Figure 10-6. *Eye movement can be controlled through positioning type and illustration elements.*

It is possible to lead a reader's eye in a desired direction by placement of type and illustrations. Figure 10-6 shows how this is done.

UNITY. *Unity* is the harmonious relationship among the various type and illustration elements in a printed job.

Two or more typefaces should be combined in a single job only if they look right together. Typefaces with similar shapes and weights may be combined if done with care. Using several different type sizes and styles in a single layout distracts from the clarity of the message and should be avoided, Figure 10-7.

POOR
(7 DIFFERENT SIZES)

BETTER
(3 DIFFERENT SIZES)

Figure 10-7. *The use of a variety of type sizes and styles distracts from the clarity of the message.*

The use of illustrations of various sizes and shapes can also distract from the harmony of a job. Unity is achieved by using the same basic shape throughout, Figure 10-8.

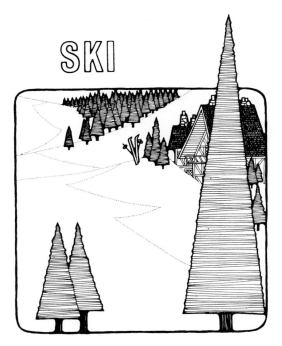

Figure 10-8. *Unity is achieved by using the same basic shape throughout the layout.*

COLOR. Selecting ink color and paper color for a printed job is part of the design process. We have already seen how color can be used to emphasize a word, a series of words, or an illustration. Color can do much more than just provide emphasis, however. Ink and paper colors can attract attention, hold attention, and even communicate directly with the viewer.

Color Attracts Attention. A visual message cannot be successfully sent if the intended receiver does not look at it. Color can be used to attract attention to the message. Bright colors, for example, will draw attention to billboards and posters that are read from a distance.

Color Holds Attention. Color also holds a viewer's attention over an extended period of time. Imagine trying to read a book whose text is printed with orange ink on red paper. Your head would probably begin to ache after only a very short time. Colors that are easiest on the eyes include dark green, blue, and violet.

Besides colors that are easy on the eyes, there should be sufficient contrast between paper color and ink color. Black or blue ink on white paper are the combinations most often used.

Color Communicates. Colors are classified as warm or cool. Red, orange, and yellow are considered *warm* colors. They are the colors of sun and fire. Blue, green and violet are considered *cool* colors. These are the colors of nature: blue water, green grass, and the violet darkness of night.

People are affected by color. Warm colors tend to excite people; cool colors tend to calm them down.

Besides affecting emotions, colors can communicate directly with people. Red, for example, may say stop! Red may indicate danger. Green, however, may say that all is well; it tells the viewer to continue. Colors can be used to communicate, so choose them with care.

TEST YOUR KNOWLEDGE

1. Describe what is meant by *design.*
2. List six principles of design.
3. List three factors in determining the size and shape of a printed page.
4. Describe the difference between formal and informal balance.
5. Identify three illustrations in this book that exhibit formal balance and three that show informal balance.
6. Clip a full page advertisement from a magazine or newspaper. Locate and label the true and optical centers on this page. Where are the major type and illustration elements located?
7. List twelve techniques that can be used to add contrast to a printed message for emphasis.
8. Find an advertisement in a newspaper or magazine that contains both type and illustration elements. Place a sheet of tracing paper over the ad and outline each major design element. Using Figure 10-6 as a model, record on the tracing paper the eye movement required to read the ad. Now cut the elements out of the ad and place them on a sheet of plain paper. Rearrange the elements and note the changes in eye movement that would be required of the reader.
9. Describe what is meant by *unity.*
10. List four reasons for adding color to a printed product.

UNIT 11

JOB PLANNING AND LAYOUT

Objectives

When you have completed this unit, you will be able to:

1. Identify the starting and end points of the product planning process.
2. List five questions that are used to gather information about a job to be printed.
3. Define *layout.*
4. List the four basic types of layouts.
5. Describe the function and characteristics of a thumbnail sketch.
6. Describe the function and characteristics of a rough layout.
7. Describe the function and characteristics of a comprehensive layout.
8. Define *pasteup.*
9. Use symbols to represent the type and illustrations included in a rough layout.
10. Describe the function and characteristics of a dummy.

Terms to Know

Here are some of the words you will need to understand before reading this unit. If the meaning of a word is not clear to you, look it up in the Glossary in the back of this book.

layout	comprehensive layout	reverses
thumbnail sketch	mechanical	dummy
rough layout	pasteup	

JOB PLANNING

Communication is conveying a message from one person or group to another. INTRODUCTION TO GRAPHIC ARTS deals with the use of printed images to convey these messages. Printing is the primary vehicle for communicating graphically, Figure 11-1.

Figure 11-1. *Printing is a vehicle for communicating graphically. These printed products carry messages from sender to receiver. (Sun Chemical Co.)*

Messages are printed in order to communicate. Printed messages may serve many different purposes. The specific purpose will depend upon the need of the individual or group that is communicating. For example, printed messages can be used to inform, influence, stimulate, question, and entertain.

Planning is essential to the printing process. Careful planning will enhance the effectiveness of the printed product. Planning will also contribute to efficient production.

THE PLANNING PROCESS. Planning is a process. It is an integral part of graphic communications. Planning begins with acquiring data about the job to be done. It results in a series of decisions relating to the printed product.

In order to plan effectively, accurate information is needed. One way to obtain this information is to ask questions of yourself and others involved in producing the printed product. Some information-gathering questions that should be asked are:

• What message is being transmitted?

• Why is it being transmitted?

• Does the type of message require a particular kind of treatment? For example, must it be dignified or can it be humorous?

• How will the finished product be used?

• What audience do you wish to reach?

Information gathered in this way will help you decide important questions relating to format, style, size, method, number, schedule, and cost:

• What form will the product take? Will it be a single sheet, a booklet, an entire book?
• Are illustrations to be used? Will they be line drawings, photographs, or a combination of both?
• What size will the finished product be?
• Will the sheets be trimmed, folded, perforated?
• Will the sheets be bound? How?
• By what method will the product be printed?
• What type of paper will be used? What color paper?
• Will colored inks be used? If so, what colors?
• How many copies will be printed? Will reprints be needed?

• How long will it take to complete the job?
• How much will it cost?

After these decisions have been made, the next step is to develop a graphic plan for the printed product. This plan is called a *layout*.

PREPARING THE LAYOUT

A layout is a graphic plan for a printed product. The layout shows the arrangement of type, illustrations, and other elements to be included. It also conveys information about how the job is to be printed.

LAYOUT SYMBOLS. A layout reflects the visual appearance of a job to be printed. It need not and generally does not contain the actual elements to be included in the final product. Symbols are often used to represent these elements. See Figure 11-2.

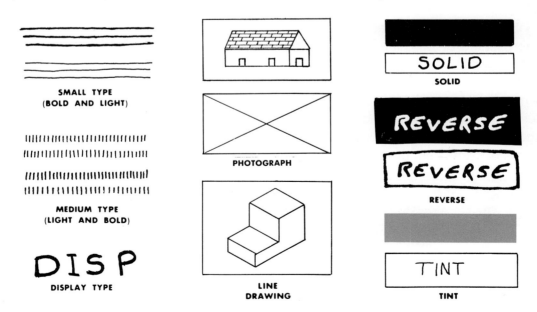

SMALL TYPE
(BOLD AND LIGHT)

MEDIUM TYPE
(LIGHT AND BOLD)

DISP

DISPLAY TYPE

PHOTOGRAPH

LINE
DRAWING

SOLID

SOLID

REVERSE

REVERSE

REVERSE

TINT

TINT

Figure 11-2. Symbols are used to represent the various elements included in a layout.

Type Matter. Parallel lines are generally used to represent small type (10 points or less). Medium type, 12 to 18 points in size, is usually depicted by a series of wavy lines. Words in 24-point type or larger are generally "roughed in" to size.

The weight of a typeface can be conveyed by the heaviness of the lines drawn. Spacing requirements can be suggested by changing the distance between the parallel or wavy lines.

Solids, Reverses and Tints. Solids may be represented in two ways. The solid area can be outlined and the word *solid* written in its center. A charcoal pencil may also be used to darken the solid area.

Reverses are treated in the same manner as solids. Either outline and label these areas or darken the reversed areas with a charcoal pencil.

Tints and shaded areas are usually represented by outlining or by shading with a pencil.

Photographs and Line Drawings. Illustrations can be indicated by outlining the areas they will occupy. Diagonal lines or sketches of the illustrations should be included in the outlined areas.

Colored Effects. Color can be represented in a layout with pastel chalks, colored pencils, or colored felt-tip pens.

LAYOUT TOOLS AND SUPPLIES. Items essential for preparing a layout are paper, pencils, a straightedge, a line gage, and a place to work. Two or three charcoal pencils of different hardness are especially useful. These pencils can be used to suggest not only the shape but also the tone of the printed image. Felt tip pens can also be used for this purpose.

Drafting instruments, especially a triangle, T-square, and drawing board are helpful. However, they are not absolutely essential for preparing a layout. Other useful items are a type catalog, a clip art book, an ink-color chart, and a variety of paper samples.

TYPES OF LAYOUTS

There are four basic types of layouts. They are the thumbnail sketch, the rough layout, the comprehensive layout, and the mechanical layout. Characteristics of the first three types of layouts are summarized in Figure 11-3.

MAJOR LAYOUTS					
TYPE	**FUNCTION**	**SIZE**	**CARE IN PREPARATION**	**COLORS**	**DEGREE OF REALISM**
THUMBNAIL	**TO EXPLORE AND DEVELOP IDEAS**	**REDUCED**	**NOT CRITICAL**	**ANY AVAILABLE**	**SUGGESTIVE**
ROUGH	**TO VISUALIZE SPACE AND TYPE RELATIONSHIPS**	**100%**	**REASONABLE**	**CLOSE AS CONVENIENT**	**APPROXIMATE**
COMPREHENSIVE	**TO SHOW FINISHED PRINTED PIECE**	**100%**	**EXPERT, GREAT DETAIL**	**EXACT PAPER AND INK**	**DUPLICATE FINISHED JOB**

Figure 11-3. *Layout characteristics.*

THUMBNAIL SKETCHES. *Thumbnail sketches* are used to explore and develop ideas. Thumbnail sketches are made rapidly to present overall design features rather than design details.

Thumbnail sketches are generally prepared in a reduced size that approximates the finished proportions of the printed product. Several thumbnail sketches are shown in Figure 11-4.

Figure 11-4. Thumbnail sketches are used to explore and develop ideas.

ROUGH LAYOUT. The *rough layout* is used to show space relationships among all elements in a printed job. It is made by refining the best of the thumbnail sketches.

A rough layout is drawn the same size as the finished job. It is more detailed than the thumbnail sketch. Large type is "roughed in." Small type is shown by drawing parallel lines about the same density that the type will be. The content of illustrations is suggested in and their positions are indicated.

A rough layout is illustrated in Figure 11-5. From this layout a printer could begin to put a simple job together. For more complex jobs, however, a more detail layout is needed.

Figure 11-5. The rough layout is used to show space relationships among all of the elements in a printed job.

COMPREHENSIVE LAYOUT. The *comprehensive layout* is a prototype of the proposed product. It should come as close as possible to duplicating the final product, even though actual type and illustrations are not yet available. Figure 11-6 shows a comprehensive layout.

Figure 11-6. *The comprehensive layout is a prototype of the proposed product. It serves as a guide or blueprint to those who produce the printed item.*

A comprehensive layout allows everyone involved with the product to see it before it is printed. It provides an opportunity to make final changes and serves as a guide or blueprint for the printer.

MECHANICAL LAYOUT. The *mechanical layout,* or *pasteup* as it is sometimes called, is an exact duplicate of the printed job. It contains the actual illustrations used. Type matter is also included. Figure 11-7 shows a mechanical layout.

A mechanical layout is very expensive to produce. It can be prepared only after

---

ART PREPARATION AND PHOTOGRAPHY/UNIT 15

CREATING, OBTAINING, AND USING PHOTOGRAPHS/UNIT 15

Focusing is accomplished with a lens. The lens is probably the most important part of the enlarger. It is usually connected to the enlarger head with an accordian-like bellows. The distance between the lens and negative is adjusted to focus the image. Most lenses come equipped with a built-in diaphragm for controlling aperture size.

Raising or lowering the head of the enlarger adjusts the distance between the light and the paper. This adjustment is usually made with a hand crank in order to vary the size of the projected image.

Exposing the Projection Print. First, thoroughly clean the enlarger. Remove all traces of dust and dirt from the negative, the negative carrier, and the lens.

Turn off the room lights and turn on the safelights before you load and expose photographic paper. Be sure the filters in the safelight are correct for the paper being used.

Insert the negative in the negative carrier, emulsion side face down toward the lens.

(15-35)

Figure 15-35. A photographic easel. (Brodhead-Garrett Co.)

An easel is used to hold the light-sensitive paper during exposure, Figure 15-35. Adjust the easel to the size of the desired enlargement. Then cut a piece of plain white paper to the size of the desired print. Insert this paper into the easel and position the easel on the base of the enlarger. Adjust and focus the image on the plain, white paper prior to exposing the photographic paper.

Open the lens to the widest aperture and turn the enlarging lamp on. Raise or lower the head of the enlarger until the image is the correct size. Focus until the image is sharp and clear. If the size of the image changes, readjust the head and refocus. When the image is the correct size and in focus, close the lens

diaphragm until fine detail just begins to disappear but still remains visible.

Determining Exposure Time. Use a 1-inch strip of photographic paper from a sheet of the same type that will be used for the projection print. Remove the plain, white paper from the easel and replace it with the light-sensitive strip. Be sure the emulsion (shiny) side of the photographic paper faces up toward the lens.

Expose the test strip as follows. Turn on the enlarger and expose the entire strip for five seconds. Then cover one quarter of the strip with opaque cardboard and expose for five more seconds. Move the cardboard to the midpoint of the strip and expose the uncovered half for an additional ten seconds. Finally, move the cardboard to cover three

quarters of the test strip and expose for twenty more seconds. A test strip prepared in this way is pictured in Figure 15-36. The four sections of the strip represent exposures of five, ten, twenty, and forty seconds.

Process the test strip in the same way as described for contact prints. Once the proper exposure has been determined, full-size projection prints can be made.

(15-36)

Figure 15-36. A test strip is made in order to determine correct exposure time for each enlargement.

114

115

Figure 11-7. *A mechanical is an exact duplicate of the job to be printed. It contains all type, illustrations, and ornamentation.*

all type, illustrations and ornamentation are ready. Procedures for preparing mechanical layouts are described in Unit 19.

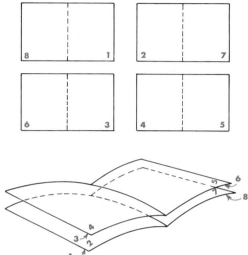

Figure 11-8. *An eight-page booklet. Note the location of each page.*

MULTI-PAGE LAYOUTS

Dummy layouts indicate the general design and content of booklets, pamphlets, or any other multi-page printed product. The dummy shows the size, shape, form, and general style of such products.

To prepare a dummy layout, sheets of paper are first folded to obtain the desired number and size of pages. The pages are then numbered. An eight-page booklet can be made by folding two sheets of paper as shown in Figure 11-8. Finally, page layouts are attached to these blank pages to form the dummy layout.

TEST YOUR KNOWLEDGE

1. Identify the starting and end points of the product planning process.
2. Prepare a list of five questions for gathering information to be used in planning the production of a printed product.
3. Describe what is meant by *layout*.
4. List four basic types of layouts.
5. Explain the function and characteristics of a thumbnail sketch.
6. Explain the function and characteristics of a rough layout.
7. Explain the function and characteristics of a comprehensive layout.
8. Describe what is meant by *pasteup*.
9. Prepare a rough layout for a one-page, 8½″ × 11″ flyer that will advertise a product of your choice. The layout should contain both type and illustration elements. Use the symbols in Figure 11-2 to represent these elements.
10. Explain the function and characteristics of a dummy.

SECTION 4

MANUSCRIPT PREPARATION AND TYPOGRAPHY

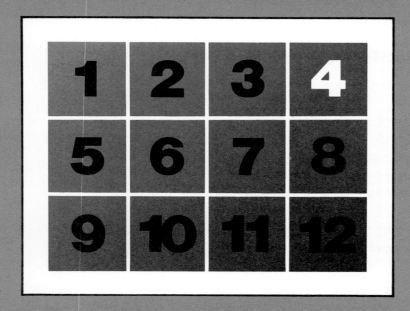

UNIT 12

TYPE, TYPEFACES, TYPE MEASUREMENT, AND TYPOGRAPHY

Objectives

When you have completed this unit, you will be able to:

1. Explain the difference between hot type and cold type composition methods.
2. List three kinds of hot type.
3. Describe three techniques for generating cold type.
4. Identify the six major classes or styles of type.
5. Select appropriate typefaces for six different printed products.
6. Describe the relationship among the units of measurement that comprise the printer's point system.
7. Identify ascender and descender letters.
8. Define *typography*.
9. Describe what is meant by a font, a series, and a family of type.

Terms to Know

Here are some of the words you will need to understand before reading this unit. If the meaning of a word is not clear to you, look it up in the Glossary in the back of this book.

hot type composition	typeface	roman type	novelty type
cold type composition	body	serif	point system
foundry type	text type	sans serif type	point
Linotype	Old English	square serif type	pica
Monotype	blackletter	script type	line gage

TYPE

As we have seen in Unit 9, symbols, photographs, and drawings are used to convert thoughts and ideas of the message sender into visual form. Type provides the means for including symbols in a visual message. Letters of the alphabet and numbers are the most important of these symbols. They are the communication link between sender and receiver.

The two basic methods of composing type for graphic communication are: hot type composition and cold type composition.

HOT TYPE COMPOSITION. In general, hot-type composition methods employ type made from molten metal. Multiple copies of a message can be printed directly from hot type. Handset foundry type, Figure 12-1, is considered hot type. Linotype slugs containing an entire line of symbols on a single body and machine-set monotype also fall into the hot type category. A linotype slug is shown in Figure 12-2. Hot type composition methods are discussed in detail in Unit 16.

COLD TYPE COMPOSITION. Letters and numbers produced by cold type

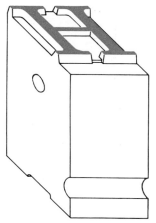

Figure 12-1. Foundry type is used for hot type composition.

Figure 12-2. A Linotype slug contains an entire line of symbols on a single body. Linotype is a hot type composition method.

composition methods are not made from molten metal. Cold type symbols can be produced in three ways:

1. By hand-assembling preprinted paper and plastic letters. Figure 12-3 illustrates one kind of preprinted alphabet.

Figure 12-3. *A preprinted alphabet used for cold type composition. (Zipatone Inc.)*

Figure 12-5. *The StripPrinter. Symbols are generated on photographic paper through a strip of plastic containing characters in negative form. (StripPrinter, Inc.)*

Techniques for hand assembling a variety of types of preprinted alphabets are covered in Unit 17. Typewriter composition is also discussed in Unit 17. Unit 18 describes how photographic cold type composing machines are used.

TYPEFACES

Originally the term *face* referred to the printing surface of a piece of hot type. That face determined the size and characteristics of the printed symbol, Figure 12-6.

Today the term *face* refers to the specific, unique characteristics of each

Figure 12-4. *An IBM Selectric Composing typewriter used for cold type composition. Typing elements (arrow) can be changed to provide different typefaces. (IBM Office Products Division)*

2. By using a typewriter. A commonly used cold type composition typewriter is shown in Figure 12-4.

3. By photographic techniques. Figure 12-5 shows a machine capable of composing type by photographic means. Symbols are generated on photographic paper by exposing the paper through a strip of plastic which contains characters in negative form.

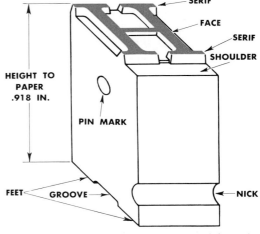

Figure 12-6. *Parts of a piece of foundry type.*

style of type, hot or cold. Each typeface has a name by which it is identified in graphic arts and printing industries.

A printer has many typefaces from which to choose. Although thousands of typefaces exist, all can be categorized into six major classes or styles: text, roman, sans serif, square serif, script and novelty.

TEXT TYPE. Text typefaces, Figure 12-7, are difficult to read. Letter shapes resemble the hand-drawn letters of early scribes. Text type is also called *Old English* and *Blackletter.* These faces connote a feeling of age, reverence, and formality. Text type should never be set in all capital letters. Such a message would be almost impossible to read.

𝕰𝖓𝖌𝖗𝖆𝖛𝖊𝖗𝖘 𝕺𝖑𝖉 𝕰𝖓𝖌𝖑𝖎𝖘𝖍
𝕬𝕭𝕮𝕯𝕰𝕱𝕲𝕳𝕴𝕵𝕶

𝕮𝖑𝖔𝖎𝖘𝖙𝖊𝖗 𝕭𝖑𝖆𝖈𝖐
𝕬𝕭𝕮𝕯𝕰𝕱𝕲𝕳𝕴𝕵𝕶𝕷𝕸

Figure 12-7. *Common text typefaces. (Typographic Sales, Inc.)*

ROMAN TYPE. Roman typefaces are generally easy to read. There are three different styles of roman type: oldstyle, modern, and transitional. Each is characterized by the shape of its serifs and the thick and thin strokes that make up its symbols. *Serifs* are short crosslines located at the ends of the main strokes.

Several kinds of serifs are shown in Figure 12-8.

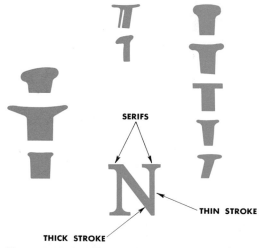

Figure 12-8. *Examples of various serifs. Serifs are the short crosslines located at the ends of main strokes.*

Oldstyle Faces. The oldstyle roman faces, Figure 12-9, are patterned after letters used in early roman inscriptions. They are open, rounded and very readable. The contrast between thin and thick strokes is only moderate. Serifs are pointed.

GARAMOND BOLD abc

COCHIN 1234567890 ab

GOUDY Old Style abcde

TRUMP MEDIAEVAL

Figure 12-9. *Oldstyle roman typefaces. (Typographic Sales, Inc.)*

Modern Faces. The term *modern* refers to a style of roman faces designed approximately 200 years ago. Letters are quite readable. There is extreme contrast between thin and thick strokes.

Serifs are generally thin and delicate. Modern roman faces are shown in Figure 12-10.

BAUER BODONI BOLD a

MELIOR 1234567890 a

AMERICANA BOLD 1

BAUER BODONI Italic

Figure 12-10. *Modern roman typefaces. (Typographic Sales, Inc.)*

Transitional Faces. These faces fall halfway between oldstyle and modern in terms of contrast between thin and thick strokes. Transitional roman faces are shown in Figure 12-11.

BASKERVILLE 123456

CLARENDON abcdef

CALEDONIA 12345678

Century Schoolbook 12

Figure 12-11. *Transitional roman typefaces. (Typographic Sales, Inc.)*

SANS SERIF TYPE. Sans serif typefaces do not have serifs at the ends of their main strokes, Figure 12-12. There is little variation in the thickness and weight of letter strokes. Uniform strokes are used throughout.

FUTURA LIGHT 12345

SPARTAN BOLD 123456

HELVETICA 1234567

Gil Sans Italic 123 abcdefgh

Figure 12-12. *Sans serif typefaces do not have serifs. There is little variation in the thickness of letterstrokes. (Typographic Sales, Inc.)*

Sans serif typefaces are popular today. They are used in headlines, captions, and even in the body of books and magazines. They work well wherever simplicity of design is desired.

SQUARE SERIF TYPE. Square serif typefaces, Figure 12-13, are geometric in design. Letters are made from uniform strokes. Square serifs are added to the ends of strokes.

SERIFA 1234567890 a

STYMIE EXTRA Bold

LYONS EGYPTIAN ABCD

Figure 12-13. *Examples of square serif typefaces. (Typographic Sales, Inc.)*

Square serif typefaces are used mainly for headlines, advertisements, and short pieces of reading matter. They should not be used where large amounts of copy must be read.

SCRIPT TYPE. Script typefaces resemble handwriting, Figure 12-14. Like handwriting, script type is characterized by variety in the thickness of character strokes.

Script type is also referred to as *cursive* type. Script faces are used to produce special effects. They are also appropriate for invitations and announcements.

Script type should never be composed in all capital letters. It would be very diffi-

Figure 12-14. *Script typefaces resemble handwriting and hand lettering. (Typograpic Sales, Inc.)*

cult to read a message set in this manner.

NOVELTY TYPE. Novelty typefaces are also called *decorative* typefaces, Figure 12-15. They are usually used to get attention or to establish a mood. Some faces attract attention by their boldness. They are very useful in advertising. Others affect the mood of the receiver. For example, they may make him happy or sad.

Figure 12-15. *Novelty typefaces can be used to get the receiver's attention and to establish a mood. (Typographic Sales, Inc.)*

TYPE MEASUREMENT

Our linear system of measurement using inches and fractions of inches is not used to measure type. It is too cumbersome. Instead a specially developed system of measurement is used. It is called the *point system* of measuring type.

POINT SYSTEM. The basic unit of the point system is the *point.* One point is equivalent to $1/72$ inch. There are 72 points in one inch.

Twelve points equal one *pica*. Six picas, then, equal one inch. A half of a pica (6 points) is called a *nonpareil*. There are 12 nonpareils in an inch.

In addition to points and picas, newspaper printers commonly use a measurement called an *agate*. One agate is equal to 5½ points. Figure 12-16 shows the relationship among the units comprising the printer's point system and the linear inch.

```
            1 POINT = 1/72 INCH
            1 INCH = 72 POINTS
        12 POINTS = 1 PICA
          6 PICAS = 1 INCH
6 POINTS (1/2 PICA) = 1 NONPAREIL
      5 1/2 POINTS = 1 AGATE
```

Figure 12-16. *The printer's point system of measurement.*

LINE GAGE. A *line gage* is a printer's ruler. It is used to determine point and pica measurement. A line gage is pictured in Figure 12-17. Note that it contains two scales, an inch scale and a nonpareil/pica scale. Some line gages contain an agate scale as well.

TYPE SIZES. Type is measured in points. The common sizes of type range from six through 72 point. Other sizes are available, however.

Type larger than 72 points is sized by the *line*. A line is equal to 12 points. A piece of 8-line headline type measures 8 picas or 96 points high.

Hot Type Size. The body of a piece of type determines its size. The relationship between type body and typeface is shown in Figure 12-18. Common type

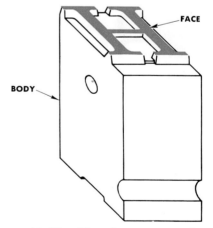

Figure 12-18. *The face on a piece of foundry type is always smaller than the type body.*

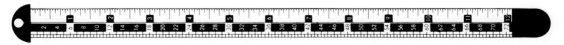

Figure 12-17. *A line gage is a printer's ruler. Note the scales that are included.*

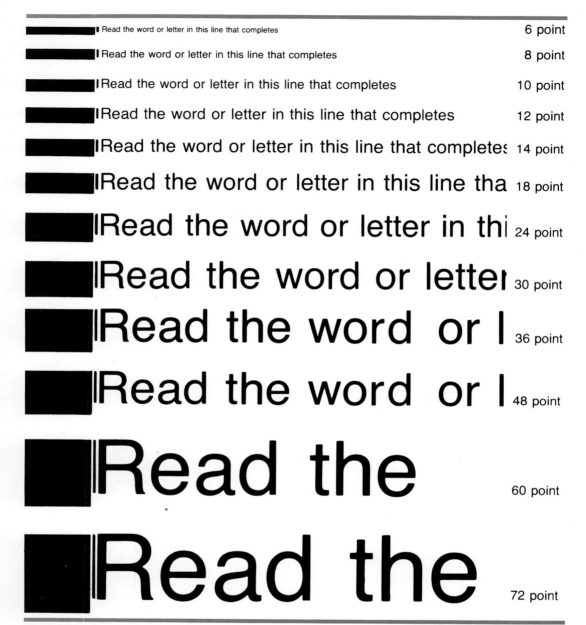

Read the word or letter in this line that completes — 6 point

Read the word or letter in this line that completes — 8 point

Read the word or letter in this line that completes — 10 point

Read the word or letter in this line that completes — 12 point

Read the word or letter in this line that completes — 14 point

Read the word or letter in this line tha — 18 point

Read the word or letter in thi — 24 point

Read the word or letter — 30 point

Read the word or l — 36 point

Read the word or l — 48 point

Read the — 60 point

Read the — 72 point

Figure 12-19. Common type sizes. Point size designates the body of the type on which the character sits. (Typographic Sales, Inc.)

sizes are pictured in Figure 12-19. Note that letters are smaller than the actual body size.

Cold Type Size. Several sizes of cold type are shown in Figure 12-20. Cold type size is determined by measuring from the top of a tall *ascender* letter to the bottom of a *descender* letter. Ascender letters are b, d, f, h, k, l, and t. Descender letters are g, j, p, and q.

TYPOGRAPHY

Typography refers to the overall design of the printed page. It deals mostly with the selection and arrangement of type elements. A designer or printer skilled in typography is called a typographer.

A typographer must understand several terms relating to type, typefaces, and type measurement. In addition to those already covered in this unit are the terms *font, series, family, legibility, readability,* and *appropriateness.*

FONT. A *font* is a complete assortment of characters of one size and style of type. A font of type includes capital and lowercase letters, numbers, and punctuation marks. An example of a type font is 30 point century schoolbook bold, Figure 12-21.

GRAPHIC A
GRAPHIC AR1
GRAPHIC ARTS
GRAPHIC ARTS
GRAPHIC ARTS

Figure 12-20. *Cold type comes in various sizes.*

Century Schoolbook Bold
ABCDEFGHIJKLMNOPQRS
TUVWXYZ&.,:;"''"!?()-abcdef
ghijklmnopqrstuvwxyz
$1234567890

Figure 12-21. *A font of type includes capital and lowercase letters, numbers, and punctuation marks of one size and style. (Typographic Sales, Inc.)*

Figure 12-22. *A particular type style available in several sizes is called a type series. (Typographic Sales, Inc.)*

SERIES. The term *series* is used when a type style is available in several sizes. All available sizes of the font shown in Figure 12-22 make up a type series.

FAMILY. A *family* is a group of related typefaces. Each member of a type family has the same basic name. Members also have the same general design characteristics. They differ, however, in the weight of the face, the amount of space allotted to each character, and the angle of each character. Members of a typical family are pictured in Figure 12-23.

LEGIBILITY. *Legibility* refers to the speed with which a type character can be identified by the reader. Some typefaces are more legible than others. For example, roman type characters are generally easier to identify than are square serif characters.

Anyone responsive to the beauty of fine typography will appreciate the flexibility of spacing offered by Alphatype. ABCDEFGHIJKLMNOPQRSTUVWXYZ

Trade Gothic

Anyone responsive to the beauty of fine typography will appreciate the flexibility of spacing offered by Alphatype. ABCDEFGHIJKLMNOPQRSTUVWXYZ

Trade Gothic Italic

Anyone responsive to the beauty of fine typography will appreciate the flexibility of spacing offered by Alphatype. ABCDEFGHIJKLMNOPQRSTUVWXYZ1234

Trade Gothic Bold

Anyone responsive to the beauty of fine typography will appriciate the flexibility of spacing which is offered by the Alphatype system. ABCDEFGHIJKLMNOPQRSTUVWXYZ12345

Trade Gothic Condensed

Anyone responsive to the beauty of fine typography will appreciate the flexiblity of spacing which is offered by the Alphatype system. ABCDEFGHIJKLMNOPQRSTUVWXYZ1234

Trade Gothic Bold Condensed

Figure 12-23. *A family is a group of related typefaces. (Typographic Sales, Inc.)*

READABILITY. *Readability* refers to the ease with which a printed page can be read. Some typefaces are easy on the eyes. They can be read for long periods of time without tiring the reader's eyes. The readability of a page also depends upon the arrangement of type used and the amount of white space on the page.

APPROPRIATENESS. The *appropriateness* of a typeface for a particular job is determined by the intended message and the intended audience. Some typefaces are said to talk; others shout. Some faces make us think of antiquity; others convey the impression of newness. In addition, characteristics such as masculinity, femininity, and formality can be suggested by the typeface used.

TEST YOUR KNOWLEDGE

1. Describe the difference between hot type composition and cold type composition.
2. List three kinds of hot type.
3. Identify three techniques available for producing cold type.
4. Using newspapers and old magazines, locate an example of each of the six major classes or styles of type. Clip these examples and paste them in your notebook. Label each type style.
5. Select an appropriate typeface for each of the following: poster headline, invitation to a party, business card, newspaper headline, textbook page, church program. Select the typefaces from those pictured in this unit.
6. With a chart, show the relationship among the units of measurement in the printer's point system.
7. Identify seven ascender letters and four descender letters.
8. Describe what is meant by *typography.*
9. Define the terms *typefont, type series,* and *type family.*

UNIT 13

PREPARING COPY FOR THE COMPOSITOR

Objectives

When you have completed this unit, you will be able to:

1. Explain the meaning of specifications that have been added to a manuscript page.
2. Define *copyfitting*.
3. Calculate the number of typeset lines that a manuscript page will fill.
4. Identify the three categories of errors that are discovered by proofreading.
5. Use standard proofreading marks to indicate changes and corrections that have to be made to a manuscript.

Terms to Know

Here are some of the words you will need to understand before reading this unit. If the meaning of a word is not clear to you, look it up in the Glossary in the back of this book.

copy	leading	em
manuscript	typeface	copyfitting
type size	measure	proofreader's marks

COPY PREPARATION

Copy is the manuscript that is furnished to a compositor. The compositor then composes or sets the copy in type. Careful preparation of the manuscript will help insure that the type is set correctly.

MANUSCRIPT FORM. The form of the manuscript that is submitted to the compositor should meet certain physical requirements. Use good quality 8½″ × 11″ bond paper. Type on one side of the sheet only. Double space and leave wide margins. Corrections should be typed or made neatly in ink. Be sure to number and identify all manuscript pages.

MANUSCRIPT SPECIFICATIONS. Specifications for type size, typeface, and measure must be clearly written on the manuscript. Specifications controlling the arrangement of type and instructions for changing typefaces should also be given. Figure 13-1 illustrates a manuscript page with specifications added.

Type Size. The size of the type and amount of leading (vertical space between lines) should be indicated. This is done by using two numbers separated by a slash. For example, 10/12 (read "10 on 12") means that 10 point type will be printed within 12 points of vertical space. This leaves 2 points of space between each line of type. Type set 8/9 (8 on 9) means 8 point type with one point of space between lines.

Typeface. In manuscript specifications always give the complete name of the typeface selected.

Measure. *Measure* means the width to which the line of type is set. Line width (measure) is usually given in picas.

Arrangement of Type. Paragraph indentions are indicated in *ems* of the type size. An em is equal to the square of the type size being used. A 10 point em, then, measures 10 points square. A 12 point em measures 12 points on each side.

Specifications to position headings must also be given. The compositor must be told to set the heading flush left, flush right or on center.

Changing Typefaces. Instructions to the compositor for changing typefaces include:

1. Underscoring a word or words once means set the underscored in *italic*.

2. Underscoring a word or words twice means set it in SMALL CAPS.

3. Three underscores mean set in all CAPITALS.

4. A wavy underscore means set in **boldface**.

Planographic or Lithographic Printing

☐☐☐You have already learned how printing can be done from a raised surface and from a lowered surface. Do you think it's possible to print from a flat surface? The answer is yes. Planographic and lithographic are terms used to describe such methods of printing.

☐☐☐ Lithographic printing is based on the principle that grease and water do not mix, Figure 5-1. The process works this way. First, a greasy image is placed on a flat plate. The image may be drawn directly on the plate with a grease pencil or it may be placed on the plate by photographic means. Next, water is applied to the plate. This water will cover the non-image area of the plate. The water will not cover the greasy image because water and grease do not mix! The entire plate is then coated with ink. Ink is a greasy substance and adheres to the greasy image. The ink does not adhere to the wet portions of the plate because grease and water do not mix! Paper is then pressed against the surface of the plate and the inked image is transferred to the paper, Figure 5-2. Two planographic printing methods are shown in Figures 5-3 and 5-4.

Offset Printing

Note to Compositor
10/12 Century Schoolbook
20 Pica Measure

Figure 13-1. *Specifications have been added to this manuscript page. These specifications serve as instructions to the compositor.*

COPYFITTING

Copyfitting is a technique to determine before typesetting if copy will fit into a given area. With copyfitting, a typographer can get a good idea as to what typeface and type size to use in order to fill available space.

Copyfitting consists of two steps: copy measurement and type calculation.

COPY MEASUREMENT. Copy measurement involves counting the number of characters in a typewritten manuscript. Punctuation marks and spaces

Elite types |12 characters per inch

Pica types| 10 characters per

Figure 13-2. *The relationship between elite and pica type. Note the size of each typewriter character.*

are also included in the character count.

A regular ruler can simplify counting characters. Generally, either an elite or a pica typewriter is used to prepare manuscript copy. Copy typed on an elite machine measures twelve characters per inch. Pica typewriters type ten characters per inch. Spacing between words on both machines is equal to a single character. Figure 13-2 shows the relationship between elite and pica type. An accurate character count can be determined by measuring the length of each manuscript line.

TYPE CALCULATION. The result of the character count is used to calculate the number of typeset lines the manuscript will fill. Type specimen books are used for this purpose. Type books often list the number of characters per pica for all sizes of common typefaces. Examples are included in Figure 13-3.

12 pt. Times Roman (194)

ABCDEFGHIJKLMNOPQRSTUVWXYZ& ABCDEFGH
abcdefghijklmnopqrstuvwxyz abcdefghijklmn 1234567890
( ) fi fl ⅛ ¼ ⅜ ½ ⅝ ¾ ⅞ — & ? ! $, . ; : ' ' - /

2.36 charactrers per pica

10 pt. Times Roman (194)

ABCDEFGHIJKLMNOPQRSTUVWXYZ& ABCDEFGHIJKLMNOP
abcdefghijklmnopqrstuvwxyz abcdefghijklmnopqrstuvwxy 1234567890
( ) fi fl ⅛ ¼ ⅜ ½ ⅝ ¾ ⅞ — & ? ! , . ; : ' ' - /

2.80 characters per pica

8 pt. Times Roman (194)

ABCDEFGHIJKLMNORQRSTUVWXYZ& ABCDEFGHIJKLMNOPQRSTUVWXYZ
abcdefghijklmnopqrstuvwxy abcdefghijklmnopqrstuvwxy abcdefghijklmnop 1234567890
( ) fi fl ⅛ ¼ ⅜ ½ ⅝ ¾ ⅞ — & ? ! , . ; : ' ' - /

3.40 characters per pica

Figure 13-3. *Type specimen books list the number of characters per pica for all sizes of the common typefaces. (Typographic Sales, Inc.)*

Multiply the number of characters per pica by the width or measure of the line (in picas) to find the number of characters that will be contained in each printed line of type. Charts such as the one shown in Figure 13-4 are also available for this purpose.

By dividing the total number of characters in the manuscript by the number of characters in a single typeset line, you can determine the number of printed lines the copy will fill. The amount of vertical space needed is easily calculated by multiplying the point size of the type plus the leading (in points) by the total number of lines to be set.

Once the total vertical space requirement is known, we can determine whether or not the copy will fit into the

space that is available. Adjustments can be made by either changing type size and/or typeface or by changing the amount of leading between lines. Cutting or adding to the manuscript provides another means of adjustment.

PROOFREADING
Proofreading is done both before and after a manuscript is set in type. The purpose of proofreading is to discover errors and mark them for correction.

DISCOVERING ERRORS. Errors generally fall into three categories: typographical, spelling and punctuation, and grammar.

Typographical Errors. These are mistakes made by the typist who prepared the manuscript. For example, *an* instead of *and* or *thsi* instead of *this*.

Spelling and Punctuation Errors. These mistakes can be attributed to the author. Some words may be misspelled. There may be sentences that are punctuated incorrectly.

Errors in Grammar. Grammar errors reflect improper use of the language. The author may have disregarded rules of correct grammar or may have poorly structured sentences.

HELVETICA CHARACTER COUNT PER PICA						
PICAS	**SIZE IN POINTS**					
	6	**7**	**8**	**9**	**10**	**12**
10	35	33	31	28	24	21
12	42	39	37	34	29	25
14	49	46	44	40	34	29
16	56	52	51	45	39	34
18	63	59	56	51	44	38
20	70	66	62	56	48	42
22	77	72	68	62	53	46
24	84	78	74	68	58	50
26	91	84	81	74	63	54
28	98	92	88	79	68	58
30	105	99	93	84	72	63

Figure 13-4. *A chart for determining the number of characters of Helvetica type contained in line widths from 10 through 30 picas.*

PROOFREADING MARKS. Standard proofreading marks are used to indicate changes and corrections to be made by the compositor. Common proofreading marks are illustrated and explained in Figure 13-5.

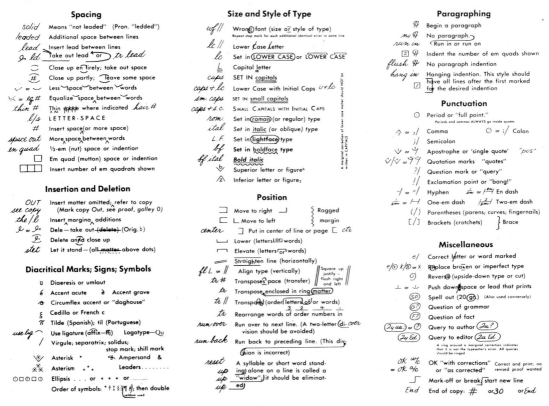

Figure 13-5. *Common proofreading marks.*

TEST YOUR KNOWLEDGE

1. Explain the meaning of each of the specifications that have been added to the manuscript page pictured in Figure 13-1.
2. Describe what is meant by *copyfitting.*
3. Count the number of characters on the manuscript page shown in Figure 13-1. Use a ruler for this purpose. Now calculate the number of typeset lines that this manuscript page will fill when set in 10 point Century Schoolbook (2.70 characters per pica). The measure of typeset line will be 20 picas.
4. Identify three categories of errors found by proofreading.
5. Proofread a page in your notebook. Use standard proofreading marks to indicate changes and corrections that need to be made.

SECTION 5

ART PREPARATION AND PHOTOGRAPHY

UNIT 14

CREATING, OBTAINING, AND USING DRAWINGS

Objectives

When you have completed this unit, you will be able to:

1. Define *pictorial drawings*.
2. Outline the procedures for creating pictorial drawings.
3. Define *technical drawings*.
4. List the materials and tools used to prepare technical drawings.
5. Prepare a three-view orthographic projection from a pictorial drawing.
6. Prepare a pictorial technical drawing from a three-view orthographic projection.
7. Define *clip art*.
8. Describe how to crop an illustration.

Terms to Know

Here are some of the words you will need to understand before reading this unit. If the meaning of a word is not clear to you, look it up in the Glossary in the back of this book.

pictorial drawings	mechanical drawing	pasteup
technical illustrations	clip art	diagonal-line method
scaling	cropping	proportional scale

CREATING DRAWINGS

Drawings are pictures used to communicate graphically. They are created to add clarity or interest to a visual message. In certain situations, illustrations express the sender's ideas more effectively than words.

Drawings may be either pictorial or technical.

PICTORIAL DRAWINGS. *Pictorial drawings* are usually prepared by artists using freehand techniques. They are created on white paper with black ink. Generally, specialized drawing instruments are not needed for pictorial drawings, Figure 14-1.

Materials and Tools. A good quality white paper or board should be used to

Figure 14-1. *A pictorial drawing. It was prepared by an artist using freehand techniques.*

prepare the picture. Paper can influence the quality of a drawing. Avoid uncoated papers. They tend to absorb ink and give a ragged edge to an inked line. Coated stock gives a clean, sharp line.

Use light-blue pencils to make guidelines and notes. Press lightly on the pencil. You do not have to erase guidelines and notes prepared in this manner. Light-blue lines do not photograph. They are seen by film as though they were white. The reason for this is explained in Unit 19.

Inking pens and felt-tip pens are used to draw opaque black lines. Pencil images should be avoided because they do not photograph well. Small paint brushes and a good quality black drawing ink can be used to fill in large areas or create special effects.

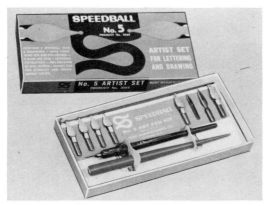

Figure 14-2. *A set of interchangeable pen points used for freehand lettering and sketching. (Hunt Manufacturing Co.)*

A set of interchangeable pen points for freehand lettering and sketching is shown in Figure 14-2. The points can be changed to control line width. A ruling pen is pictured in Figure 14-3. It can also be used with several different points.

Freehand Drawing Techniques. An outline of procedures for creating pictorial drawings is provided in the following paragraphs.

Determine the Message. A good illustrator is able to create drawings that present accurate visual messages. To do this the artist must fully understand the material to be illustrated. Discussions with the message sender are quite helpful. Reading the text associated with the illustration is also a must. In addition, the artist should know how the printed product will be used and who will be using it.

Prepare Sketches. It is often a good idea to explore possible ways of illustrating the text material by preparing several rough pencil sketches. Additional details can then be pencilled in on the most promising sketches. The best sketch is then selected.

Figure 14-3. *This ruling pen comes with interchangeable points for controlling line width. (Koh-I-Noor Rapidograph, Inc.)*

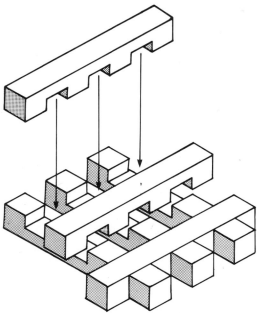

Figure 14-4. *A technical drawing. It was prepared with the aid of drawing instruments.*

Size the Illustration. The illustration must be prepared to fit the space allotted to it. Generally, the layout for the product is prepared larger than the final product. This allows the layout to be reduced by a photographer. Photographic reduction makes errors and poor quality lines less noticeable. Be sure your illustration is the proper size.

Create the Artwork. Pictures can be drawn directly in ink. It is often easier, however, to draw the illustrations first in pencil. Pencil lines can be drawn and erased if necessary.

If a light-blue pencil is used, stray marks or guidelines do not have to be erased. Light-blue lines do not photograph.

After the pencil drawing is complete, trace the lines with ink. Use a pen with good quality, opaque black ink.

TECHNICAL DRAWINGS. *Technical drawings* are usually prepared with drawing instruments. Often these illustrations are included in service and operation manuals to show parts and assemblies. Figure 14-4 shows a technical drawing.

Materials and Tools. A variety of additional tools is used to create technical illustrations.

A drawing board or a light table is essential for copy preparation. In addition, a T-square is needed for drawing horizontal lines. A drawing board and a T-square are pictured in Figure 14-5. A scale for measuring, Figure 14-6, is also helpful.

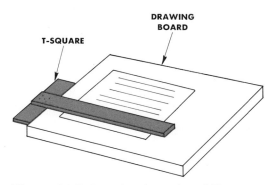

Figure 14-5. *Drawing board and T-square.*

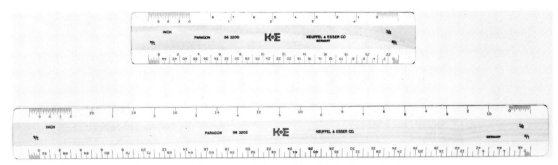

Figure 14-6. *A scale is used for measuring. (Keuffel & Esser Co.)*

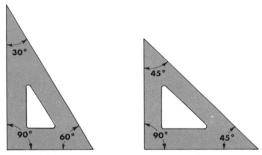

Figure 14-7. *A 45° or a 30°-60°-90° triangle is used to draw vertical and sloping lines.*

Along with a T-square, triangles are used to draw vertical and slanted lines. Figure 14-7 shows a 45° and a 30°-60°-90° triangle. Irregular curved lines are made with french curves, Figure 14-8.

Drawing instruments are used to make arcs and circles. A set of instruments including compasses, dividers, and ruling pens is shown in Figure 14-9.

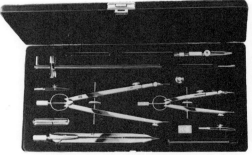

Figure 14-9. *A set of drawing instruments includes compasses, dividers, and ruling pens. (Keuffel & Esser Co.)*

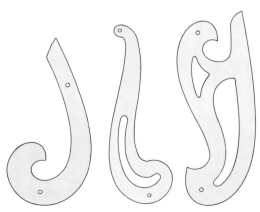

Figure 14-8. *French curves are used to produce curved lines.*

Mechanical Drawing Techniques. Technical drawings prepared with

Sometimes only two views are required to completely illustrate the size and shape of an object, Figure 14-11. Note how dashed lines are used to indicate lines present but not visible in a view.

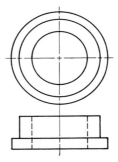

Figure 14-11. A two-view orthographic projection. Dashes are used to indicate hidden lines.

instruments are called mechanical drawings. The three basic types of mechanical drawings are: orthographic projection, pictorial, and schematic.

Orthographic Projection. Orthographic projection is used to show accurate details and dimensions of an object. This is done by showing different views of the object. Top, front, back, bottom, and left and right sides can be shown. Normally, though, only those views needed to completely picture the object are provided. This can usually be done in three views: top, front, and right side. A three-view orthographic projection is shown in Figure 14-10.

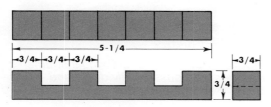

ORTHOGRAPHIC PROJECTION

Figure 14-10. A three-view orthographic projection.

Pictorial. Pictorial technical drawings show an object in three dimensions. The object is pictured as if it were photographed. The basic types of pictorial technical drawings are perspective, isometric, and oblique drawings.

Perspective drawings show the object as it would actually appear. Parts of the object in the foreground are larger than those in the background. Lines showing depth are not parallel, but rather, they converge. Figure 14-12 is a perspective drawing.

Isometric drawings also show three adjacent faces of the object pictured. They do not, however, show the object exactly

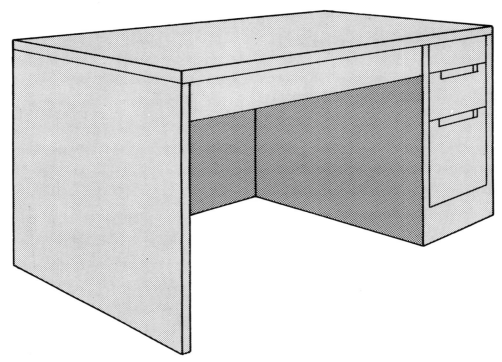

Figure 14-12. *A perspective drawing. The object is shown as it would actually appear to the eye.*

as it would appear to the eye. All sides of the object are shown in true size and shape. Lines do not converge. Figure 14-13 shows an isometric drawing.

Oblique drawings are not as realistic looking as perspective or even isometric ones. Note in Figure 14-14 how the object is placed. Lines representing length and width make right angles with each other. Depth lines can be made at any convenient angle.

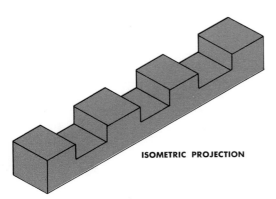

ISOMETRIC PROJECTION

Figure 14-13. *In an isometric drawing, all sides of the object are shown in true size and shape. Lines showing depth do not converge as in perspective drawings.*

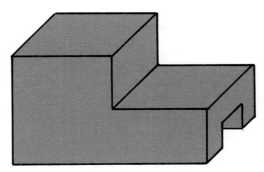

Figure 14-14. *An oblique drawing. Depth lines can be made at any angle that is convenient.*

Schematic. Schematic drawings make use of special symbols to describe a variety of different things. A schematic which shows the arrangement of components in an electrical circuit is pictured in Figure 14-15. Figure 14-16 is an example of a production flow chart. Industry uses this type of schematic to describe how its products are produced.

OBTAINING PICTURES

It is not always necessary to create drawings from scratch in order to add clarity or interest to a visual message. Often, commercially preprinted artwork, called *clip art,* can be used.

CLIP ART. Clip art is available in sheets and books. Generally, each sheet or book page contains several black and white illustrations. Often the pictures are provided in several sizes. Some clip art books contain multicolor artwork as

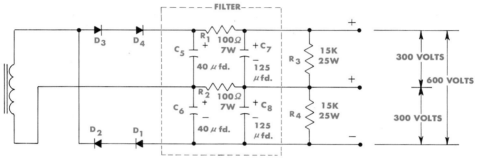

Figure 14-15. *Electrical circuit schematic.*

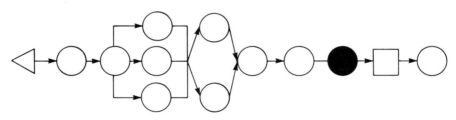

PRODUCTION STAGE	DESCRIPTION	SYMBOL
STORAGE	NOTHING DONE TO PRODUCT FOR EXTENDED TIME	◁
OPERATION	WORK PERFORMED ON PRODUCT	○
TRANSFER	PRODUCT MOVED TO NEXT STAGE	→
DELAY	TEMPORARY STORAGE	●
INSPECTION	QUALITY CHECK AGAINST ORIGINAL SPECIFICATIONS	☐

Figure 14-16. *Production flow charts are schematic drawings. Note the meaning of each symbol.*

well. Clip art samples are shown in Figure 14-17.

A variety of preprinted clip art covers a wide range of situations. The purchase price of clip art usually includes permission to reproduce the pictures.

Clip art is easy to use. Simply choose a picture, cut it out of the sheet or book and paste it into position on the mechanical.

USING ILLUSTRATIONS

Sometimes parts of an illustration are eliminated in order to emphasize or highlight other areas. This is done by *cropping*.

Illustrations must fit into an allotted space in the final printed product. Some illustrations may have to be reduced or enlarged. Determining the amount of reduction or enlargement of an illustration is called *scaling*.

Figure 14-17. *A page from a clip art book.*

Figure 14-18. *Crop marks are used to identify the area of an illustration to be printed.*

After illustrations are cropped and scaled, they can be added to a mechanical layout by *pasting up.*

CROPPING. Identifying an area of an illustration to be printed will eliminate some unwanted areas. Cropping can emphasize important areas of a picture or change the final shape.

Crop Marks. An area of a picture to be printed is identified with crop marks, Figure 14-18. Sometimes crop marks are made on a tissue overlay, Figure 14-19. The overlay sheet is attached to the illustration.

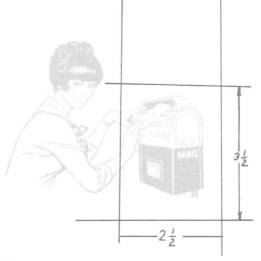

Figure 14-19. *Crop marks can be indicated on a tissue paper overlay sheet that is attached to the illustration.*

SCALING. Determining the proper enlargement or reduction is called *scaling.* Scaling changes the size of an illustration without changing its shape.

Diagonal-Line Method. The diagonal-line method of scaling, Figure 14-20, is an easy and quick way of reducing and/or enlarging pictures.

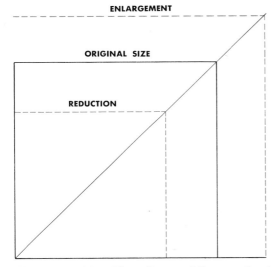

Figure 14-20. *The diagonal-line method of scaling illustrations. A ruler is used to determine the length and width of the reduction or enlargement.*

To enlarge or reduce an illustration by this method, first draw a box around the illustration or part of the illustration to be used. (Do not mark the actual illustration. Use a transparent overlay sheet.)

To enlarge, extend either the top or bottom and one side of the box, Figure 14-21. Next, draw a diagonal line from the intersection of the two extended lines through the opposite corner of the box. Construct a perpendicular line from either extended side to the diagonal line. Complete the enlargement by dropping a second perpendicular from the intersected point on the diagonal to the other extended side of the box.

To reduce an illustration, you do not have to extend the box. All other steps are the same as for enlarging. See Figure 14-21.

Proportional Scale Method. A proportional scale is a tool to determine enlargements and reductions. A typical proportional scale is shown in Figure

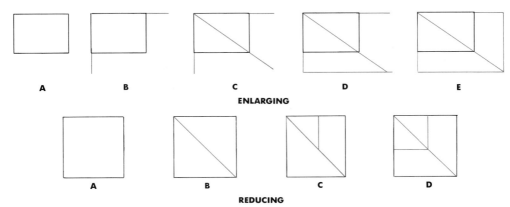

Figure 14-21. *Steps in enlarging or reducing an illustration using the diagonal-line method.*

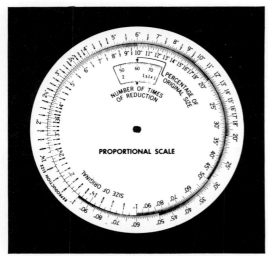

Figure 14-22. *A proportional scale can be used to determine reductions and enlargements.*

14-22. It is made of two circular pieces of cardboard fastened together at their centers. The outside, larger disc indicates the finished size of the reduction or enlargement. The inner, smaller disc indicates the size of the original.

Suppose you have a 7″ x 5″ picture to fit in a space 3 inches high. To find the width of the final art, line up the length of the original (5″) on the smaller wheel with the length of the finished reduction or enlargement (3″) on the larger wheel. Without moving the wheel, look up the original width (7″) on the small wheel. The final width on the large wheel will be lined up (4³⁄₁₆″).

To find the finished length, line up the widths and read across from the original length.

Many proportional scales come with a small window diecut into the inner disc. When widths or lengths are lined up, the window shows the percentage of reduction or enlargement.

PASTING UP. Scaled and cropped illustrations are added to a mechanical layout by *pasting up.* The mechanical layout, or pasteup as it is sometimes called, is an exact copy of how the final printed job will look. It contains all elements to be included in the final product. Preparing mechanical layouts is described in Section 8 of this book.

TEST YOUR KNOWLEDGE

1. Describe what is meant by *pictorial drawing.*
2. Prepare an outline of the procedures for creating pictorial drawings.
3. Describe what is meant by *technical drawing.*
4. List the materials and tools needed to prepare technical drawings.
5. Sketch a three-view orthographic projection of the object pictured in Figure 14-13.
6. Prepare an isometric sketch of the object shown in Figure 14-10.
7. Describe what is meant by *clip art.*
8. Describe two ways crop marks can be added to an illustration to identify the area of the picture to be printed.

UNIT 15

CREATING, OBTAINING, AND USING PHOTOGRAPHS

Objectives

When you have completed this unit you will be able to:

1. Explain the purpose of each of the four ingredients needed to produce a photograph.
2. List the names of six different types of cameras and one advantage of each.
3. Describe the difference between slow and fast speed films.
4. Define *focusing* and identify three devices used to focus a camera.
5. Explain how light intensity and duration of exposure is controlled.
6. Identify three ways to determine correct exposure.
7. List the steps in processing a roll of black and white film.
8. Describe the functions of the developer, stop, and fixing solutions used in processing photographic films and papers.
9. List the steps in exposing and processing contact prints.
10. Explain the procedures for drying glossy, matte, and resin-coated photographic papers.
11. List the steps in exposing and processing a projection print.
12. Describe the function of each of the major parts of an enlarger.

Terms to Know

Here are some of the words you will need to understand before reading this unit. If the meaning of a word is not clear to you, look it up in the Glossary in the back of this book.

lens	focusing	changing bag	enlarger
latent image	film speed	contact printing	easel
developer	ASA number	emulsion	bellows
stop bath	aperture	continuous tone copy	line copy
fixer	film processing	test strip	safelight
negative	developing tank	projection printing	halftone

CREATING PHOTOGRAPHS

Like drawings, photographs are used to communicate graphically. They add clarity or interest to a visual message. In some instances one picture is truly worth a thousand words.

Photographs are made by exposing film in a camera, processing the film to make a negative, and converting the negative into a positive print by contact or projection printing.

PRINCIPLES OF PHOTOGRAPHY. Four ingredients are needed to make a photograph: light, optics, silver compounds, and mechanics.

Light. Whatever we see is due to the reflection of light. A camera does not take pictures of objects; it takes pictures of light reflecting from objects.

Figure 15-1 shows how light is reflected from objects with smooth and with rough surfaces. Some objects reflect most of the light that strikes them. Mirrors and white shirts fall into this category. Objects that are dark do not reflect as much light. Instead they absorb light like a sponge absorbs water.

Optics. Objects and portions of objects reflect different amounts of light. The

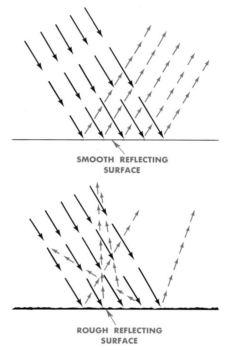

SMOOTH REFLECTING SURFACE

ROUGH REFLECTING SURFACE

Figure 15-1. Reflection of light from smooth and rough surfaces.

angle at which a single ray of light will reflect off an object is equal to the angle at which the light ray strikes the object, Figure 15-2. Because light strikes an object from many different directions, light reflecting from the object will travel in just as many different directions. This is true for light reflecting from every single point on the object.

If the different rays of light reflecting from a point on an object are to make visual sense, they must come together inside the eye or camera at a single point. Millions of these pinpoints of light then form a complete picture of the entire object.

Optics is the technical field that deals with lenses and what they do. A lens is used to collect the light reflecting from each point on an object. It then organizes the light so it will focus at a single point within the eye or camera. A lens focuses light into a sharp picture.

Lenses focus light into a sharp picture by bending light rays. This is called *refraction.* Normally, light rays travel in a straight line. However, when rays pass from a medium of one density, such as air, into a medium of another density, such as glass, they bend.

Figure 15-3 demonstrates how a single light ray passing from air into a glass prism and then back again into air is bent or refracted. Figure 15-4 shows

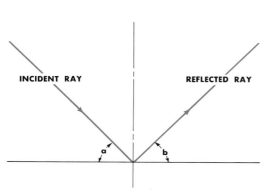

Figure 15-2. *The angle at which a single light ray reflects off an object is equal to the angle at which the light ray strikes the object. Angle a equals angle b.*

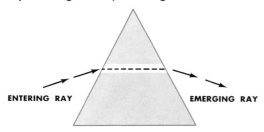

Figure 15-3. *A single light ray is bent or refracted when it passes through a glass prism.*

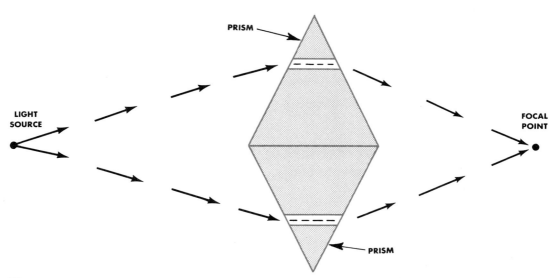

Figure 15-4. *Two glass prisms can act as a simple lens by focusing light rays at a single point.*

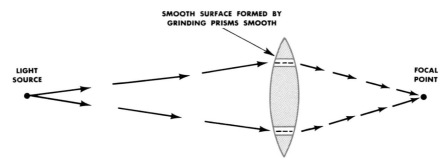

Figure 15-5. *A simple lens.*

how two glass prisms can act as a simple lens. A refined lens is pictured in Figure 15-5.

Silver Compounds. Light creates a picture inside a camera by striking a material that is very sensitive to light. This something is a silver compound. Generally, the silver compound used is silver bromide. The silver bromide crystals are suspended in gelatin which is spread smoothly across a transparent plastic base.

If you could look at a piece of film before and then after it is exposed to light, you wouldn't notice any difference. There is a difference, however. Sub-microscopic specks of pure silver are produced within the crystals that have been exposed to light. These tiny specks of silver form a *latent image.* It allows the film to "remember" where it was struck by light. Figure 15-6 illustrates how the crystals on a piece of film look before and after exposure.

The silver specks act as development centers. When the exposed film is placed in a special chemical solution (developer), all of the crystals that were exposed to light turn into grains of black

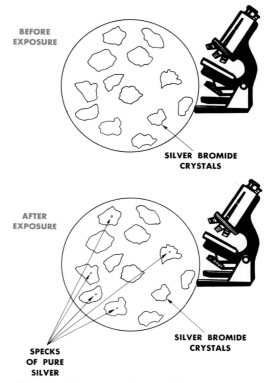

Figure 15-6. *A piece of film before and after exposure. Note the tiny specks of silver that have formed on the exposed silver crystals.*

silver. A developed piece of film is shown in Figure 15-7.

Another chemical solution (fixer) is then used to remove those crystals that were not developed, Figure 15-8.

AFTER
DEVELOPMENT

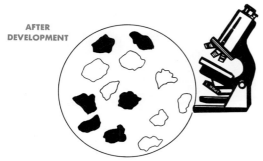

Figure 15-7. *The light-struck crystals turn black after the film is developed.*

AFTER
FIXING

Figure 15-8. *Fixer removes the unexposed and undeveloped crystals from the developed film.*

The resulting picture is called a negative, Figure 15-9. It is darkest where the object was lightest and lightest where the object was darkest.

Mechanics. The camera keeps the film in total darkness until the photographer takes the picture. Almost all cameras consist of a light-tight box, a lens and devices for controlling exposure. A *shutter* controls the amount of time that the film is exposed to light. A *diaphragm* controls the intensity of the light that strikes the film.

TYPES OF CAMERAS. Many types of cameras are used today. Those used most often for graphic reproduction are: box, folding, reflex, miniature, and press cameras.

Figure 15-9. *A photographic negative. It is darkest where the object was lightest and lightest where the object was darkest.*

97

Folding Cameras. Folding cameras are like box cameras. The major difference is that the folding camera can be compressed when not in use. A modern folding camera is shown in Figure 15-11.

Box Cameras. Box cameras are relatively inexpensive. Many models are available, and all are easy to operate. One popular model box camera is pictured in Figure 15-10.

Figure 15-10. A modern box camera. (Eastman Kodak Co.)

Figure 15-11. *The Polaroid SX-70 instant camera is a folding camera. (Polaroid Corp.)*

Some folding cameras contain controls for the intensity and/or duration of exposure. Some provide a way of adjusting the distance between the lens and the film. Adjusting the distance between lens and film is called *focusing.*

Box cameras usually have a fixed shutter speed. This means that all pictures are exposed for the same amount of time. Focusing is usually not possible. Sharp enlargements cannot be made from box camera negatives because of the poor quality of lenses used in this type of camera.

Reflex Cameras. The two types of reflex cameras are the single lens reflex and the twin lens reflex. Both offer the advantage of seeing the picture in the viewfinder as it will appear when printed. When the picture is focused in the viewfinder, it will be just as sharp on the film.

Figure 15-12. *A single lens reflex camera. The photographer sees the object to be photographed through the camera lens. (Braun North America)*

Figure 15-13. *A twin lens reflex camera. (Yashica, Inc.)*

Single Lens Reflex. A popular single lens reflex (SLR) camera is pictured in Figure 15-12. The photographer sees the object to be photographed through the taking lens of the camera. Many single lens reflex cameras will accept a variety of interchangeable lenses. SLR cameras are available in 35mm and 120mm sizes.

Twin Lens Reflex. A twin lens reflex camera, Figure 15-13, has two lenses, one above the other. The lower lens is the taking lens. Figure 15-14 shows the relationship between the two lenses.

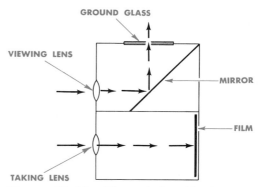

Figure 15-14. *The relationship between the two lenses on a twin lens reflex camera. The upper lens is for viewing. Film is exposed through the lower lens.*

Miniature Cameras. Miniature cameras are popular. They are small and compact. Miniature cameras generally use 35mm film packaged in cassettes of 20, 24, or 36 pictures. Per picture cost for this type of camera is relatively inexpensive. A wide variety of available accessories also makes the miniature camera popular. Figure 15-15 shows a 35mm SLR camera. It is a "miniature" camera because of the size of the film it uses.

Figure 15-16. *A press camera. The large negatives allow very large prints to be made without loss of detail. (H. P. Marketing Corp.)*

Figure 15-15. *35mm cameras are relatively small and compact. (Vivitar Corp.)*

Press Cameras. A press camera, Figure 15-16, was once very popular with news photographers. Today they are seldom used by the press. Instead press cameras are used to produce large negatives, usually on 4″ × 5″ film. Large negatives allow very large prints to be made without loss of detail.

CAMERA HANDLING. Because of the diversity of types and models of cameras, only general handling suggestions will be given here. Check the instruction manual for your camera for specific handling instructions.

Selecting the Film. Black and white film is usually used to produce photographs for graphic reproduction. Choose a brand name, general purpose film. General purpose film has good latitude. This means it can be slightly overexposed or underexposed and still produce a usable negative.

Film Speed. Film speed is the sensitivity of the film to light. It is indicated by an

ASA (American Standards Association, now the American National Standards Institute) number printed on the package and instruction sheet that comes with the film. The higher the ASA number, the more sensitive the film is to light. A slow speed film has an ASA number of 100 or less. A fast film has an ASA number of 300 or more. Medium speed films have ASA numbers between 100 and 300.

Fast films are used to take pictures in dim light without a flash. Slower films may be used for outdoor exposures in bright sun.

Slow films contain smaller silver bromide crystals and produce photographs with greater detail than fast films do. It is a good idea to select a film with the lowest possible ASA number that will permit proper exposure.

Loading the Camera. Always load and unload the camera in subdued light. If you use a roll film with a paper backing, place the film in the supply side of the camera before breaking the seal. Remove the seal completely. After the film has been exposed, make sure the paper wrapper is taut before resealing.

When you load 35mm film be sure the sprocket holes on both sides of the film are engaged in the sprockets. After 35mm film has been exposed, it must be rewound into the cassette before you open the camera.

Focusing the Camera. Focusing means adjusting the distance between the film and the camera lens. As the subject to be photographed nears the camera, the lens must be moved farther and farther from the film plane in order to bring the subject into sharp focus.

Fixed Focus Cameras. The lenses on such cameras are fixed. They render objects from about six feet to infinity in reasonably sharp focus. Photographing subjects closer than six feet with fixed focus cameras should not be attempted.

Scale Focusing. The lens-to-film distance on this type camera is adjusted by turning the lens mount a predetermined amount. The amount is indicated by a scale which is graduated in feet.

Rangefinders. Rangefinders are used on some cameras to determine the subject-to-camera distance. There are two types of rangefinders: split-field and coincidental. Split-field focusing is accomplished by aligning the top and bottom halves of the image seen through a rangefinder. A split-field image is shown in Figure 15-17. Coincidental rangefinders focus by superimposing one image on top of another, Figure 15-18.

IMAGE IS
OUT OF FOCUS

THE CAMERA
IS PROPERLY
FOCUSED

Figure 15-17. The image seen through a split-field rangefinder. When the two image halves are aligned, the subject will be sharply focused on the film.

IMAGE IS
OUT OF FOCUS

THE CAMERA
IS PROPERLY
FOCUSED

Figure 15-18. *Focusing with a coincidental rangefinder.
When the two images become one, the subject will be
sharply focused on the film.*

Ground-Glass Focusing. Reflex cameras use a ground glass screen as the principal means of focusing. The object to be photographed is in focus when it appears sharp and clear on the ground-glass screen.

Controlling Light Intensity. A diaphragm controls the intensity of the light that passes through the lens and strikes the film. The iris diaphragm, Figure 15-19, is the one most used today. It consists of a series of adjustable metal plates. The plates are adjusted by rotating a ring on the lens housing or by moving a lever. This, in turn, forms a larger or smaller opening as desired. The opening is called the *aperture.*

IRIS
DIAPHRAGM

Figure 15-19. *The iris diaphragm is used to control the intensity of the light striking the film. (Berkey Marketing Co.)*

The size of an aperture or lens opening is indicated by an *f*/number. The higher the *f*/number, the smaller the aperture. Closing the diaphragm from one *f*/number to the next higher number reduces the amount of light passing through the lens by one half.

Controlling Exposure Time. The length of exposure is determined by the amount of time the shutter remains open. Simple cameras have only one shutter speed. This speed is relatively slow. Be sure to hold the camera steady during exposure.

Shutter speeds on more expensive cameras are controlled by setting a dial or moving a lever. The numbers on the dial or lever refer to fractions of a second. The numerator of each fraction is 1. A shutter speed of 1 means $1/1$ or 1 second, 2 means $1/2$ second, 5 means $1/5$ second, 10 means $1/10$ second, 25 means $1/25$ second, 50 means $1/50$ second, 100 means $1/100$ second, etc. Shutter speeds are graduated so that each speed is approximately one-half as long as the previous one.

Determining Correct Exposure. A correctly exposed negative is neither too dark nor too light. An overexposed negative will be too dark to make a good print. A print made from such a negative is very light. An underexposed negative is too light. A print made from an underexposed negative will be too dark.

The amount of blackening of a negative is determined by three things. The first is the sensitivity of the film itself indicated by its ASA number. The second is the intensity of the light striking the film. This is regulated by adjusting the lens aperture. The third is the length of time that light strikes the film. This is regulated by adjusting the shutter speed.

Correct *f*/numbers and shutter speeds for various lighting conditions are given on the instruction sheet that comes packed with each roll of film. An exposure calculator, Figure 15-20, is helpful as well.

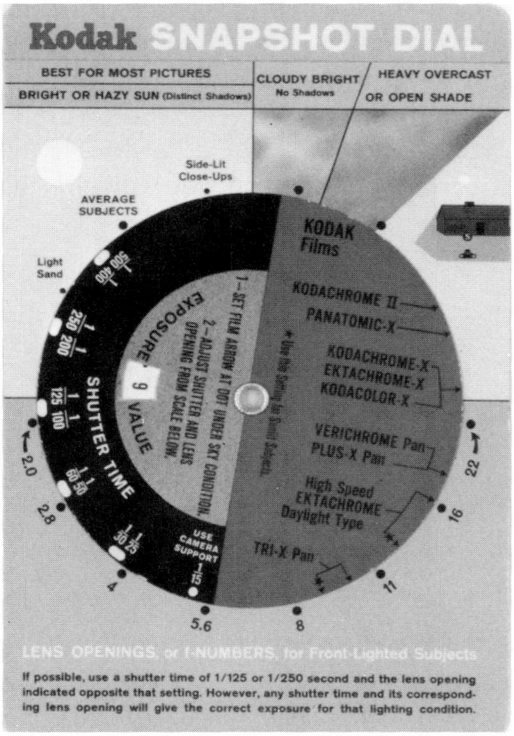

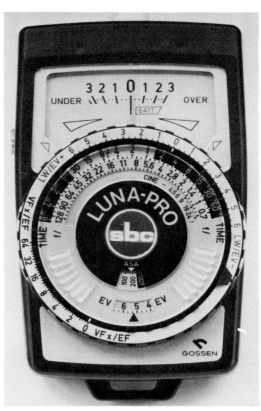

Figure 15-20. *Exposure calculators may be used to determine correct f/numbers and shutter speeds. (Eastman Kodak Co.)*

Correct exposures can be determined also with the aid of a light meter. A light meter measures available light. A typi-

cal light meter is shown in Figure 15-21. Many modern cameras have light meters built directly into their housing. Consult the instruction sheet that came with the meter or camera for directions on how to use the light meter.

Figure 15-21. *A light meter can also be used to determine correct exposure. (Berkey Marketing Co.)*

FILM PROCESSING. After it is exposed, the film contains a latent image. The film must be processed to make this latent image visible.

Developing Tanks. A developing tank is a light-tight container. Its cover is designed to permit processing chemicals to be poured in and out of the tank without permitting light to enter.

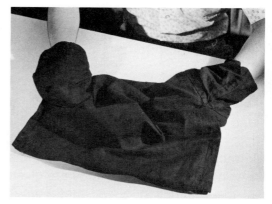

Figure 15-23. *A changing bag may be used to keep film in total darkness while it is being loaded into the developing tank.*

Exposed film is wound onto a reel or apron. This must be done in total darkness. The reel and film are then placed into the tank for processing. Once the film is in the covered tank, processing can take place with room lights on. Several types of developing tanks are pictured in Figure 15-22.

Loading the Tank. Practice loading the tank with a dummy roll of film before actually loading the film in the tank. Do this several times.

Ratchet type reels, Figure 15-24, are loaded from the outside toward the

Figure 15-22. *Several types of developing tanks.*

The developing tank must be loaded in total darkness. This can be done in a darkroom or in a changing bag, Figure 15-23. Place the tank and film in the changing bag and close the zippers. Put both hands through the sleeves of the bag to load the film. The tank is in total darkness, while the person loading the film may be in a lighted room.

Figure 15-24. *Loading a ratchet-type reel. Feed the film in as far as it will go. Then turn one side of the reel back and forth while holding the other side stationary.*

center of the reel. Feed the film into the reel as far as it will go. Then turn one side of the reel back and forth while holding the other side stationary. The film will feed itself onto the reel. Be sure the film is completely on the reel before placing it into the tank.

Stainless steel reels, Figure 15-25, are loaded from the inside out. Attach one end of the film to the clip at the center of the reel. This will tend to curl the film. Maintain this curl by pressing on the film's edges with thumb and forefinger. Keep the tips of your thumb and forefinger in contact with the outer edges of the reel, while turning the reel counterclockwise with your other hand. The film should snap into the spirals formed by the sides of the reel. Be sure the film does not touch itself at any point before placing the reel into the tank.

Figure 15-25. *A stainless steel reel. Attaching the film to the clip at the center of the reel will cause the film to curl. The film must snap into the spirals formed by the sides of the reel. (Rollei of America, Inc.)*

Aprons such as the one shown in Figure 15-26 are easy to use. Select an apron that is the same width as the film. Place the end of the film under the center loop of the apron and roll the apron and film up together in total darkness. Then place the apron and film into the light-tight developing tank.

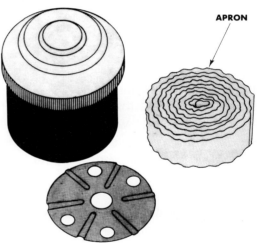

Figure 15-26. *Some tanks come with aprons rather than reels. The apron and film are wound together and then placed into the developing tank.*

Developing the Film. A special chemical is used to reduce the exposed silver bromide crystals to pure silver. This chemical is called the developer. Several different types of developers are available. Usually they come as a concentrate in either dry or liquid form. The concentrate must be mixed with water according to the manufacturer's recommendations. Developers should be stored in sealed brown glass containers to prevent oxidation.

The temperature of the developer must be carefully controlled during the development process. Consult the instruction sheet packed with the developer to determine the required temperature. The temperature of the developer can be raised or lowered by placing the bottle of developer into a bath of running water set at the desired development temperature.

Once the developer is at the proper temperature, pour it into the tank as quickly as possible. The developer should remain in the tank for the time specified in the instructions.

Agitate the film in the developer according to the manufacturer's recommendation. This insures that fresh developer will be in contact with the film at all times. Pour the developer out of the tank after the required developing time has elapsed.

Stopping the Action of the Developer. A mild acetic acid solution is used to stop the action of the developer. This solution is called *stop.* The temperature of the stop should be about the same as the developer.

Pour the stop solution into the tank immediately after removing the developer. The film should remain in the stop bath for approximately one minute.

Removing the Unexposed Silver Crystals. A fixing solution is used to remove all of the unexposed and undeveloped silver crystals from the developed film. The fixer also hardens the film's emulsion. The temperature of the fixer should be about the same as that of the developer. Follow manufacturer's recommendations for time and agitation requirements.

Washing the Negatives. After the film is fixed, the cover of the tank can be removed and the film washed. Washing removes all traces of the processing chemicals.

Wash the film by placing the uncovered tank under running water. Set the water at about the same temperature as the developer was. Allow the film to wash for a minimum of 20 minutes.

After it is washed, remove the film from the reel. The film may now be put into a wetting agent such as Kodak Photo-Flo for about one minute. This will help prevent water spots from forming while the film is drying.

Drying the Negatives. Dry the negatives by hanging the developed film in a dust-free area. Attach clips to both ends of the film. The clip at the top is used to hang the film. The weight of the bottom clip helps prevent the film from curling.

Protecting the Negatives. Protect negatives from being scratched and collecting dust. Cut the film into strips and store them in glassine envelopes.

CONTACT PRINTING. Contact printing produces photographic prints that are the same size as the negatives used to make them. The image on a contact print is a positive image rather than a negative one. It is light where the original subject was light and dark where the subject was dark.

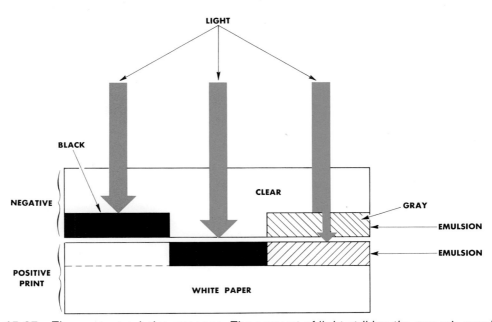

Figure 15-27. *The contact printing process. The amount of light striking the paper's emulsion is determined by the silver image on the negative.*

Figure 15-27 illustrates how contact prints are made. The emulsion side of a film negative is placed in direct contact with the emulsion side of a piece of photographic paper. The emulsion sides of the film and paper are the sides containing the silver bromide crystals. A contact printing frame or printer is used to maintain tight contact.

The photographic paper is then exposed through the negative to a source of light. Light passing through the clear areas of the negative will produce a black area on the print after it is processed. Light passing through the gray areas will produce grays in the positive. Because no light passes through the opaque areas of the negative, the paper below is not exposed and will remain white in these areas.

Contact Frames and Contact Printers. Contact printing frames and print-

The frame or printer is loaded in a darkroom with only safelights on. The light coming from a safelight will not expose the emulsion on photographic paper. Be sure that the filters on the safelights are correct for the paper being used. Popular types of safelights are shown in Figure 15-30.

ers keep the film negative and photographic paper in tight contact. Figure 15-28 shows a contact printing frame. A contact printer is shown in Figure 15-29.

Figure 15-30. *Typical safelights. The light coming from a safelight will not expose the emulsion on photographic paper. (nuArc Co., Inc.)*

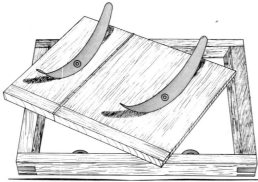

Figure 15-28. *A contact printing frame is used to maintain tight contact between the emulsion of the negative and the emulsion on the photographic print paper.*

To load the contact printing frame, place the base of the negative on the glass plate. The emulsion side (dull side) faces up. Then place the photographic paper over the negative. Its emulsion side (glossy side) contacts the emulsion side of the negative. After the back of the frame is closed, expose the photographic paper through the negative.

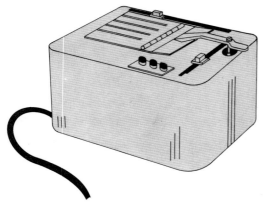

Figure 15-29. *A contact printer can also be used to make contact prints.*

Contact printers come equipped with a built-in light source for exposing the paper. Most printers also contain a built-in safelight to aid in positioning the film and the paper.

To load the contact printer, place the base of the negative on the glass plate. Then place the photographic paper emulsion side down on the negative. When the cover of the contact printer is closed, a light goes on and the paper is exposed.

If you use a contact printing frame, place it on the baseboard of an enlarger. The light from the enlarger exposes the print. Adjust the head of the enlarger so that the projected light just surrounds the frame. Set the lens aperture to an *f*/stop number in the middle of the scale. You may turn the enlarger lamp on and off manually or with a timer.

With a contact printer, an external light source is not needed. Closing the cover turns the lamp on. Opening it turns the lamp off. Some contact printers come equipped with a built-in timer for controlling exposure.

Determining Exposure Time. A strip of photographic paper one inch wide is used to determine correct exposure time. Cut the strip from a sheet of photographic paper and load it into the frame or printer. Expose the test strip for exactly 10 seconds.

Process the test strip according to the instructions given in the following paragraphs. If the image on the developed test strip is too light, repeat the exposure using a longer time. If the image is too dark, shorten the exposure time. Adjust and repeat the process until a satisfactory test strip is obtained. Once you have determined the proper exposure time, full-size contact prints can be made.

Processing the Contact Print. Contact prints are generally processed in three trays. The first tray is filled with developer, the second contains stop, and the third tray is filled with fixer. A large tray or tank in which to wash the processed prints is also required. A typical setup is illustrated in Figure 15-31.

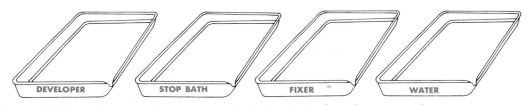

DEVELOPER STOP BATH FIXER WATER

Figure 15-31. *Suggested arrangement of chemicals for print processing.*

Developing the Print. The developing solution should be prepared according to the manufacturer's recommendations. Developer temperature is usually between 68 and 75 degrees.

You may develop photographic paper by time or inspection techniques. If the paper is to be developed for a specific period of time, follow the manufacturer's instructions concerning temperature and agitation. If the paper is to be developed by inspection, remove it from the developer when the image looks right.

Stopping the Action of the Developer. After the print is developed, transfer it to a stop bath with a pair of tongs. The stop neutralizes the action of the developer. The print should remain in the stop bath for at least 30 seconds. The tray containing the stop should be agitated continuously.

Removing the Unexposed Silver Crystals. Use a second pair of tongs to transfer the print from the stop bath to the fixing solution. This solution removes all the unexposed and undeveloped silver crystals from the developed print. The print should remain in the fixer for about 10 minutes.

Washing the Prints. Wash prints under clear running water for approximately one-half hour. Improperly washed prints will discolor in a relatively short period of time.

Drying the Prints. A ferrotype plate is used to produce a shiny finish on glossy photographic paper. After you drain the excess water from the print, place it face down on the polished surface of the ferrotype plate. Cover the print with a blotter and use a roller to obtain tight contact between the plate and the print, Figure 15-32. Stand the plate on edge. The print will fall away from the plate when it is dry.

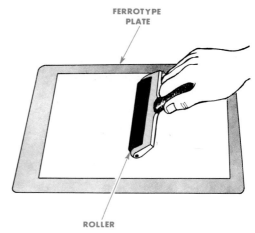

FERROTYPE PLATE

ROLLER

Figure 15-32. *A roller is used to ensure complete contact between print and ferrotype plate.*

Matte or dull finish papers are dried by placing them between blotters. Photographic blotters can be purchased in book and roll forms.

Resin-coated papers are dried by placing them face up on a table. Simply remove excess water with a squeegee. Resin-coated photographic papers dry in a matter of minutes.

PROJECTION PRINTING. Projection printing makes photographic prints larger than the negatives used to make them. These prints are called enlargements. Like contact prints, the image of an enlargement is light where the original subject was light and dark where the subject was dark. It is a positive image.

Enlargers. Although enlargers come in a variety of styles and sizes, they all have the same essential elements: a light source, a negative carrier, a device for focusing, and a means of adjusting the distance between the lens and the light-sensitive paper. The parts of an enlarger are illustrated in Figure 15-34.

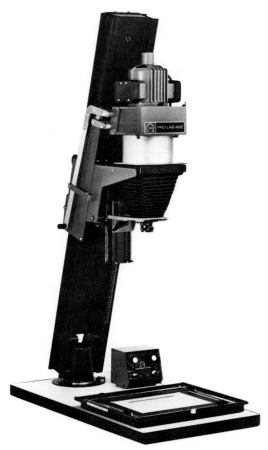

Figure 15-33. A photographic enlarger is used to make projection prints. (Berkey Marketing Co.)

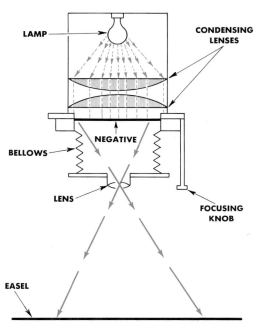

Figure 15-34. The parts of a typical enlarger.

An enlarger such as the one pictured in Figure 15-33 is used for projection printing. The negative is placed, emulsion side down, in the head of the enlarger between the light source and the lens. Light-sensitive paper is generally held in an easel placed on the base of the enlarger. The enlarger works like a projector. When it is turned on, the light passes through the negative and lens. It projects the negative image onto light-sensitive paper rather than on a screen. The size of the enlargement is controlled by raising or lowering the enlarger head.

The light source used in an enlarger is usually an incandescent bulb. It may be clear or frosted. The bulb is located in the head of the enlarger. A means of distributing the light evenly over the negative, such as a piece of ground glass, is also provided. A special condensing lens may also be used.

A negative carrier holds the negative. It is between the light source and the lens. Many enlargers have several carriers for use with different size negatives.

Insert the negative in the negative carrier, emulsion side face down toward the lens.

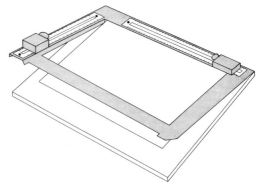

Figure 15-35. *A photographic easel. (Brodhead-Garrett Co.)*

Focusing is accomplished with a lens. The lens is probably the most important part of the enlarger. It is usually connected to the enlarger head with an accordian-like bellows. The distance between the lens and negative is adjusted to focus the image. Most lenses come equipped with a built-in diaphragm for controlling aperture size.

Raising or lowering the head of the enlarger adjusts the distance between the light and the paper. This adjustment is usually made with a hand crank in order to vary the size of the projected image.

Exposing the Projection Print. First, thoroughly clean the enlarger. Remove all traces of dust and dirt from the negative, the negative carrier, and the lens.

Turn off the room lights and turn on the safelights before you load and expose photographic paper. Be sure the filters in the safelight are correct for the paper being used.

An easel is used to hold the light-sensitive paper during exposure, Figure 15-35. Adjust the easel to the size of the desired enlargement. Then cut a piece of plain white paper to the size of the desired print. Insert this paper into the easel and position the easel on the base of the enlarger. Adjust and focus the image on the plain, white paper prior to exposing the photographic paper.

Open the lens to the widest aperture and turn the enlarging lamp on. Raise or lower the head of the enlarger until the image is the correct size. Focus until the image is sharp and clear. If the size of the image changes, readjust the head and refocus. When the image is the correct size and in focus, close the lens diaphragm until fine detail just begins to disappear but still remains visible.

Determining Exposure Time. Use a 1-inch strip of photographic paper from a sheet of the same type that will be used for the projection print. Remove the plain, white paper from the easel and replace it with the light-sensitive strip. Be sure the emulsion (shiny) side of the photographic paper faces up toward the lens.

Expose the test strip as follows. Turn on the enlarger and expose the entire strip for five seconds. Then cover one quarter of the strip with opaque cardboard and expose for five more seconds. Move the cardboard to the midpoint of the strip and expose the uncovered half for an additional ten seconds. Finally, move the cardboard to cover three quarters of the test strip and expose for twenty more seconds. A test strip prepared in this way is pictured in Figure 15-36. The four sections of the strip represent exposures of five, ten, twenty, and forty seconds.

Process the test strip in the same way as described for contact prints. Once the proper exposure has been determined, full-size projection prints can be made.

40 SECONDS   20 SECONDS   10 SECONDS   5 SECONDS

Figure 15-36. A test strip is made in order to determine correct exposure time for each enlargement.

Processing and Drying the Projection Print. Projection prints are processed and dried in the same manner as contact prints. Complete instructions are provided earlier in this unit under "Processing the Contact Print."

OBTAINING PHOTOGRAPHS
It is not always necessary to take your own photographs. Often, you may purchase photographs for reproduction from professional sources. Sometimes photographs can also be obtained at no cost from industrial concerns and advertising agencies.

USING PHOTOGRAPHS
Photographs must fit into their allotted spaces in the printed product. Like other illustrations, photographs may have to be reduced or enlarged in size. Procedures for scaling or determining the amount of reduction or enlargement are the same as those described in the previous unit.

Photographs are often cropped to highlight the most important part of each picture. Cropping photographs is the same as cropping other types of illustrations as described in Unit 14.

CONVERTING PHOTOGRAPHS INTO HALFTONES. Most pictorial and technical illustrations are made up of black lines and black shapes on white paper.

Everything is black and white. There are no shades of gray. Printers refer to such illustrations as *line copy.*

Photographs are different. They consist of black and white plus intermediate tones of gray. Printers call photographs *continous tone copy.*

Before photographs can be printed, all of the gray areas must be converted into black dots. This process is called halftone photography. The product of halftone photography is a halftone.

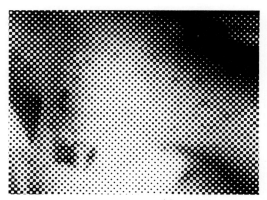

Figure 15-37. *An enlarged section of a halftone. The image is formed by dots of various sizes.*

A halftone is a reproduction of the continuous tone photograph with the image formed by dots of various sizes. An enlarged section of a halftone is shown in Figure 15-37. Procedures for converting photographs into halftones are described in Unit 20.

TEST YOUR KNOWLEDGE

1. Describe the parts that light, silver compounds, optics, and mechanics play in creating a photograph.
2. List six different types of cameras and an advantage of each.
3. Explain the difference between slow and fast speed film. Refer to ASA numbers, size of silver bromide crystals, and uses for each type of film.
4. Describe what is meant by *focusing,* and list three devices that are used to focus a camera.
5. Explain how a diaphragm is able to control the intensity of light entering a camera. Also describe how a shutter can control the duration of exposure.
6. Give three methods for determining correct f/numbers and shutter speeds when taking pictures under various lighting conditions.
7. List in proper order the major steps in processing a roll of black and white film.
8. Describe the functions of the developer, stop, and fixing solutions used to process photographic films and papers.
9. List in order the major steps in exposing and processing contact prints.
10. Explain how to dry glossy, matte, and resin-coated photographic papers.
11. List in sequence the major steps in exposing and processing a projection print.
12. Describe briefly the function of each of the labeled parts of the photographic enlarger pictured in Figure 15-34.

SECTION 6

COMPOSITION

UNIT 16

HOT TYPE COMPOSITION

Objectives

When you have completed this unit, you will be able to:

1. Identify the parts of a piece of foundry type.
2. Locate uppercase and lowercase letters, punctuation marks, figures, spaces and quads in the California job case.
3. Recognize demon letters.
4. Define *em quad* and illustrate the relationship among the various spaces and quads found in a California job case.
5. Illustrate how to set type flush left, flush right, on center, and how to justify a line of type.
6. List the basic steps involved in dumping, tying, and proofing a type form.
7. Explain the difference between hand-set and machine-set hot type.
8. Describe the type produced by the Monotype, Linotype and Ludlow typecasting machines.

Terms to Know

Here are some of the words you will need to understand before reading this unit. If the meaning of a word is not clear to you, look it up in the Glossary in the back of this book.

wood type	spaces	borders	dumping
foundry type	quads	hand miterer	brayer
composing stick	em	type bank	distribution
galley	ligature	nick	Monotype
proof press	diphthong	flush left	Linotype
reproduction proof	leads	flush right	matrix
California job case	slugs	centering	Ludlow
demons	rule	justification	

HAND-SET HOT TYPE

Wood and foundry type are both classi-fied as "hot type." An individual piece of wood or foundry type consists of a single character resting on a wood or metal body. All of the characters needed to form words and sentences are stored in special type cases.

Wood type and foundry type are both set by hand. Individual characters are taken from the type case and set or assembled in a *composing stick* to form lines of type. The assembled type is called a *type form.* A composing stick used to set type is shown in figure 16-1.

Once set, the type is transferred from the composing stick to a three-sided tray called a *galley.* String is used to hold the assembled form together.

After it is tied, the form is printed on a proof press. The print obtained is called a *proof.* The proof is then read and, if necessary, corrections are made in the type form.

The corrected type form can be used for direct reproduction on a platen or cylin-der press. (See Units 22 and 27.) Re-vised proofs may also be made from the

Figure 16-1. *A composing stick is used to set foundry type. (Brodhead-Garrett Co.)*

corrected type form for use in other methods of printing. Such proofs are called *reproduction proofs* or *repros.*

WOOD TYPE. Wood type is generally used for poster printing. Characters are large and are carved into the end grain of specially treated hardwoods. Wood type is much lighter in weight than metal type of the same size. Pieces of wood type are pictured in Figure 16-2.

Figure 16-2. *Wood type used for poster printing.*

FOUNDRY TYPE. Foundry type is made from lead with some antimony and tin added. This mixture of metals is called an alloy. The alloy is heated to a molten state (850°F) and poured into typeface molds. When cool, the hardened type is removed from the molds.

Each piece of foundry type is exactly

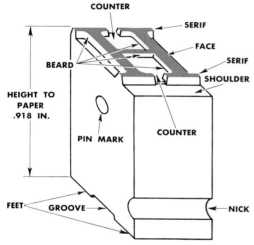

Figure 16-3. *The parts of a piece of foundry type.*

0.918 inch high. This is called *type high.* The face of the character, which carries the ink, is a mirror image of the symbol to be printed. Figure 16-3 illustrates the parts of a piece of foundry type.

Unit 12 describes the various typefaces that are available in foundry type. Information concerning type sizes and procedures for measuring type is also provided in Unit 12.

CALIFORNIA JOB CASE. Type is stored in shallow drawers or cases. Each case, approximately 1 × 16 × 32 inches, is divided into compartments. The California job case is used most. It contains 89 compartments, as shown in Figure 16-4. The California job case provides storage for uppercase and lowercase letters, punctuation marks, numerals, and spaces and quads. It also provides compartments for special characters that are called ligatures and diphthongs.

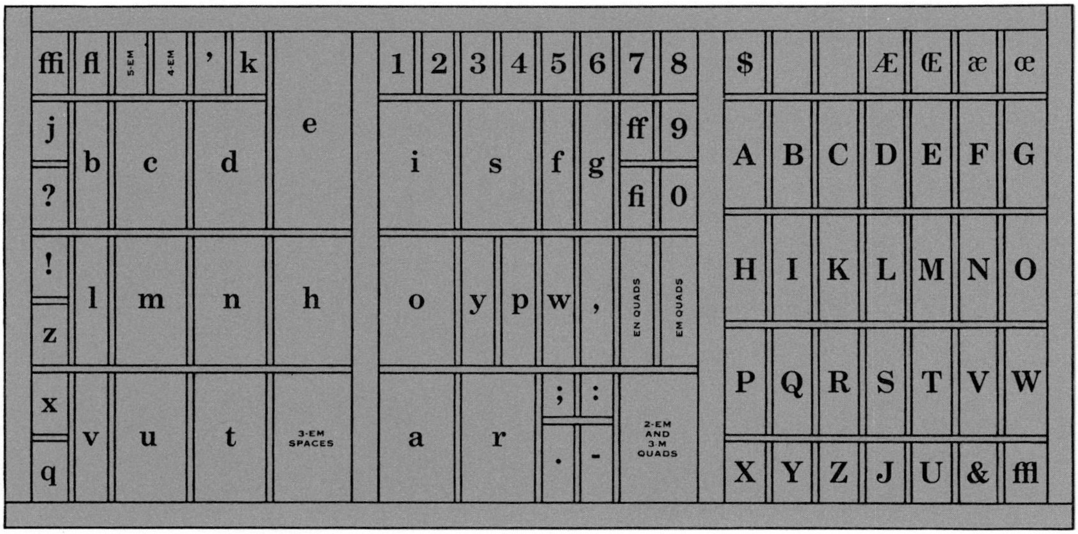

Figure 16-4. *Lay of California job case.*

Uppercase and Lowercase Letters. Uppercase or capital letters are stored in the compartments located at the right-hand side of the job case. With two exceptions, they are arranged in alphabetical order. Capital *J*'s and capital *U*'s follow the *Z*.

Lowercase or small letters are stored in compartments located in the left and center sections of the job case. The letters used most are stored in larger, more centrally located compartments.

Demons. Typefaces are cast in reverse of how they print. Because of this, some letters are difficult to distinguish. They look like other letters. Letters that are difficult to distinguish are called *demons*. Figure 16-5 illustrates the demon letters and how they will appear when printed.

Punctuation Marks. The apostrophe is located to the left of the lowercase *k* in the left-hand third of the case. Commas, semicolons, colons, periods, and hyphens are located in the center compartments of the California job case.

Numerals. The numerals *0* through *9* are located in compartments at the top of the center section of the case. Individual numbers can be combined to form any desired number.

Spaces and Quads. *Spaces* and *quads* are pieces of type metal that are shorter than the other pieces of type. Because they are shorter, they will not print when the assembled type is inked and printed. Instead they form white spaces on the printed copy.

All spaces and quads are based on the *em* which is equal in measurement to the square of the type body size in the

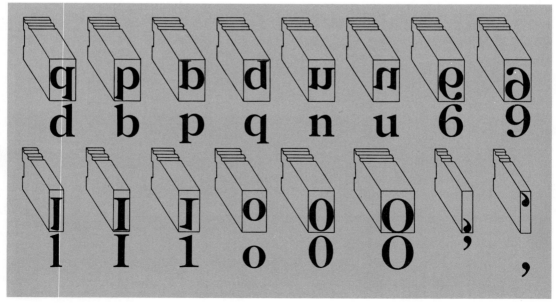

Figure 16-5. Demon type characters.

case. Figure 16-6 illustrates several different sizes of em quads. The relationship among spaces, en quads, and em quads is shown in Figure 16-7. Figure 16-8 shows the comparative sizes of spaces and quads contained in a case of 12-point type.

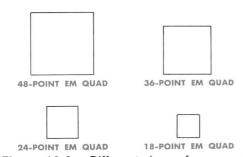

Figure 16-6. *Different sizes of em quads. An em is equal in size to the square of the type body.*

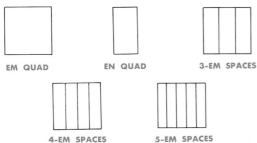

Figure 16-7. *The relationship among spaces, en quads, and em quads.*

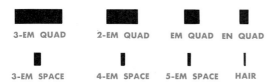

Figure 16-8. *Sizes of spaces and quads contained in a font of 12-point type.*

Ligatures and Diphthongs. A *ligature* consists of two or more letters cast on a single type body. Some italic types include ligatures to prevent letters that overhang their body from breaking. The common ligatures are: *fi, ff, fl, ffi,* and *ffl.*

Diphthongs consist of two vowels joined on one type body. Some styles of type include diphthongs to improve the appearance of the printed product. The common diphthongs are *AE, OE, ae,* and *oe.*

COMPOSING STICK. A composing stick is used to hold the type while it is being set or assembled into words and sentences. The stick is adjustable in pica and half-pica graduations. The parts of a composing stick are shown in Figure 16-9.

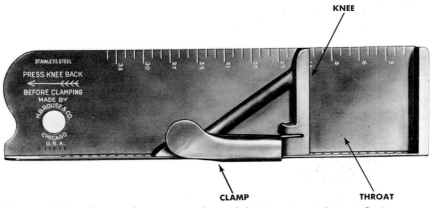

Figure 16-9. *Parts of a composing stick. (Brodhead-Garrett Co.)*

Spacing Between Lines. Thin strips of type metal are used to provide space between the lines of type in a type form. These strips of metal do not print and are called leads and slugs. A *lead* is generally one or two points thick and may be cut to any desired length. A *slug* is usually six points thick. It also can be cut to any desired length. A *lead and slug cutter* such as the one pictured in Figure 16-10 is used to cut leads and slugs to length.

Figure 16-10. *Lead and slug cutter. (Brodhead-Garrett Co.)*

Figure 16-11. *Hand miterer used to miter border strips. (H. B. Rouse & Co.)*

Rules. Strips of type-high metal are used to print straight lines of various thicknesses. Such strips are called *rules* and are made from brass or type metal. A lead and slug cutter is used to cut rules to length.

Borders. Borders are individual pieces of type or strips of type-high metal used to provide decoration within or around a type form. A *hand miterer* is shown in Figure 16-11. It is used to miter or cut the corners of the border strips at an angle when it is necessary to completely surround the type form.

FOUNDRY TYPE COMPOSITION. Carefully remove the California job case from the type bank (cabinet) and place it on top of the bank. Be sure to position the case behind the lip of the slanted top. The lip prevents the case from sliding to the floor. A California job case properly positioned on a type bank is pictured in Figure 16-12.

Adjust a composing stick to the desired line length or measure of the job. The pica and half pica graduations on the throat of the composing stick help posi-

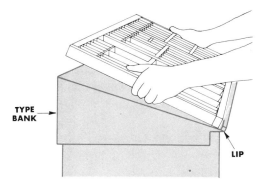

Figure 16-12. *Be sure to position the case behind the lip of the slanted top. Otherwise it may slide to the floor.*

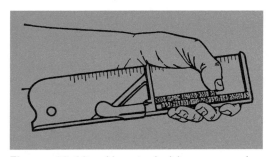

Figure 16-13. *How to hold a composing stick.*

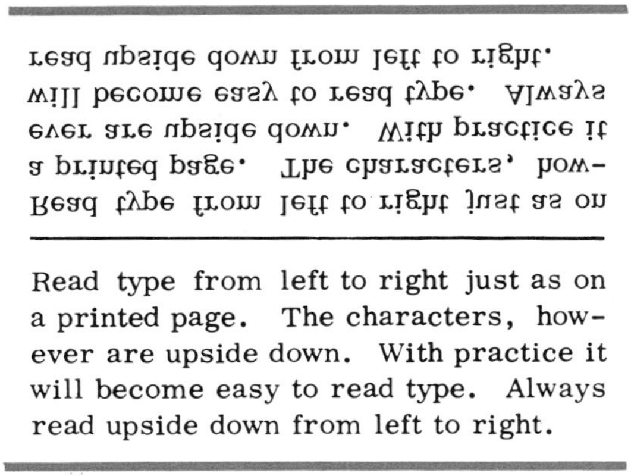

Read type from left to right just as on a printed page. The characters, however are upside down. With practice it will become easy to read type. Always read upside down from left to right.

Figure 16-14. *How a type form looks in a stick and how it looks after it is printed.*

tion the movable knee of the stick. Be sure to lock the knee in position before proceeding.

Cut a slug on the lead and slug cutter. To prevent binding, cut the slug slightly shorter than the measure of the job. Then place the slug in the stick.

Set foundry type by removing individual characters from the California job case and placing them into the composing stick. Hold the stick in the left hand as shown in Figure 16-13. With the right hand pick up the type from the case and transfer it to the composing stick.

Set type from left to right with the characters upside down. Always start at the knee of the stick and work toward the solid end. The nick on each piece of type must face up toward the open side of the composing stick. Figure 16-14 illustrates how a type form looks in the stick and after it is printed.

Setting Type Flush Left. *Flush left* means that all characters that begin each line will be aligned at the left when printed. Insert the first letter of the first word next to the knee of the stick. The nick must face up toward the open side. Repeat this process until the first line is completed.

Use quads and spaces to fill or "quad out" the line. Small spaces should be placed next to the last word. Large spaces or quads are used to end the line. This will prevent the small spaces from falling when the type is removed from the stick.

Try various combinations of spaces and quads to accurately control line length. It should never be necessary to force a space or quad into the composing stick. A properly set line can stand alone in the stick without movement when the entire line is tilted forward.

After the first line is completed, insert a lead or slug. Repeat the above procedure when setting the second line of type. Continue this process until the stick is full or until all of the required type has been set. Figure 16-15 shows several lines of type that have been set flush left.

This copy is set flush left.
All lines start at the left margin.
Quads and spaces are used to
fill out each line.

Figure 16-15. *Type set flush with the left-hand margin.*

Setting Type Flush Right. The procedures for setting type flush right are quite similar to those used when setting type flush left. There are two basic differences, however. First, after the words have been set and before the line is quadded out, the entire line of type is pushed away from the knee and moved toward the solid side of the stick. The second difference is that spaces and quads are added at the beginning rather

than at the end of each line of type. Figure 16-16 shows several lines of type that have been set flush right.

This copy is set flush right.
All lines end at the right margin.
Spaces and quads are added at
the beginning of each line of type.

Figure 16-16. *Type set flush with the right-hand margin.*

Setting Type on Center. Figure 16-17 shows several lines of type that have been set on center. Again the proce-

This copy is set on center.
Place an equal number of spaces
and quads at the beginning
and end of each line.

Figure 16-17. *Type set on center.*

dures are similar to those used when setting type flush left. This time, however, the lines are centered within the composing stick by placing an equal number of spacing units at the beginning and end of each line. Spaces and quads used at the end of a line must match the spaces and quads placed at the beginning.

Justification. Type is justified when all lines of type are exactly the same width. Justification is done by adjusting the spaces between words so that all lines begin flush left and end flush right. The comparative widths of spaces are shown in Figure 16-18. Several lines of type are pictured in Figure 16-19.

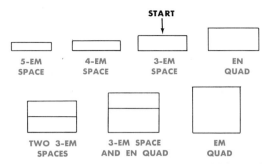

START

| 5-EM SPACE | 4-EM SPACE | 3-EM SPACE | EN QUAD |

| TWO 3-EM SPACES | 3-EM SPACE AND EN QUAD | EM QUAD |

Figure 16-18. Comparative widths of spaces used to justify a line of type.

When type fills a measure and a part of a word still remains to be set within the line, spacing between several words may have to be reduced. This is accomplished by substituting 4-em and 5-em spaces for the 3-em spaces used between words. Some letters, because of their ending and beginning letter shapes, appear to be closer or farther

apart than others. Place the thinnest spaces between those words that appear to be farthest apart. For example, note how a thin space was used between the words *Printing* and *Art* in Figure 16-20.

A short line of type may be made to fill the measure by increasing the size of the spacing units used between certain words. Place the thickest spaces between those words that, because of their ending and beginning letter shapes, appear to be closest together. For example, note how a thick space is used between the words *the* and *father* in Figure 16-20.

This copy is justified. Justification is accomplished by adjusting the spaces used between words. All lines of type are exactly the same length.

Figure 16-19. Justified type.

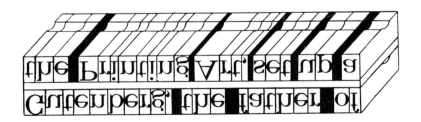

Gutenberg, the father of
the Printing Art, set up a

Figure 16-20. Foundry type is justified by adjusting the size of the spaces used between words.

Sometimes a complete word cannot be included in a single line even after adjusting the spaces between words in that line. When necessary, such words can be hyphenated. Words can be hyphenated only between syllables. The first part of a word, followed by a hyphen, ends the original line. The second part of the same word starts the next line. Places where a word may be hyphenated are given in a dictionary.

DUMPING AND TYING UP THE TYPE FORM. After the necessary lines have been set or when the composing stick is full, type is removed from the stick and tied with string. Removing the type form from the composing stick is called *dumping.* Procedures for dumping and tying up a type form are described in the following paragraphs.

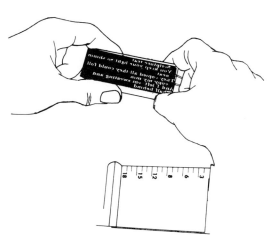

Figure 16-21. *How to remove type from the composing stick.*

Dumping. Place the composing stick in a three-sided metal tray called a *galley.* Grasp the type form as shown in Figure 16-21 and slide it out of the stick. Carefully move the type to a corner of the galley so that two of its sides are supported by two sides of the galley.

Tying. Tie a knot at one end of a piece of string. The string should be long enough to wrap around the type form five or six times. Hold the knotted end of the string in your left hand. Position this end of the string at the upper left-hand corner of the form. Wind the string with your right hand in a clockwise direction around the form. When you come to the knot, cross over it. Overlapping the knot in this way helps to bind the string in position. Continue to wind the string around the form. Secure the end of the string by tucking it under the other layers of string with a lead or piece of rule. A tied-up type form is shown in Figure 16-22.

TYPE FORM

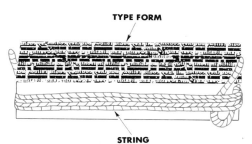

STRING

Figure 16-22. *Use a lead to tuck the end of the string under the layers of string wrapped around the type form.*

PROOFING THE TYPE FORM. A proof press, Figure 16-23, is used to make the first print of a type form. The resulting print is called a *proof.* Proofs are pulled to check for errors in the type form before the job goes to press.

To pull a proof, place the galley on the bed of the proof press. The open end of the galley should face the cylinder.

Carefully apply ink to the typeface with a *brayer* (inking roller). The procedure is

Figure 16-23. Proof press. (The Challenge Machinery Co.)

as follows: place a small amount of ink on the ink plate. Run the brayer over the ink plate several times. Place the inked brayer on the type form and pass it lightly over the form. Make sure that all areas of the form are inked. The inking process is pictured in Figure 16-24.

Next, place a clean sheet of paper on the inked form. Be careful not to move this paper once it contacts the form. Now roll the cylinder over the form. The resultant pressure will cause the ink to be transferred to the paper. Carefully strip the paper from the form, Figure 16-25. The proof should be sharp and legible. Turn the open end of the galley toward the cylinder and re-ink the type form for each additional proof.

Figure 16-24. Inking a type form with a brayer.

Figure 16-25. To avoid smudging, use care when stripping the proof from the type form.

Cleaning the Type Form. After a proof is pulled, the form must be cleaned with a cloth pad moistened with type wash, Figure 16-26. Type wash is a solvent

Figure 16-26. *Wash the type form after proofing. Be sure to place all rags containing solvents in special metal safety cans.*

and is used to remove the ink that remains on the form. Type wash is flammable so be sure to place all rags containing solvents in special metal safety cans.

Distributing the Type Form. After a proof is pulled and the form corrected, the form is either printed on a platen or cylinder press or used to prepare reproduction proofs. Reproduction proofs are used as camera copy for other methods of printing.

When the form is no longer needed, each piece of type must be returned to

Figure 16-27. *Foundry type must be carefully distributed after it is printed.*

its proper location in the California job case. This is called distributing the type.

The proper technique for holding the type form during distribution is shown in Figure 16-27. Hold two or three lines of type, nicks up, in the left hand. Remove the top slug and pick off several characters from the right end of the form with the right hand. Then drop one character at a time into its proper compartment. Also return leads and slugs to their proper places.

MACHINE-SET HOT TYPE

Hand-set type is cast in a foundry and then stored in a California job case for future use. Typesetting machines do not store type. They store molds used to make type. Typesetting machines cast and set their own type. After the form has been printed, the type is generally melted down and the metal reused.

Monotype typesetting machines cast and set individual pieces of type. Each type body contains a single character. Other machines, such as the Linotype, Intertype and Ludlow, each produce a complete line of characters, all cast on a single body. These lines of type are called *slugs.* A linotype slug is shown in Figure 16-28.

Figure 16-28. *A Linotype slug.*

MONOTYPE. Two basic machines make up the Monotype typesetting system: a keyboard and a caster. A Monotype keyboard unit is pictured in Figure 16-29. Figure 16-30 shows a Monotype casting unit.

Monotype Keyboard. The keyboard unit is controlled by an operator who types out the desired copy. Keys are provided for uppercase and lowercase letters, numbers, punctuation marks, and other necessary instructions. The keyboard produces a perforated paper tape. Each character is represented by its own set of perforations.

Monotype Caster. The casting unit is controlled by the perforated tape that was produced by the keyboard unit.

Compressed air reads the perforation code and positions the desired mold in the caster. A Monotype matrix or mold case is shown in Figure 16-31.

Molten metal is then injected into the mold and immediately solidifies. In this way, individual characters are formed. The characters are delivered by the machine in sequence and properly spaced and justified. Spacing between

Figure 16-30. *Monotype casting unit. (Monotype International)*

Figure 16-31. *Monotype matrix case. (Monotype International)*

Figure 16-29. *Monotype keyboard unit. (Monotype International)*

Figure 16-32. *A type form set in Monotype. (Monotype International)*

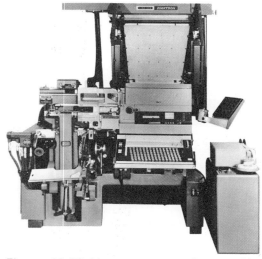

Figure 16-33. *Linotype typesetting machine. (Mergenthaler Linotype Co.)*

lines is accomplished by adding leads and slugs. A sample of a type form produced by a Monotype caster is shown in Figure 16-32.

LINOTYPE AND INTERTYPE. Linotype and Intertype machines operate in a similar manner. Both are line-casting machines. A Linotype machine is pictured in Figure 16-33.

Line-casting machines are controlled by either a keyboard or a punched tape. At the touch of a key or at the direction of the tape, a matrix (mold) is released from its storage case (magazine). Each size, kind, and style of type has its own magazine.

After all of the matrices for a single line are assembled within the machine, the line is automatically justified. Spacebands are used for this purpose. Assembled matrices and spacebands are shown in Figure 16-34.

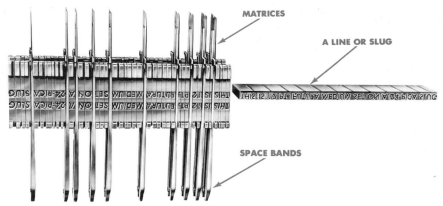

Figure 16-34. *Assembled matrices and spacebands are used to produce a Linotype slug. (Mergenthaler Linotype Co.)*

The assembled matrices and space-bands are then moved to the machine's casting mechanism. There, molten metal injected into the molds immediately solidifies. The slug is then ejected from the mold and delivered to a galley at the front of the machine. The matrices and spacebands are automatically returned to the magazine for reuse.

LUDLOW. The Ludlow system combines both hand and machine operations to produce a line of type. A Ludlow casting unit and matrix cabinets are pictured in Figure 16-35. Each drawer contains a complete font of matrices or molds.

Individual matrices are removed from the drawer and placed into a special composing stick, Figure 16-36. Two sizes of Ludlow matrices are pictured in Figure 16-37.

Figure 16-36. *Setting Ludlow matrices. (Ludlow Typographic Co.)*

Figure 16-35. *Ludlow casting unit and matrix cabinets. (Ludlow Typographic Co.)*

Figure 16-37. *Two sizes of Ludlow matrices. (Ludlow Typographic Co.)*

The justified line of matrices is next inserted into the Ludlow machine. Molten metal is injected into the mold and solidifies. The line of type is then removed from the mold and is delivered on a galley at the front of the machine.

The Ludlow system is used mostly for display composition. Any number of duplicate slugs may be cast from a single line of matrices.

TEST YOUR KNOWLEDGE

1. Draw a picture of a piece of foundry type. Identify and label each of its major parts including: serif, face, shoulder, body, face, and nick.
2. Refer to Figure 16-4 and locate in alphabetical order each uppercase and each lowercase letter. Then note the location of punctuation marks, numerals, spaces and quads.
3. Illustrate what each of the following printed letters would look like if it was cast in reverse on a piece of foundry type: d b p q n u 6 9 1 l l o O 0 ' , .
4. Describe what is meant by *em quad.* Using simple diagrams, illustrate the relationship among the various spaces and quads found in a California job case.
5. Using X's to represent type characters and O's to represent spacing materials, draw three lines of type flush left, three lines flush right, three lines on center, and three justified lines. Base your illustrations on a line length of 3 inches (18 picas).
6. Outline procedures for dumping, tying, and proofing a type form.
7. Explain the differences between hand-set and machine-set hot type.
8. Describe the differences in type produced by Monotype, Linotype, and Ludlow typecasting machines.

UNIT 17

MECHANICAL COLD TYPE COMPOSITION

Objectives

When you have completed this unit, you will be able to:
1. Identify three kinds of preprinted types.
2. Define *dry-transfer type* and explain how it is used.
3. Define *pressure-sensitive type* and explain how it is used.
4. Describe how to make corrections in dry-transfer and pressure-sensitive composed type matter.
5. Describe the procedures for using hand-set paper type.
6. Explain how lettering devices are used to create display letters.
7. Identify three processes of typewriter composition.
8. Indicate two limitations of a standard typewriter.
9. Outline the procedures for justifying type matter on a standard typewriter.
10. Describe the major difference between type composed on standard and proportional spacing typewriters.
11. List three kinds of interchangeable typeface typewriters.

Terms to Know

Here are some of the words you will need to understand before reading this unit. If the meaning of a word is not clear to you, look it up in the Glossary in the back of this book.

cold type	composing stick	justification
composition	typewriter	keyboarding
dry-transfer type	composition	

PREPRINTED TYPES AND LETTERING DEVICES

A variety of preprinted types and lettering devices is available for composing small amounts of type by hand. These materials and devices are relatively inexpensive, but, if properly used, produce professional looking copy. Because preprinted types and lettering devices do not need molten metal to generate type, they are classified as cold type composition techniques.

DRY-TRANSFER TYPE. Dry-transfer types are preprinted characters attached to transparent plastic or translucent paper sheets called carriers. Each

carrier usually contains a single size and style of type.

The characters are printed in reverse on the back of the carrier sheet. They are right reading when viewed through the top surface of the carrier. Figure 17-1 shows samples of dry-transfer type.

Dry-Transfer Composition. The backs of the letters printed on the carrier sheet are coated with a wax-like adhesive. Position each letter on the mechanical and rub or burnish the top surface of the carrier over the letter with a blunt tool. Burnishing transfers the character to the mechanical. The transfer process is shown in Figure 17-2.

You may add guidelines to the mechanical to aid in positioning the letters. If you use a light blue pencil, you will not have to erase the guidelines. Light blue lines do not photograph when the mechanical is converted to a negative.

If a letter is improperly transferred or if it is damaged during the transfer process, it may be removed from the mechanical with the edge of a razor blade or with tape. After the type is in place, cover the copy area with the protective backing sheet supplied with the carrier. Rub the

Figure 17-1. *Dry-transfer type. The preprinted characters are attached to a carrier sheet. (Zipatone Inc.)*

Figure 17-2. Dry-transfer composition. The character is placed over the mechanical, rubbed, and the carrier sheet is pulled away. (Zipatone Inc.)

Figure 17-3. Pressure-sensitive type composition. The letter is cut out of the carrier sheet and adhered to the mechanical. (FORMATT Cut-Out Acetate Art Aids)

copy with a blunt tool. This helps to improve the adhesion between the letters and the mechanical.

Pressure-sensitive type consists of letters printed on the top surface of clear plastic carriers. Each carrier usually contains a single size and style of type. The backs of the plastic carriers are coated with adhesive and are protected by paper backing sheets.

Pressure-Sensitive Type Composition. Cut letters out of the carrier sheet with a sharp knife. Position each letter on the mechanical and rub with a blunt

tool to make it adhere. Figure 17-3 shows the procedure for setting pressure-sensitive type.

If you transfer a letter improperly or if the letter is damaged, you may remove it with a knife point from the mechanical and replace it.

HAND-SET PAPER TYPE. Hand-set paper type comes as preprinted letters on paper pads. Each sheet of the pad contains a single letter. Pads are available in a wide variety of type styles and sizes. Hand-set paper type pads are pictured in Figure 17-4.

Figure 17-4. *Hand-set paper type is supplied as preprinted letters on paper pads.*

Hand-Set Paper Type Composition. Remove letters from the pads and assemble in a special composing stick. Start at the closed end of the stick and push each successive letter against the one before it. The blue letters that are printed on the top side of the pad sheets should face up. Letters on the other side

of the sheets are printed in black ink. Blank pad sheets are used to space between words. The correct procedure for composing hand-set paper type is shown in Figure 17-5.

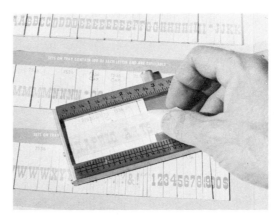

Figure 17-5. *Hand-set paper type is set by removing characters from their pads and assembling them in a special composing stick.*

Remove completed lines of type from the composing stick with the aid of masking tape. Cut a piece of tape a little longer than the line and lay it over the assembled letters. Remove the type from the stick and turn it over so that the black printed letters face up.

Next trim the composed line to within ⅛ inch of the letters. Use rubber cement to adhere the trimmed line of type to the mechanical.

LETTERING DEVICES. Several lettering devices are available for creating display letters using pen and ink. One of the most versatile of these devices is the Varigraph Headwriter, Figure 17-6.

Letters cut into a plastic strip guide a pen which produces characters on paper. Letters can be produced in various sizes and may be condensed or ex-

***Figure** 17-6.* *The Varigraph Headwriter uses a pen and ink to produce type matter. (Varigraph Inc.)*

panded. Italic and backslanted letters can also be produced with this device.

TYPEWRITER COMPOSITION

Typewriters are cold-typesetting machines. Impact, strike-on, and direct impression composition are names used to describe type set in this manner.

An operator depresses keys on the typewriter keyboard. As each key is depressed, a raised character strikes an inking ribbon. This causes the ribbon to contact a sheet of paper. The desired image is formed when ink is transferred from the ribbon to the paper.

Figure 17-7 illustrates the impressions made by three different types of ribbons. The image produced by the carbon ribbon is the best of the three. It is sharp and dense. If possible, use a carbon ribbon when setting type with a typewriter.

Composition should be done on a good quality white paper. A smooth-finished paper is best.

Standard typewriters can compose type matter. They are limited, however, in that they do not provide for proportional spacing of characters. A second limitation, being restricted to a single typeface, has been recently overcome with the development of interchangeable typeface typewriters.

STANDARD TYPEWRITERS. Each character on a standard typewriter occupies the same amount of space. The lowercase *i* is the same width as the uppercase *W.* A period occupies the same amount of space as an *M.* Because all characters occupy the same amount of space, type set on a standard typewriter lacks the esthetic appeal of hot type. Readibility is also lessened.

Standard typewriters are commonly used to prepare copy for letters and similar documents. Generally, such copy is set flush left.

If necessary, standard typewriters can produce justified type matter. However, the copy must be typed twice.

Justifying Type Matter on a Standard Typewriter. Decide on a maximum line length and begin typing. Do not exceed the desired line length on any line typed.

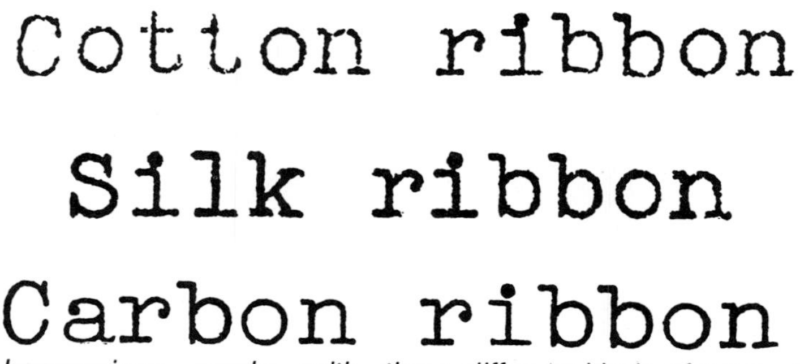

Cotton ribbon

Silk ribbon

Carbon ribbon

Figure 17-7. Impressions made with three different kinds of typewriter ribbons.

```
Standard typewriters can beXX
used to produce justifiedXXXX
type matter.  This isXXXXXXXX
accomplished by typing theXXX
copy twice.  Decide on aXXXXX
maximum line length and begin
typing.  Do not exceed theXXX
desired line length on anyXXX
line typed.  Stop typing when
you near the end of a lineXXX
and there is not enough roomX
to add another full word.XXXX
Fill in the space remainingXX
on each line with a series of
X's.  The X's representXXXXXX
spaces to be added betweenXXX
words during the secondXXXXXX
typing.
```

```
Standard  typewriters  can be
used   to   produce   justified
type   matter.   This    is
accomplished   by typing   the
copy    twice.  Decide    on   a
maximum line length and begin
typing.   Do    not   exceed the
desired   line   length   on any
line typed.  Stop typing when
you   near   the end of a   line
and   there is not enough room
to   add   another   full word.
Fill   in   the space remaining
on each line with a series of
X's.    The    X's    represent
spaces   to   be   added between
words   during   the   second
typing.
```

Figure 17-8. *Justifying type matter with a standard typewriter. Two typings are required. The X's represent spaces to be added during the second typing.*

Stop typing when you near the end of a line and there is not enough room to add another full word.

Fill in the space remaining on each line with a series of X's. The X's represent spaces to be added between words during the second typing. During the second typing, distribute the extra spaces between words throughout the line so that the final word will be flush right. Justifying type matter with a standard typewriter is shown in Figure 17-8.

PROPORTIONAL SPACING TYPE-WRITERS. The spaces filled by characters typed on a proportional spacing typewriter vary. Individual characters have varying widths and occupy varying amounts of space, Figure 17-9.

Type set on a proportional spacing typewriter looks more like hot type than does type set on a standard machine. One

Each letter on an ordinary typewriter fills exactly the same amount of space. On a proportional spacing typewriter, however, the width of letters varies and appropriate space is automatically allowed, resulting in copy that is visually pleasing and similar to hot type.

Figure 17-9. *The spaces filled by characters typed on a proportional spacing typewriter vary. Different characters fill different amounts of space.*

Figure 17-10. *A proportional spacing typewriter. (IBM Office Products Division)*

example of a proportional spacing typewriter is the IBM "Executive" typewriter, Figure 17-10. Justifying copy on the Executive typewriter also requires two typings.

RECORDER   REPRODUCER

Figure 17-11. *A Justowriter recorder and reproducer. The reproducer automatically justifies the copy during a second typing. (Friden)*

The Friden "Justowriter", Figure 17-11, is one proportional spacing machine capable of automatic justification. The Justowriter consists of two units: a recorder and a reproducer.

Copy is keyboarded on the recorder. The recorder produces a typed sheet of paper which is checked for errors. It also produces a perforated tape. The tape controls the reproducer which automatically retypes and justifies the copy at a rate of approximately 100 words per minute.

INTERCHANGEABLE TYPEFACE TYPEWRITERS. As the name indicates, typefaces on these machines can be changed or replaced as desired. Several sizes and styles of type may be mixed in a single job.

IBM Selectric Typewriter. A "Selectric" typewriter, pictured in Figure 17-12, does not contain typebars. Instead a single sphere-shaped element contains all of the letters, numbers, and symbols. The element is about the size of a golf ball, Figure 17-13.

Figure 17-12. *An IBM Selectric type-writer. (IBM Office Products Division)*

Figure 17-13. *A single sphere-shaped Selectric element contains all uppercase and lowercase letters, numbers, and punctuation marks. (IBM Office Products Division)*

12 pt. Pyramid Medium
11 pt. Univers Bold
11 pt. Univers Medium
10 pt. Press Roman Italic
10 pt. Pyramid Medium
10 pt. Aldine Roman Italic
8 pt. Pyramid Medium
8 pt. Pyramid Italic
8 pt. Aldine Roman Medium
8 pt. Bodoni Book Medium
8 pt. Aldine Roman Italic

Figure 17-14. *Samples of typefaces and sizes used on the Selectric typewriter. (IBM Office Products Division)*

Figure 17-15. *The VariTyper features proportional spacing and interchangeable typefaces. (Addressograph Multigraph Corp.)*

Type elements can be changed in seconds. Some samples of typefaces and sizes available for use with the Selectric typewriter are shown in Figure 17-14.

Varityper. A VariTyper composing machine is pictured in Figure 17-15. It is capable of proportional spacing. Type fonts are interchangeable. A VariTyper type font is shown in Figure 17-16.

Figure 17-16. *VariTyper type font.*

3	4	5	6	7	8	9
i ;	I (	J	P y	B	A Y	M
j '	f)	a	S *	C	D w	W
l '	r !	c	b †	E	G ¾	m
. -	s /	e	d $	F	H ½	
,	t	g	h +	L	K &	
	:	v	k =	T	N %	
		z	n]	Z	O @	
		?	o		Q ¼	
		[	p		R −	

Figure 17-18. *Seven different letter widths are provided by the IBM Selectric Composer. (IBM Office Products Division)*

IBM Selectric Composer. A Selectric Composer, Figure 17-17, justifies lines of type automatically during a second typing. Like the Selectric Typewriter, the Composer uses interchangeable sphere-shaped type elements.

Figure 17-19. *An IBM Electronic Selectric Composer. (IBM Office Products Division)*

Figure 17-17. *An IBM Selectric Composer features proportional spacing, interchangeable typefaces, and will automatically justify type matter during a second typing. (IBM Office Products Division)*

Characters are proportionally spaced. Each fills three, four, five, six, seven, eight, or nine units of horizontal space. Figure 17-18 shows letter widths.

A more advanced version of the Selectric Composer is pictured in Figure 17-19. This machine can hold up to 8,000 keyboarded characters in electronic memory. While held in memory, text can be altered and formats changed. Then, at the touch of a button, an error-free, formatted proof is automatically generated. Copy can be set flush left or right, on center, or justified with only one keyboarding.

TEST YOUR KNOWLEDGE

1. Name three kinds of preprinted types.
2. Describe what is meant by *dry-transfer type* and explain the process of dry-transfer composition.
3. Describe what is meant by *pressure-sensitive type* and explain how it is used.
4. Explain how to correct type matter that has been composed with dry-transfer type and with pressure-sensitive type.
5. Explain how to compose type matter with hand-set paper type.
6. Describe how to make display letters with a lettering device.
7. List three names for the process of setting type with a typewriter.
8. Identify two important limitations of standard typewriters when used for cold type composition.
9. Outline how to compose justified type matter on a standard typewriter.
10. Explain the major difference between type composed on a standard typewriter and type composed using a proportional spacing machine.
11. Identify three different kinds of interchangeable typeface typewriters.

UNIT 18

PHOTOGRAPHIC COLD TYPE COMPOSITION

Objectives

When you have completed this unit, you will be able to:
1. Illustrate the basic principle behind phototypesetting.
2. Identify the procedures for setting type with a StripPrinter.
3. List the basic steps in setting type with a Headliner.
4. Illustrate the difference between the contact and projection methods of photocomposition.
5. Define *display type* and *text type*.
6. Describe the major characteristics of first, second, third, and fourth generation text phototypesetters.

Terms to Know

Here are some of the words you will need to understand before reading this unit. If the meaning of a word is not clear to you, look it up in the Glossary in the back of this book.

cold type composition	display type	projection printing
phototypesetter	contact printing	text type

PHOTOCOMPOSITION

Typesetting by means of photography is called *photocomposition.* Characters are generated by exposing photographic paper through a series of negatives. Each negative contains a transparent image of a desired character. The basic principle behind photocomposition is shown in Figure 18-1. Photocomposition is a cold type composition technique.

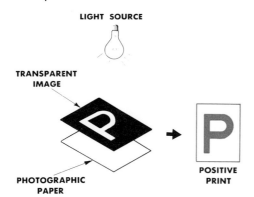

LIGHT SOURCE

TRANSPARENT IMAGE

PHOTOGRAPHIC PAPER

POSITIVE PRINT

Figure 18-1. The basic principle of photo-typesetting. Light-sensitive paper is exposed through a film negative of the desired character to a source of light.

After the photographic paper is exposed, it must be processed. The steps in processing are the same as those described in Unit 15 for producing contact and projection prints. They include developing, stopping, fixing, washing, and drying the exposed print. Once processed, the photographic paper can be trimmed to size and positioned on the mechanical.

Phototypesetting machines are used for photocomposition. Some phototypesetters produce display type. Others generate text copy.

DISPLAY PHOTOTYPESETTERS.

Display phototypesetters produce display type. Display type measures 14 points and larger and is used for headings and to attract attention.

There is a variety of display phototypesetters available on the market. They vary widely in terms of their design and operation. Some require hand positioning and spacing of each letter; exposure is made by contact printing on the photographic paper. More complex machines automatically provide the correct amount of space between letters. A third type of phototypesetter produces its copy through projection printing techniques. The most sophisticated phototypesetters are operated by a keyboard.

StripPrinter. A StripPrinter, Figure 18-2, uses contact printing to produce an image. Each letter must be positioned by hand in order to obtain the desired spacing between letters.

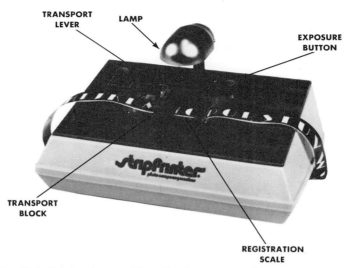

Figure 18-2. *The StripPrinter is used for display composition. (StripPrinter Inc.)*

A filmstrip containing one size and style of type serves as the negative. A roll of light-sensitive paper is positioned within the unit's housing, directly below the lamp which controls exposure.

Registration marks for letter spacing are provided on the filmstrip, Figure 18-3. Each character has a left and right registration mark. The distance between left and right registration marks is slightly larger than the width of the actual character.

Figure 18-3. *Registration marks on the StripPrinter filmstrip serve as an aid in letter spacing.*

Setting Type with a StripPrinter. Position the filmstrip so that the first character to be set is between the lamp and the sensitized paper. Align the left registra-

tion mark of the character with the zero mark on the registration scale. Lock the transport block with the transport lever. Then move the transport block to the left until the registration mark at the right of the character aligns with the zero mark on the registration scale. Locking and moving the transport block also advances the light-sensitive paper.

Exposure is made by pressing the exposure button. Repeat the positioning and exposure process until all desired characters have been set. Then remove the exposed paper from the StripPrinter and process it according to directions given in Unit 15 for processing contact prints.

Headliner. A Headliner, Figure 18-4, like a StripPrinter produces images by means of contact printing. Unlike the StripPrinter, however, it automatically provides the right amount of space between characters.

149

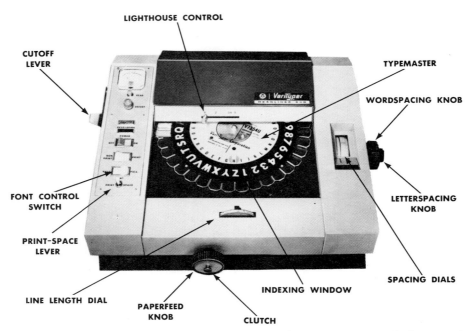

Figure 18-4. *The Headliner automatically provides the correct amount of space between display characters. (Addressograph Multigraph Corp.)*

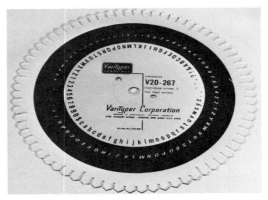

Figure 18-5. *The depth of the slots along the edge of a Headliner Typemaster controls letter spacing.*

A plastic disc containing one size and style of type serves as the negative. Slots of varying depth are located along the circumference of the disc. These slots control letter spacing. A Headliner Typemaster® disc is illustrated in Figure 18-5.

Setting Type with a Headliner. Position the typemaster on the Headliner and set the wordspacing dial, the lighthouse setting, and the full or half font control switch. To set these controls refer to the information printed on the Typemaster.

Turn the Typemaster until the desired character appears in the indexing window. Then expose the light-sensitive paper, which is located below the lighthouse, by moving the print-space lever to the print position. The light-sensitive paper advances automatically when the print lever is moved. Repeat this procedure until all of the desired characters have been set.

After composition, cut off the exposed paper by lifting the cut-off lever. Then feed the paper into a self-contained, three-compartment processing tank. In the tank it is developed, fixed, and washed before emerging from the side of the Headliner. Once processed, the photographic paper can be trimmed to size and accurately positioned on the mechanical.

Photo-Typositor. A Photo-Typositor, Figure 18-6, is a photosetting machine that produces type by projection printing. It can compose single and multiple lines of display type.

Figure 18-6. *The Photo-Typositor generates display type by projection printing techniques. (Visual Graphics Corp.)*

A filmstrip containing one size and style of type serves as the negative. Because the image is projected on light-sensitive paper, each font of type can be resized, condensed, expanded, italicized, back-

slanted, distorted, overlapped, angled, shadowed, or even set in a circle.

The strip of exposed light-sensitive paper is processed within the Photo-Typositor. Once processed, the photographic paper can be trimmed to size and positioned on the mechanical.

Compugraphic. The Compugraphic CG 7200 is a keyboard-operated display phototypesetting machine, Figure 18-7. The operator adjusts the machine for proper word and letter spacing and then composes the type at the keyboard. The exposed photographic paper must be processed before it is pasted up on the mechanical.

Figure 18-7. *The Compugraphic CG 7200. (Compugraphic Corp.)*

past thirty to thirty-five years. Literally hundreds of machines have been developed during this time. It would be impossible to review all or even many of these machines here. Instead we will examine four machines representative of the four generations of phototypesetters.

First Generation Phototypesetters. The Intertype Fotosetter, though no longer manufactured, is a first generation phototypesetter. The unit itself looks like a hot metal line casting machine. The operating principle of the Intertype Fotosetter is illustrated in Figure 18-8. Circu-

TEXT PHOTOTYPESETTERS. Text phototypesetters are used to compose text type. Text type measures 12 points or smaller and is used for the body of a page or book.

Four generations of text phototypesetting machines have evolved during the

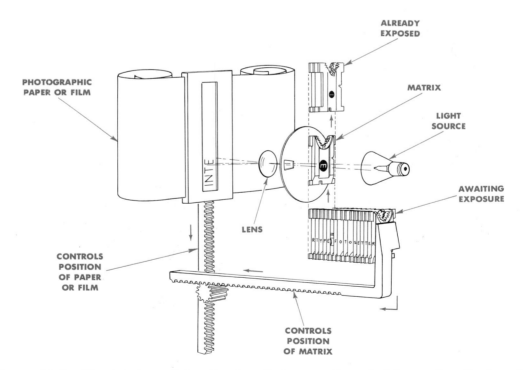

Figure 18-8. *The Intertype Fotosetter is a first generation phototypesetter. Each matrix contains a negative of a single character.*

lating matrices contain negatives of the character. The matrices are positioned between the light source and photographic paper during exposure.

An operator at the keyboard or a perforated paper tape controls input on the Fotosetter. Several different lenses make it possible to change the point size of the type. After exposure, the paper or film is developed in a darkroom.

Second Generation Phototypesetters. The Mergenthaler Linofilm, Figure 18-9, represents second generation phototypesetters. Second generation machines are operated automatically by tape produced on one or more separate keyboards. This results in faster composition. The Linofilm photographic unit generates up to 40 newspaper lines per minute.

Negative images of the characters to be generated on the Linofilm are contained on font grids. Each grid contains 88 characters. A single Linofilm turret can carry eighteen grids. Figure 18-10 shows a Linofilm turret and font grid.

Figure 18-9. *The Mergenthaler Linofilm is a tape-operated second generation phototypesetter. (Mergenthaler Linotype Co.)*

Figure 18-10. *Linofilm turret and font grid. (Mergenthaler Linotype Co.)*

153

Third Generation Phototypesetters. The Linotron 606, Figure 18-11, manufactured by Mergenthaler, represents third generation phototypesetters. The Linotron 606 can set 3000 lines of type per minute from a computer tape. Thousands of characters can be generated during each second of this machine's operation.

A third generation phototypesetter forms the image electronically on the face of a cathode ray tube. Complete pages of type are formed at one time.

A cathode ray tube (CRT) is similar in design to the picture tube of a television set. The image formed on the screen is focused through a lens and then projected onto photosensitive paper or film. The operating principle of the CRT phototypesetter is shown in Figure 18-12.

Figure 18-11. *The Mergenthaler Linotron 606 represents the third generation of phototypesetters. (Mergenthaler Linotype Co.)*

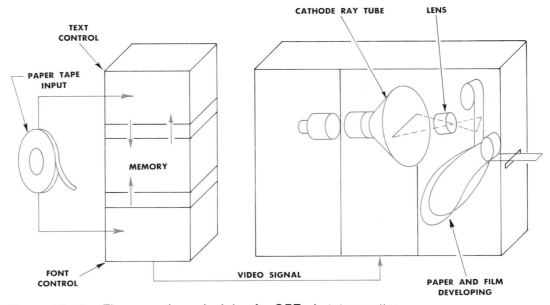

Figure 18-12. *The operating principle of a CRT phototypesetter.*

Figure 18-13. *The Monotype Lasercomp is a fourth generation phototypesetting machine. (Monotype International)*

Fourth Generation Phototypesetters. The Monotype Lasercomp shown in Figure 18-13 represents the fourth generation of phototypesetters. It makes use of an intense beam of light generated by a device called a Laser to expose photographic film or paper. A minicomputer controls the Laser beam as it moves rapidly back and forth across the light-sensitive material. Characters are generated, dot by dot, in either negative or positive form.

Input to the Lasercomp is from magnetic floppy discs, magnetic tape, or from paper tape. Output is at a rate of over 500 eight-point characters per second.

TEST YOUR KNOWLEDGE

1. Prepare a simple diagram illustrating the basic principle of phototypesetting.
2. Outline how to set type with a StripPrinter.
3. List the steps in setting type with a Headliner.
4. Illustrate with simple diagrams the basic difference between the contact and projection methods of photocomposition.
5. Explain what is meant by *display type* and *text type.*
6. Identify the differences of first, second, third, and fourth generation text phototypesetting machines.

SECTION 7

GRAPHIC ARTS PHOTOGRAPHY

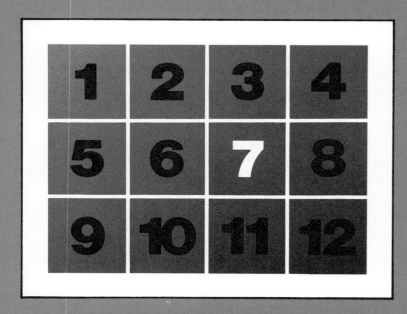

UNIT 19
LINE PHOTOGRAPHY

Objectives

When you have completed this unit, you will be able to:
1. Explain how to make a pasteup.
2. Define *line copy* and give three examples.
3. Define *continuous tone copy* and give three examples.
4. Describe the difference between a horizontal and vertical process camera and between a darkroom camera and a gallery camera.
5. Illustrate and identify the major parts of a process camera.
6. Explain the size relationships among *f*/stop openings.
7. Compute exposure times and *f*/stops for enlargements and reductions.
8. List two ways to identify the emulsion side of a piece of process film.
9. List the basic procedures for exposing a line negative.

Terms to Know

Here are some of the words you will need to understand before reading this unit. If the meaning of a word is not clear to you, look it up in the Glossary in the back of this book.

pasteup	copyboard	orthochromatic
wax coater	lens	gray scale
line copy	bellows	focusing
continuous tone copy	diaphragm	*f*/stop
veloxes	process film	emulsion
process photography		

PREPARING CAMERA COPY

Illustrations and type matter are assembled on a suitable base to produce a mechanical layout. A mechanical layout, or pasteup as it is sometimes called, is an exact duplicate of the job to be printed.

The mechanical layout is photographed in order to obtain a film negative. Film negatives are needed to produce many types of printing plates. (See Section 8).

MAKING THE PASTEUP. The comprehensive layout serves as a guide or blueprint for preparing the mechanical. It shows the location of all type matter, illustrations, and ornamentation.

A clean piece of white illustration board or white cardstock may be used as a base. Trim the base so it is at least one inch wider and one inch longer than the final page will be.

Use a light blue pencil to mark the location of the various elements on the base. Light blue lines do not have to be erased; they will not photograph.

Adhering the Elements. Illustrations and type matter may be attached to the base with rubber cement or wax. Be sure that the elements are properly positioned before adhering them.

With a small brush apply a thin, even coat of rubber cement to the back of the type matter or illustration. Position the element on the base and press lightly with your fingers. After it is dry, remove excess rubber cement by rubbing gently with your fingertips or a rubber cement pickup.

Instead of rubber cement, wax may be used to adhere the elements to the base. A wax coating machine, Figure 19-1, applies a thin layer of wax to the back of each element. The element may then be pressed in place on the base. If necessary, elements can be removed and repositioned.

Figure 19-1. *A wax-coating machine. (The Challenge Machinery Co.)*

TYPES OF CAMERA COPY. There are two general types of camera copy—line copy and continuous-tone copy. *Line* *copy* contains no shades of gray. The images are formed by lines and areas of a single tone. Examples of line copy include most type matter, pen and ink drawings, and many photographs that have already been broken into dots and printed and are to be reproduced same size. Photographs such as these are called *veloxes.*

Continuous-tone copy has gradations in tone and contains various shades of gray. Examples of continuous-tone copy include most photographic prints, airbrush renderings, and wash drawings made with india ink or water colors.

PROCESS PHOTOGRAPHY

Converting line and continuous-tone copy into the film negatives and positives needed to prepare printing plates is termed *process photography.* The equipment, materials, and techniques for process photography are similar to those used in continuous-tone photography. Continuous-tone photography was discussed in Unit 15.

PROCESS CAMERAS. Process cameras are used to convert camera copy into film negatives. The negative image may be larger, smaller, or the same size as the image on the camera copy.

Process cameras are generally located and used in the darkroom itself. Such cameras are called *darkroom cameras.* Cameras located and used outside the darkroom are called *gallery cameras.*

Types of Process Cameras. There are two types of process cameras: *horizontal* and *vertical.* Both cameras contain the same basic parts. Both operate essentially the same way. They differ only in construction.

Horizontal Process Camera. A horizontal process camera, Figure 19-2, has its parts arranged in a horizontal line. It can be located inside or outside a darkroom, but most often it is used as a darkroom camera by installing it through the darkroom wall. Only the part of the camera that holds the film needs to be inside the darkroom. The major portion of the camera may remain in a lighted room. This makes it possible to load and unload film within the darkroom and to use the darkroom for processing even while the camera's lights are turned on.

Vertical Process Camera. A vertical process camera, Figure 19-3, has its parts arranged in a vertical line. It can also be used as a darkroom or a gallery camera. However, it must be located

Figure 19-2. *A horizontal process camera. Major parts are all arranged on a horizontal axis. (nuArc Co., Inc.)*

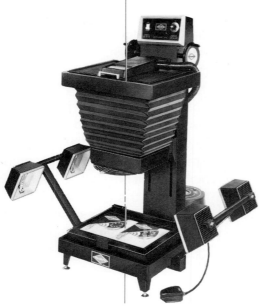

Figure 19-3. *A vertical process camera. Major parts are all arranged on a vertical axis. (nuArc Co., Inc.)*

entirely in the darkroom or entirely in a lighted room. If the vertical camera is located outside the darkroom, a light-proof film holder is needed to transport the unexposed film from the camera back to the darkroom.

Parts of a Process Camera. The major parts of a horizontal process camera are shown in Figure 19-4. A vertical process camera has the same parts arranged on a vertical axis.

Copyboard. The copy is held on the copyboard which can be moved away from or toward the lens. Most copy-boards have a glass lid to cover the copy and hold it in position.

Lights. Lights are needed to illuminate the copy. Various types of lamps can be used. The angle at which the light strikes the copy can usually be adjusted by changing the position of the lamps.

Lens. The lens is the most important part of the process camera. Usually it is the most expensive as well. The lens focuses the light reflecting from the copy onto the light-sensitive film. A *bellows* is

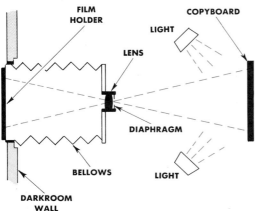

Figure 19-4. *Parts of a process camera.* (Top, *nuArc Co., Inc.*)

placed between the lens and the film to adjust the distance between the lens and the film plane.

A diaphragm is usually part of the lens housing. It regulates the amount of light entering the camera. A shutter behind the lens controls length of exposure.

Film Holder. The film holder keeps the film in place during exposure by a vacuum created with a vacuum pump. The pump is attached to the back of the film holder with a flexible rubber or plastic hose. On some cameras an adhesive is used in place of the vacuum to hold the film during exposure.

PROCESS FILMS. Many kinds of film are available for process photography. All of them produce high-contrast negatives. High-contrast negatives have black areas and clear areas; grays or tones in the camera copy are not recorded. For general process work, high-contrast orthochromatic film is used.

Orthochromatic film is sensitive to blue, green, and yellow light. It is most sensitive to blue light. Because of this sensitivity, light-blue guidelines can be left on the camera copy. Orthochromatic film cannot differentiate between the white base and the light-blue lines on the base.

Orthochromatic is not sensitive to red light. Red lines on the camera copy are seen as if they were black. Because of its lack of sensitivity to red, orthochromatic film can be handled in the darkroom under red safelight conditions.

EXPOSING A LINE NEGATIVE

All dust and dirt must be removed from the camera copyboard, the lens, and the film holder before the negative is exposed. Dust on any of these places can cause pinholes in the emulsion of the negative.

Clean the copyboard glass with glass cleaner and a paper towel. If necessary, clean the lens lightly with a lens tissue. For more stubborn spots slightly dampen the tissue with lens cleaning fluid. Be careful not to touch the lens with your fingers. Perspiration on your fingertips can permanently damage a glass lens.

POSITIONING THE COPY. Center the copy on the copyboard. Place a *sensitivity guide* or *gray scale* within the white area of the copy. Position it as close to the center of the copy as possible, Figure 19-5. This gray scale will serve as a helpful guide when the film is developed.

After the sensitivity guide is in place, close the glass cover on the copyboard. Then turn the copyboard so that the copy is parallel to the camera lens and the film holder.

FOCUSING THE CAMERA. Set the camera to obtain the reduction or enlargement desired. Adjust the distance between the lens and the film holder and between the lens and the copyboard. When the camera is properly set, the image on the film will be the correct size and in sharp focus.

Focusing controls on some cameras are calibrated directly in percentage numbers. Other cameras are equipped with digital counters for adjusting lens and copy positions. If the camera you use has a digital counter, consult the focusing chart that came with the camera for proper focusing.

ADJUSTING THE LENS APERTURE. The size of the lens aperture determines

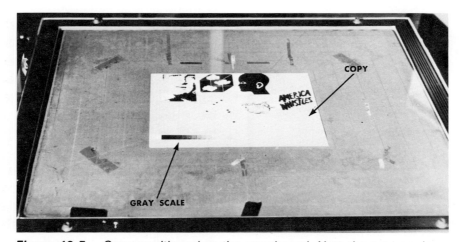

Figure 19-5.   Copy positioned on the copyboard. Note the gray scale which will serve as a guide when the film is developed.

the amount of light that will enter the camera. Aperture size is controlled by a diaphragm.

A diaphragm is a series of adjustable metal plates between the elements of the lens. They determine the size of the aperture. The plates are adjusted by rotating a ring on the lens housing or by moving a lever.

The size of a particular lens opening or aperture is indicated by an f/number. The higher the f/number, the smaller the aperture. Closing the diaphragm from one f/number to the next higher number reduces by half the amount of light passing through the lens. Aperture size relationships are shown in Figure 19-6.

Each lens has its own "best" aperture for photographic reproduction. It is the "best" aperture because it yields sharp, clear negatives while keeping exposure time to a minimum. Generally, the best

aperture will correspond to the f/stop at the midpoint of the f/scale. Use the middle f/stop for your initial exposure.

SETTING THE TIMER. A process camera generally has a timer to control the length of exposure. The timer automatically opens and closes the camera shutter. Usually, the timer controls the camera lights as well.

Exposure time depends upon the type of film being used. Consult the data sheet packed with the film to determine a suitable exposure time for your initial exposure.

Adjusting Exposure Times and f/***Stops for Enlargements and Reductions.*** Film manufacturers suggest exposure times and f/stop numbers for shooting line negatives at full size. Such negatives are exactly the same size (100%) as the copy from which they are produced.

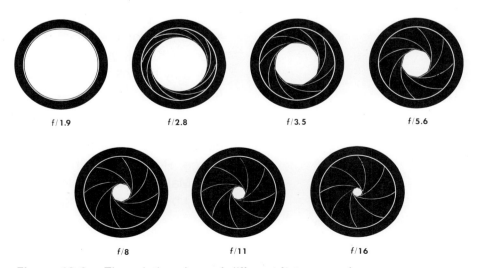

f/1.9   f/2.8   f/3.5   f/5.6

f/8   f/11   f/16

Figure 19-6. *The relative sizes of different* f/*stop openings.*

When enlarging or reducing copy, you must adjust the exposure time and/or the f/stop. To compute the new exposure, multiply the suggested exposure time at full size by an appropriate exposure factor. Consult Figure 19-7 for exposure factors at various percentages of enlargements and reductions.

EXPOSURE COMPENSATION TABLE	
% REDUCTION OR ENLARGEMENT	EXPOSURE FACTOR
25	0.40
30	0.44
40	0.47
50	0.49
60	0.54
65	0.57
70	0.61
75	0.66
80	0.74
85	0.82
90	0.88
95	0.94
100	1.00
105	1.05
110	1.10
115	1.15
120	1.19
125	1.23
130	1.27
140	1.35
150	1.42
160	1.49
170	1.56
180	1.62
190	1.68
200	1.74
210	1.82
220	1.89
230	1.98
240	2.06
250	2.16
260	2.26
270	2.36
280	2.47
290	2.58
300	2.69
400	4.00
500	5.00

Figure 19-7. *Exposure factors for enlargements and reductions.*

For example, if the basic exposure for photographing copy at full size is 22 seconds at f/16 and the copy is enlarged to 150%, the exposure factor is 1.42. Multiply this number by 22 seconds to obtain the new exposure time.

Exposure factor	1.42 seconds
Basic exposure time	× 22 seconds
New exposure time	31.24 seconds
	or 31 seconds

You may also adjust exposure by changing the f/stop setting. Opening the lens one stop (setting at the next lower f/number) while keeping the same exposure time will double the original exposure. Closing the lens one stop (setting at the next higher f/number) while keeping the same exposure time will reduce exposure by one-half.

LOADING THE FILM. Turn off all white lights in the darkroom and turn on the safelights. Be sure the safelight filters are correct for the process film being used. A Kodak Wratten Series 1A red filter may be used with most orthochromatic films.

Remove a sheet of film from the box and cut it slightly larger than the size of the image. Return the extra film to the film box. Make certain the film box is closed tightly before proceeding.

Handling the film by its edges only, place it, emulsion side up, on the center of the film holder. The emulsion side of the film must face the lens during exposure. Under a red safelight, the emulsion side of the film appears lighter than the back side of the film. Also, the emulsion side has a duller finish than does the base side.

Turn on the vacuum pump and close the film holder. The film is now ready to be exposed.

MAKING THE EXPOSURE. Press the exposure button. The camera lights will go on and the shutter will open.

Light reflecting from the white areas of the copy pass through the lens and create a latent image on the film. Because no light reflects from the black areas of the copy, corresponding parts of the film will remain unexposed.

After the exposure is completed, the shutter closes and the lights go off. At this point you can open the film holder and switch off the vacuum pump. The film is now ready for processing. Procedures for processing line negatives are described in Unit 21.

TEST YOUR KNOWLEDGE

1. Explain how to make a pasteup.
2. Define *line copy* and give three examples.
3. Define *continuous tone copy* and list three examples.
4. Explain the difference between a horizontal and a vertical process camera. What is the difference between a darkroom and a gallery camera?
5. Prepare a simple diagram to illustrate the major parts of a process camera. Label the copyboard, lights, lens, bellows, diaphragm, and film holder.
6. Show the size relationship among *f*/stop openings by drawing a series of circles of varying sizes. Include illustrations to represent *f*/stops of 8, 11, 16, 22, 32, and 45.
7. With the aid of Figure 19-7, compute the exposure times required to reduce copy by 50% and to enlarge copy to twice its original size. The exposure time required to photograph the copy at full size is 20 seconds.
8. Tell two ways the emulsion side of a piece of process film can be identified.
9. List in proper sequence the basic steps in exposing a line negative.

UNIT 20
HALFTONE PHOTOGRAPHY

Objectives

When you have completed this unit, you will be able to:

1. Identify the shadow, highlight, and middle tone areas of a photograph.
2. Describe the appearance of the dots that make up the shadow, highlight, and middle tone areas of a halftone print.
3. Define *contact screen.*
4. Illustrate how different amounts of light reflecting from the copy can determine the size of the dots formed on a halftone negative.
5. Explain why halftone photography requires a longer exposure time than does line photography.
6. Explain the differences between a main exposure and a flash exposure.
7. List the basic procedures for exposing a halftone negative.

Terms to Know

Here are some of the words you will need to understand before reading this unit. If the meaning of a word is not clear to you, look it up in the Glossary in the back of this book.

continuous tone copy	contact screen	f/stop
highlight areas	gray scale	main exposure
middle tones	focusing	flash exposure
halftone	aperture	orthochromatic

CONTINUOUS TONE COPY

Most photographic prints, airbrush renderings, and wash drawings are made up of black areas, white areas, and areas containing varying tones of gray. Such copy is called continuous tone copy. Continuous tone copy images are those that show gradations in tone.

Figure 20-1 shows a continuous tone photograph. Note that the image is made up of black areas, white areas, and areas that are gray. The black or darkest parts in the photograph are called *shadow areas.* The lightest portions of the photograph are termed *high-*

light areas. Grays in the photograph are referred to as *middle tones.*

Look again at Figure 20-1. Note the black, white, and gray areas. Now look at Figure 20-2. Figure 20-2 is an enlarged portion of Figure 20-1. Note how

Figure 20-2. *An enlarged section of Figure 20-1. Note how the image is formed by black dots. The sizes of these dots vary.*

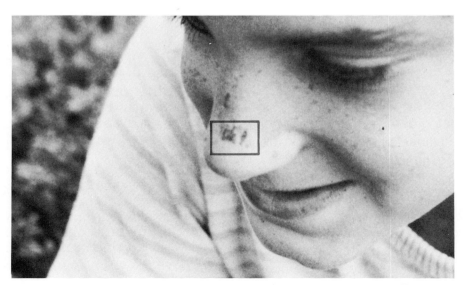

Figure 20-1. *A continuous-tone photograph contains gradations in tone. Tones range from white, through the various shades of gray, to black.*

the image is formed by various sizes of dots. The dots are printed in black ink only.

In Section 9 you will learn that printing plates can transfer ink to the paper or withhold ink from the paper. They cannot modify the color of the ink on the press to produce gradations in tone. If you ink a press plate with black ink, it will print black; it will not print gray.

Continuous tone copy is reproduced by combining printing techniques with a form of optical illusion. When black dots are large and close together, they appear as dark grays or shadow areas. Areas containing small black dots that are widely spaced appear light in tone. They form the highlight areas. Middletones are produced by controlling the size and density of the black dots. There are really no gray tones. It is an optical illusion.

Printed reproductions of continuous tone photographs, are called *halftone prints.* Halftone prints are made from *halftone negatives.*

SPECIAL TREATMENT OF CONTINUOUS TONE COPY. Continuous tone copy and line copy cannot be combined in the same mechanical layout. They must be photographed separately. Once photographed, however, a halftone negative can be com-

bined with a line negative to produce a single plate which can print both line and halftone images.

A "window" added to the line negative can aid in positioning the halftone negative. A window is formed by pasting a piece of black or red paper or film on the line mechanical, Figure 20-3. When it is

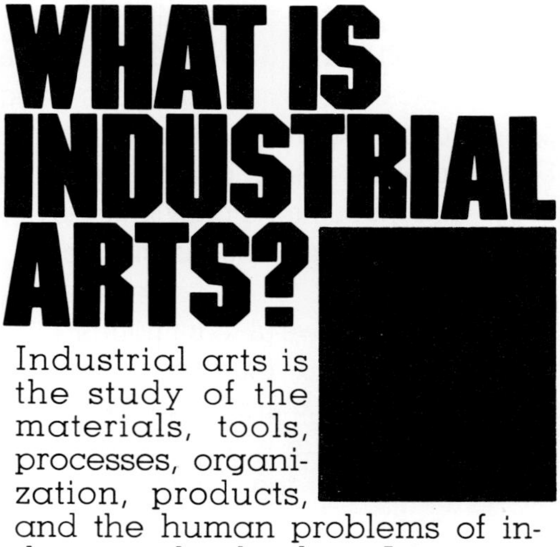

WHAT IS INDUSTRIAL ARTS?

Industrial arts is the study of the materials, tools, processes, organization, products, and the human problems of industry and technology. It is a very important part of the general education of all young people. Opportunities are provided for studying various phases of industry through technical and scientific research and in the actual use of the tools and materials of industry and technology. The junior and senior high school teacher helps provide firsthand experiences in industrial arts courses dealing with woodworking, metalworking, electricity and electronics, manufacturing, graphic arts, mechanical drawing, design, power mechanics, ceramics, plastics, and crafts.

Figure 20-3. *A negative made from this mechanical will contain a clear window. A halftone negative will be attached to this window prior to exposing the plate.*

photographed, the black or red material will form a clear window in the line negative. The halftone negative is attached to this window before making the printing plate.

HALFTONE NEGATIVES

Halftone negatives are made by exposing process film through a special contact screen to the light reflecting from continuous tone copy. The screen creates the dot pattern on the negative. A halftone negative is shown in Figure 20-4.

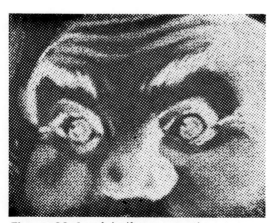

Figure 20-4. *A halftone negative.*

The image on a halftone negative is formed by dots called *halftone dots*. Halftone dots are created on the film when light reflecting from the copy passes through the contact screen.

CONTACT SCREENS. An enlarged view of a contact or halftone screen is shown in Figure 20-5. The dot structure of the screen is produced photographically on a flexible, transparent plastic. The dots are vignetted or shaded. That means they are dots with fuzzy edges.

Figure 20-5. *An enlarged section of a contact screen. The screen is made up of dots with fuzzy edges.*

Contact screens are classified according to the number of dots they produce per linear inch of film. The more dots per inch, the less noticeable will be the dot pattern in the negative and the print. Screen sizes may range from 65 to 200 lines per inch. The lines per inch can be determined by counting the number of dots along one inch of a 45 degree line.

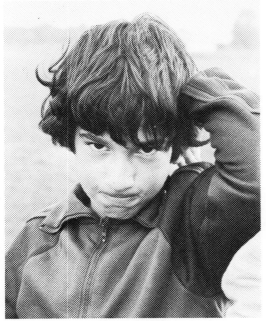

Figure 20-6. *A 65-line screen was used to produce this photograph.*

Figure 20-7. *This photograph was prepared with a 150-line screen.*

Figure 20-6 is a photograph reproduced with a 65-line screen. Figure 20-7 shows the same photograph prepared with a 150-line screen.

Contact screens are available in gray and magenta (bluish-red) colors. They are relatively expensive and may be easily scratched or spotted. Handle contact screens carefully by their edges only.

Forming the Halftone Dot. During exposure, the emulsion of the contact screen is in direct contact with the emulsion of the process film. The contact screen actually covers the process film. Both are held in the film holder. Tight contact is maintained by a vacuum pump.

Light reflecting from the continuous tone copy must pass through the contact screen in order to create a latent image on the film. Different copy areas reflect different amounts of light. The intensity of the light passing through the contact screen will determine both the size and the shape of the halftone dots.

Very little light is reflected from the shadow areas of the copy. Because of its limited intensity, this light is able to penetrate only the clear areas of the contact screen.

Light reflecting from the highlight areas of the copy is much more intense than light reflecting from shadow areas. Because of its intensity, light reflecting from highlight areas can penetrate the translucent as well as the clear portions of the contact screen. This forms large dots on the process film. Figure 20-8 shows how halftone dots are formed.

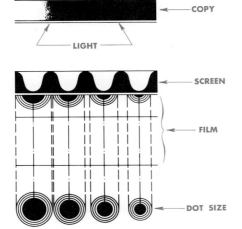

Figure 20-8. Forming the halftone dot. Light reflecting from the continuous-tone copy passes through the halftone screen and strikes the film. The size of the dot formed on the film is determined by the intensity of the light reflecting from the copy.

AUTOSCREEN FILM. Autoscreen film is manufactured by Kodak. It is a pre-screened process film for making halftones. The autoscreen film emulsion has a 133-line screen pattern already built in. Therefore, autoscreen film does not need a contact screen to produce a halftone negative.

EXPOSING A HALFTONE NEGATIVE

Shooting a halftone negative is basically the same as shooting a line negative: positioning the copy, focusing the camera, adjusting the lens aperture, loading the film and contact screen, and making the exposures.

POSITIONING THE COPY. Center the copy on the copyboard. Place a *sensitivity* guide or *gray scale* within the white area of the copy. Close the glass cover on the copyboard and turn the copy parallel to the lens and film holder.

FOCUSING THE CAMERA. Adjust the camera for the desired reduction or enlargement. On some cameras, controls are calibrated in percentage numbers. Set these controls according to the percentage of reduction or enlargement desired. On cameras with digital counters, consult the focusing chart that came with the camera. When the camera is properly set, the image on the film will be the correct size and in sharp focus.

ADJUSTING THE LENS APERTURE. Control the aperture size by setting the diaphragm with the ring or lever on the lens housing. Generally, set the diaphragm at the *f*/stop at midpoint of the *f*/numbers.

LOADING THE FILM AND CONTACT SCREEN. Turn off all white lights in the darkroom and turn on the safelights.

Remove a sheet of film from the film box and cut it slightly larger than the size of the image. Close the film box. Place the film, emulsion side up, on the center of the film holder. Turn on the vacuum pump.

Now cover the film with a contact screen larger than the film on all sides. The emulsion side of the screen should contact the emulsion side of the film. During exposure, reflected light will pass through the back of the contact screen and strike the emulsion of the film.

Complete the loading by smoothing the screen over the film. You may use a rubber roller for this purpose. Then close the film holder. The film is now ready to be exposed.

MAKING THE EXPOSURES. Two exposures are usually necessary to make a halftone negative: a main exposure and a flash exposure.

Main Exposure. During the main exposure, light reflecting from the copy must pass through the contact screen before it can expose the film. Some of the light never gets through; it is absorbed by the screen. Because so much light is lost, halftone photography requires a main exposure approximately two to four times longer than the exposure required for line copy.

Ask your teacher to help you determine the proper exposure time for photographing continuous tone copy at full size. If you are enlarging or reducing the copy, you must calculate a new exposure time based on the percentage of enlargement or reduction. Procedures for doing this are described in Unit 19. Exposure factors to be used are shown in Figure 20-9.

EXPOSURE COMPENSATION TABLE	
% REDUCTION OR ENLARGEMENT	EXPOSURE FACTOR
25	0.40
30	0.44
40	0.47
50	0.49
60	0.54
65	0.57
70	0.61
75	0.66
80	0.74
85	0.82
90	0.88
95	0.94
100	1.00
105	1.05
110	1.10
115	1.15
120	1.19
125	1.23
130	1.27
140	1.35
150	1.42
160	1.49
170	1.56
180	1.62
190	1.68
200	1.74
210	1.82
220	1.89
230	1.98
240	2.06
250	2.16
260	2.26
270	2.36
280	2.47
290	2.58
300	2.69
400	4.00
500	5.00

Figure 20-9. Exposure factors for enlargements and reductions.

You can accurately determine exposure times with a Kodak Graphic Arts Exposure Computer, Figure 20-10. It includes a *Reflection Density Guide* and an *Exposure Computer*. Instructions for using these devices are included with the kit.

After you have calculated the main exposure, set the timer and expose the film. The timer automatically opens and closes the camera shutter and operates the lights. The film is ready for the flash exposure.

Flash Exposure. The flash exposure is a supplementary exposure. It is used to strengthen the dots in the shadow areas of the negative. A flash exposure also improves detail in the negative.

Time requirements for a flash exposure can be accurately determined with the aid of a Kodak Graphic Arts Computer. Most, but not all, halftone negatives require a flash exposure.

The continuous tone copy is not used during the flash exposure. Flashing takes place within the darkroom with a flashing lamp. Figure 20-11 shows the

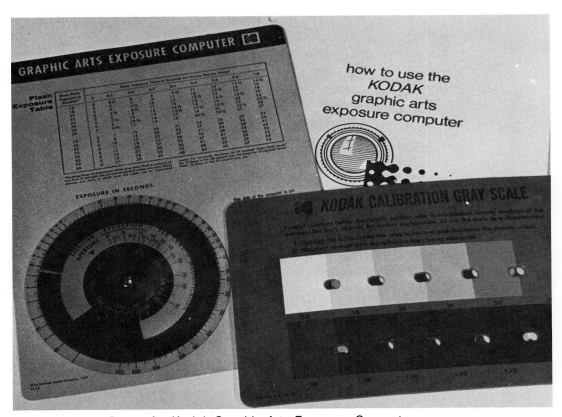

Figure 20-10. *Parts of a Kodak Graphic Arts Exposure Computer.*

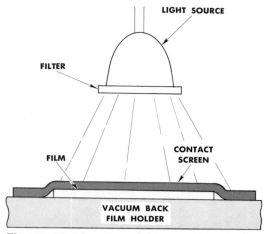

Figure 20-11. *A typical arrangement for flashing a halftone negative.*

arrangement for flashing a halftone negative. Note that the exposure is made through a contact screen while the film holder is open. The vacuum pump must remain on throughout the exposure to keep the film and screen from moving.

After the flash exposure, turn the flashing lamp and the vacuum pump off. Then remove the contact screen and return it to its protective folder. The film is now ready for processing. Procedures for processing halftone negatives are described in Unit 21.

TEST YOUR KNOWLEDGE

1. Identify the shadow areas, the highlight areas, and the middle tone areas of the continuous tone photograph shown in Figure 20-1.
2. Describe the appearance of the dots that make up the shadow, highlight, and middle tone areas of the halftone print shown in Figure 20-2.
3. Describe what is meant by *contact screen.* How are contact screens classified?
4. Prepare a simple diagram illustrating how different amounts of light pass through a contact screen. Also show how this affects the size and shape of the dots formed on a halftone negative.
5. Explain why halftone photography requires a longer exposure time than does line photography.
6. Explain the differences between a main exposure and a flash exposure, the purpose and procedures of each.
7. List in proper sequence the basic steps in exposing a halftone negative.

UNIT 21

PROCESSING LINE AND HALFTONE NEGATIVES AND MAKING FILM POSITIVES

Objectives

When you have completed this unit, you will be able to:
1. Describe the characteristics of a well-planned darkroom.
2. Illustrate three types of darkroom entrances.
3. List eight safety rules that must be followed when working in a darkroom.
4. Illustrate the tray setup for processing line and halftone negatives.
5. Describe the functions of the developer, stop, and fixing solutions used in processing negatives.
6. List the steps in processing line and halftone negatives.
7. Illustrate how film positives are made.
8. List the steps in exposing and processing a film positive.

Terms to Know

Here are some of the words you will need to understand before reading this unit. If the meaning of a word is not clear to you, look it up in the Glossary in the back of this book.

darkroom	stop bath	film positive
safelight	fixer	emulsion
developer		

THE DARKROOM

After the film is exposed, it contains a latent or invisible line or halftone image. The exposed film must be processed in order to make this image visible. Processing takes place in a darkroom, Figure 21-1.

A WELL-PLANNED DARKROOM.

Darkrooms can vary in size and shape and in the variety and sophistication of equipment they contain. However, all darkrooms must be light-tight. They have several other things in common, as well.

Size and Arrangement. Although a darkroom can be small, it must be at least large enough to house the necessary equipment. There should also be an adequate amount of working room and space to store film and chemicals.

Equipment should be arranged within the darkroom to promote a smooth work flow. Figure 21-2 shows an efficient arrangement for a small darkroom.

Cleanliness. The importance of keeping the darkroom clean cannot be over-emphasized. The darkroom must be

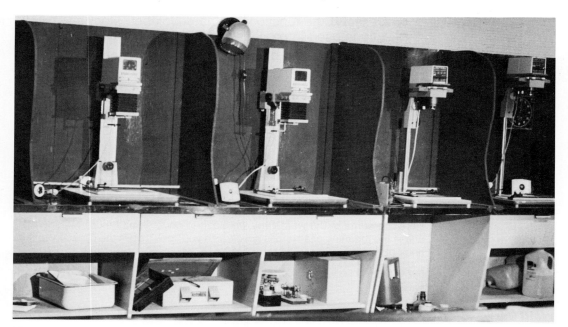

Figure 21-1. *A well-planned darkroom.*

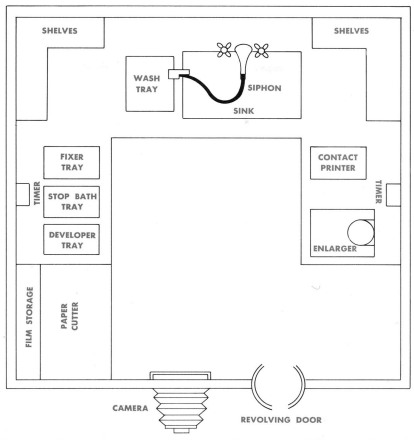

Figure 21-2. An efficient arrangement for a small darkroom. Work can flow smoothly from one work station to the next.

kept as free as possible of dirt and dust. Spilled chemicals must be cleaned up immediately. The floor should be mopped regularly.

A ventilation system that keeps dust and dirt from entering can keep the darkroom clean. Daily dusting of all equipment and work surfaces will also help.

An air conditioner, if possible, should be installed in the darkroom. Besides cooling, it will freshen and clean the air.

Entrance and Exit. The darkroom should have a door or light trap that permits people to enter and exit even while the darkroom is in use. Typical darkroom entrances are shown in Figures 21-3 through 21-5. Figure 21-3 illustrates the layout for a double door entrance. Figure 21-4 shows a typical light trap arrangement. A revolving darkroom door is shown in Figure 21-5.

Utilities. Both hot and cold water are needed. If possible, a device to accurately control the sink's water temperature should also be provided. A darkroom sink is pictured in Figure 21-6.

Electrical outlets are also necessary. To insure against an electrical overload,

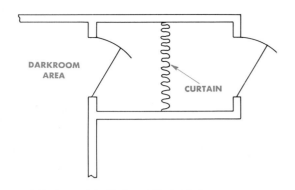

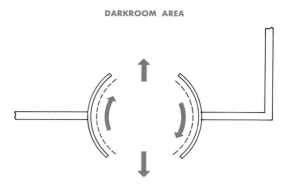

Figure 21-3. *A double-door darkroom entrance. (Bottom, Beta Screen Corp.)*

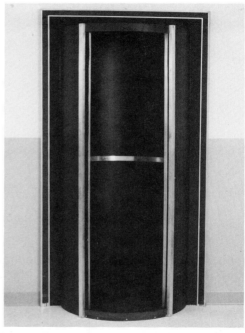

Figure 21-5. *Revolving darkroom doors consist of two cylinders. The inner cylinder turns within a stationary outer cylinder. (Bottom, Electronic Systems Engineering Co.)*

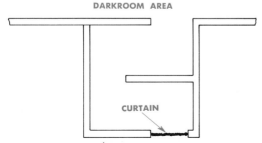

Figure 21-4. *A light trap will allow people to enter and exit even while the darkroom is in use.*

there must be an adequate number of circuits of the proper size.

Lighting. An adequate number of safelights should be located throughout the darkroom. There should be safelights at the darkroom sink and near each major piece of equipment. There should also be a safelight placed near the darkroom exit. Be sure all safelight filters are correct for the film being used.

Figure 21-6. *A darkroom sink.*
(nuArc Company, Inc.)

In addition to the safelights, a source of white light should also be available. White light is especially helpful when preparing or cleaning the darkroom.

SAFETY IN THE DARKROOM. You can minimize the chances of an accident in the darkroom if you follow basic safety rules:

1. Let your eyes become accustomed to the darkness before you start to work in the darkroom.
2. Clean up water and chemical spills immediately to prevent slipping and to reduce the danger of electrical shock.
3. Handle all chemicals with care to prevent splashing them into your eyes.
4. Never mix chemicals in the dark.

5. Store chemicals in covered containers. Use plastic containers whenever possible.
6. If darkroom chemicals irritate your hands, wear rubber or plastic gloves. Wash your hands thoroughly after placing them in any chemicals.
7. Be sure that all electrical equipment used in the darkroom is properly grounded.
8. Never handle electrical equipment when your hands are wet or when you are standing on or near a moist surface.

PROCESSING LINE AND HALFTONE NEGATIVES

Line and halftone negatives are generally processed under red safelights. Use three trays. Fill the first tray with developer, the second with stop, and the third tray with fixer. You also need a large tray or tank to wash the processed prints. A typical setup is shown in Figure 21-7.

DEVELOPING THE NEGATIVE. A special chemical, called developer, is used to reduce the exposed silver bromide crystals to pure silver. Developer is available as a concentrate in both dry and liquid forms. The concentrate must be mixed with water according to the manufacturer's recommendations.

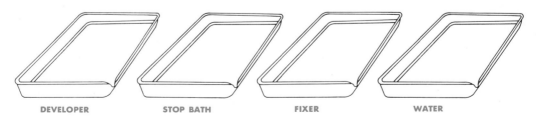

DEVELOPER   STOP BATH   FIXER   WATER

Figure 21-7. *A typical tray setup for processing line and halftone negatives.*

Figure 21-8. *The negative is developed until step 4 on the sensitivity guide turns completely black.*

Process film developer is generally prepared in two parts, Part A and Part B. These two parts are mixed just before you develop the film. Once mixed, the developer will remain usable for about one hour. The temperature of the developer should be kept between 68° and 75° F (20°-24° C).

Line and halftone negatives may be developed by time or inspection techniques. Follow the manufacturer's instructions concerning temperature and agitation if the photographic film is to be developed for a specific period of time. If the film is developed by inspection, remove it from the developer when the desired step turns black on the sensitivity guide.

You will recall that the sensitivity guide was placed on the copy before exposure. The step desired is usually a step 4, Figure 21-8. Step 5 on the sensitivity guide will appear as light gray before solid step 4 is reached.

STOPPING THE ACTION OF THE DE-VELOPER. A mild acetic acid solution, called a stop bath, is used to stop the

action of the developer. The temperature of the stop should be about the same as the developer.

After the film is developed, transfer it to the stop bath, with a pair of tongs. The stop neutralizes the action of the developer. Let the film remain in the stop bath for a minimum of 30 seconds while you continuously agitate the tray.

REMOVING THE UNEXPOSED SIL-VER CRYSTALS. Use a fixing solution to remove all unexposed and undeveloped silver crystals from the developed film. The fixer will also harden the film emulsion. Its temperature should be about the same as the developer.

Use a second pair of tongs to transfer the film from the stop bath to the fixing solution. Leave the film in the fixer for about five minutes.

WASHING THE FILM. Wash the film under clear running water for about ten minutes. Improperly washed film will begin to fog and discolor in a relatively short time.

DRYING THE FILM. Dry the film by hanging it in a dust-free area. Attach clips to opposite sides of the film. Use the top clip to hang the film. The weight of the bottom clip helps prevent the film from curling.

MAKING FILM POSITIVES

Film negatives are sometimes used to make film positives. Positives are needed to make photographic silk screen stencils or to produce certain types of offset plates.

The image on a film positive is positive rather than negative. It is clear where the original subject is light and black where the original is dark.

Figure 21-9 shows how to make film positives. Place the emulsion side of the negative against the emulsion side of the process film. Use a contact printing frame or vacuum printer to maintain tight contact.

Expose the process film through the negative to a source of light. Light passing through the clear areas of the negative will produce a black area on the film after it is processed. Because no light

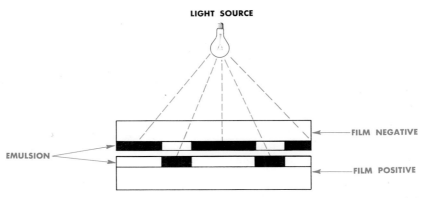

Figure 21-9. *Making a film positive. The amount of light striking the film's emulsion is determined by the silver image on the negative.*

passes throught the opaque areas of the negative, these areas of film are not exposed and will turn clear after the film is processed.

CONTACT FRAMES AND VACUUM PRINTERS.

Use a contact printing frame or vacuum printer to keep the negative and process film in tight contact. A contact printing frame is shown in Figure 21-10.

Figure 21-10. *A contact printing frame is used to maintain tight contact between the emulsion of the negative and the emulsion on the process film.*

Load the contact frame in a darkroom with only safelights on. Place the base of the negative on the glass, emulsion side (dull side) up. Then place the process film over the negative, emulsion side (dull side) down. Close the frame and expose the process film through the negative.

A vacuum printer, Figure 21-11, maintains tight contact between the film and negative with a vacuum pump. Load the vacuum printer by placing the base of the process film on the rubber blanket. Then place the negative, emulsion side down, on the process film. Close the glass cover of the printer and turn on the vacuum pump. Expose the film through the negative to a source of light.

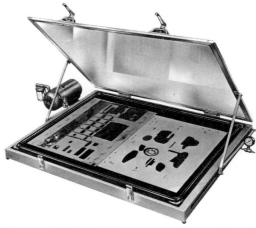

Figure 21-11. *When a vacuum printer is used, tight contact between the film and negative is maintained by means of a vacuum pump. (nuArc Company, Inc.)*

EXPOSING THE FILM POSITIVE.

If you are using a contact printing frame, place it on the baseboard of an enlarger. Use the light coming from the enlarger lens to expose the film.

When you use a vacuum printer, you will need an external light source such as the one shown in Figure 21-12.

Figure 21-12. *An external light source is used to expose the film positive. (nuArc Company, Inc.)*

Determining Exposure Time. A strip of process film one-inch wide may be used to determine correct exposure time. Cut this strip from a sheet of film and load it into the frame or printer. Expose the strip of film for exactly ten seconds.

Process the strip according to the instructions given for processing line and halftone negatives. If the image on the developed film strip is too light, expose and process another strip of film using a longer exposure time. If the image is too dark, shorten the exposure time. Repeat the process until a satisfactory image is obtained.

Once you determine the proper exposure time, a full-size film positive can be made. Process this positive the same way as you process a negative.

TEST YOUR KNOWLEDGE

1. Describe the characteristics of a well-planned darkroom.
2. Use simple diagrams to illustrate a double door entrance, a light trap entrance, and a revolving door entrance to a darkroom.
3. List eight safety rules that must be followed when working in a darkroom.
4. Illustrate a typical tray setup for processing line and halftone negatives.
5. Describe the functions of the developer, stop, and fixing solutions in processing line and halftone negatives.
6. List in sequence the major steps in processing line and halftone negatives.
7. Prepare a simple diagram to illustrate how film positives are made.
8. List in proper order the major steps in exposing and processing a film positive.

SECTION 8

PLATEMAKING

UNIT 22

PLATES FOR RELIEF (LETTERPRESS) PRINTING

Objectives

When you have completed this unit, you will be able to:

1. Identify the difference between original and duplicate letterpress plates.
2. Name three types of original and three types of duplicate letterpress plates.
3. List the basic steps in locking up a type form.
4. Illustrate the chaser method of locking up a type form.
5. Define *imposition*.
6. List the steps in preparing a linoleum block.
7. Select linoleum block plate designs that are suitable for reproduction.
8. Explain how to safely cut a linoleum block.
9. Define *photoengraving*.
10. Describe the differences between stereotypes and electrotypes.
11. List the basic steps in making a rubber stamp.

Terms to Know

Here are some of the words you will need to understand before reading this unit. If the meaning of a word is not clear to you, look it up in the Glossary in the back of this book.

letterpress printing	galley	imposition	electrotype
image carrier	head	linoleum block	rubber stamp press
plates	furniture	type-high gage	proof press
original plates	quoins	photoengraving	flexography
chase	reglets	presensitized plate	matrix
imposing stone	planer	stereotype	
chaser method	testing for lift		

TYPES OF RELIEF OR LETTERPRESS PLATES

Printing from a raised surface is called *relief* or *letterpress printing*. The image carriers or plates used in letterpress printing are called letterpress plates. There are two basic types of letterpress plates: *original* plates and *duplicate* plates.

Original plates are formed by locking up hand-set or machine-set hot type in a special metal frame called a *chase*. They may also be made by hand cutting linoleum or wood blocks. Letterpress plates produced photographically are also original plates which are called *photoengravings*.

Molds are made from original plates to duplicate letterpress plates. Several duplicates can be made from a single mold. Stereotypes, electrotypes, and rubber plates are all forms of duplicate letterpress plates.

HAND-SET AND MACHINE-SET HOT TYPE.
Hot type must be locked up in a special metal frame called a chase before it can be used on a press, Figure 22-1.

Type forms are locked up in a chase on an *imposing stone,* Figure 22-2. Below

Figure 22-1. *The form is locked up in a chase prior to being printed on a letterpress.*

Figure 22-2. *An imposing stone is a steel-topped table on which type forms are locked up. (Hamilton Industries)*

the stone are compartments for storing tools and materials used in locking up the type form.

Locking up a Type Form. The most common method of lock up is the *chaser* method. Begin by cleaning the surface of the imposing stone. Wipe the stone with a clean cloth to remove particles of dirt so that all type characters will rest squarely on the stone's surface while the form is locked up.

Carefully slide the type form from the galley onto the stone. The *head* or top of the form should be nearest you or to your left. The position of the head is determined by the layout of the job. Try to place the form so that it will print in the desired location on the paper when the long side of the paper is parallel with the long side of the chase.

Next surround the type form with a chase. If you will be printing on a small piece of paper, try to place the form slightly above the center of the chase. This will make it easier to feed the press with paper when the form is printed.

When the form is positioned in the chase, surround the form with furniture, Figure 22-3. Furniture consists of wood or metal blocks used to fill the space between the type form and chase during lockup. First place four pieces of furniture clockwise around the form, overlapping at each corner. Each piece of furni-

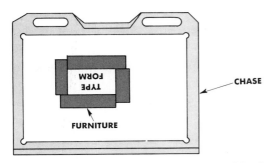

Figure 22-3. *The chaser method of lock up. The type form is completely surrounded by wood or metal furniture.*

ture should be slightly larger than the side against which it is placed. Each piece overlaps or *chases* the next piece of furniture around the form.

Then fill the space to the bottom and left of the type form with additional furniture. Use longer pieces of furniture as you approach the chase. Small spaces at the bottom and left of the chase can be filled by simply sliding the type form and furniture down and toward the left, Figure 22-4.

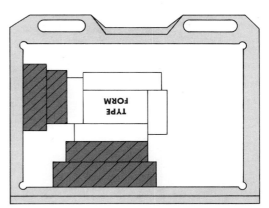

Figure 22-4. *Fill in the space at the bottom and left of the type form with furniture.*

Next, position *quoins* against the furniture at the top and right-hand side of the form. Quoins are locks used to hold the form securely in the chase. Properly positioned quoins are shown in Figure

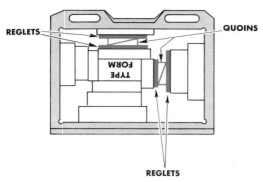

REGLETS

QUOINS

TYPE FORM

REGLETS

Figure 22-5. *Quoins are positioned at the top and right side of the type form. Reglets are used to protect the furniture.*

22-5. Place *reglets,* strips of wood 6 or 12 points thick, on both sides of each pair of quoins. Reglets protect the furniture when the quoins are tightened.

Once the quoins and reglets are in place, carefully remove the string from around the type form. Shift the furniture and quoins located at the top and right so that they rest firmly against the form. Fill in the remaining space at the top and

QUOIN KEY

PAIR OF QUOINS

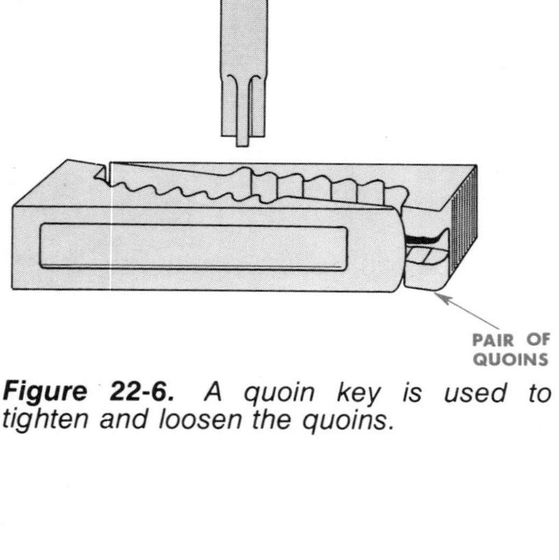

Figure 22-6. *A quoin key is used to tighten and loosen the quoins.*

at the right of the form with additional furniture.

Before using a quoin key, Figure 22-6, tighten each pair of quoins with your fingers by pushing the wedges toward each other. Then make sure that all type characters are resting squarely on the surface of the stone. A *planer,* Figure 22-7, is used for this purpose. Place the flat surface of the planer on the type form and tap gently with the back of the quoin key. Be sure that all parts of the form rest solidly on the stone.

Figure 22-7. *Plane the form to insure that all type characters are resting squarely on the stone.*

After the form is planed, tighten the quoins with the quoin key. Tighten each quoin alternately, a little at a time. Repeat until the form is tight in the chase. Do not overtighten. Too much pressure on the quoins will crack the chase.

Test the lockup for tightness by carefully placing the end of the quoin key under one edge of the chase, Figure 22-8. Press down with your fingers on each line of type to determine any looseness.

Figure 22-8. *Testing for lift.*

This is called *testing for lift*. Loose lines of type must be rejustified before the form is printed. Usually this is done by adding brass or copper spaces while the form is still in the chase.

After the lockup is completed, the chase is placed in the press and printed. Procedures for printing are described in Unit 27.

If the job will not be printed immediately, store the lockup in the chase rack pro-

vided in the imposing stone. Because wood furniture may expand or contract due to varying temperature and humidity, check the tightness of the form again before it is printed.

Imposition. Imposition means positioning one or more type forms within a chase. The contents of the chase is then printed on a single sheet of paper. Several forms are printed on a single sheet so that the paper can be folded and trimmed to form a booklet. If the type forms have been properly imposed, the pages of the booklet will appear in their correct order.

Figure 22-9 shows a chase containing four pages of type. Furniture has been added between each form to provide the necessary margins on each printed page. Note that several quoins are used to hold the type forms securely in the chase.

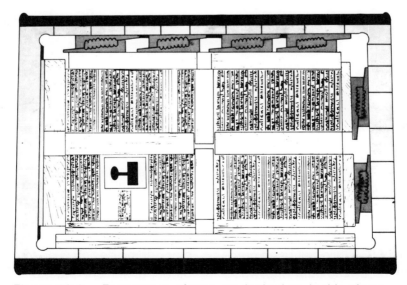

Figure 22-9. *Four pages of type are locked up in this chase.*

The layout for a four-page booklet to be printed using a form of lockup called work-and-turn is shown in Figure 22-10. First all four forms are printed on one side of the sheet. The paper is then turned over and run through the press a second time. During this second run, the forms for pages 2 and 3 print on the backs of pages 1 and 4. Forms for pages 1 and 4 print on the backs of pages 2 and 3. The printed sheets are then cut and folded as shown in Figure 22-10. The result is two complete four-page booklets. With this work-and-turn lockup, only 500 sheets of paper are needed to produce 1000 booklets.

Several duplicate type forms may also be locked up in a chase and printed on a large sheet of paper. The large printed sheet is then cut to form several duplicate printed pieces. This procedure also reduces the number of sheets that have to be fed through the press to obtain the desired number of printed copies.

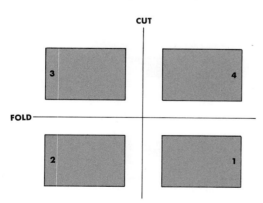

Figure 22-10. Layout for a four-page work-and-turn lock up.

HAND-CUT LINOLEUM AND WOOD BLOCK PLATES. While not used commercially, hand-cut linoleum and wood block plates can reproduce multiple

images on a letterpress. Linoleum and wood plates are made by carving into the flat surface of a linoleum block or a wood block. Areas not to print are cut away. The image to be printed is left raised on the surface of the block.

Linoleum and wood block plates are prepared using the same basic procedures. Because linoleum is easier to cut than wood, its preparation will be discussed here.

Preparing a Linoleum Block. Begin by creating or selecting a design to be reproduced. The design should have solid areas of a single color and heavy lines. Avoid designs containing fine lines. Fine lines are difficult to cut and tend to collapse or break during the printing process. A suitable linoleum block design is shown in Figure 22-11.

Figure 22-11. A design suitable for linoleum block printing. It consists of heavy lines and solid areas of color.

The design must be transferred in reverse onto the surface of the linoleum block. If the design is on tracing paper or other translucent material, carbon paper may be used to reverse the image. Tape the carbon paper, carbon side down, on the surface of the block. Place the design face down over the carbon paper. Use tape to hold the design in place on the block. By tracing over the back of the original design, you will transfer the image in reverse onto the surface of the linoleum.

At this point, it is wise to ink the carbon image that has been placed on the block. Use india ink and an inking pen. Inking is done to insure that the entire image will remain on the block without smudging during the carving process.

Figure 22-13. *Linoleum block carving tools. (Hunt Manufacturing Co.)*

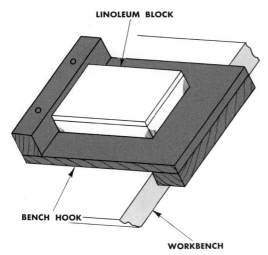

Figure 22-12. *Use a bench hook to hold the linoleum block while it is being cut.*

When the india ink is dry, place the linoleum block on a wooden bench hook, Figure 22-12. The bench hook holds the block while it is being carved.

Figure 22-13 shows a set of linoleum block carving tools. The set includes a single handle and several cutting tools. Three basic types of cutting tools are included: the knife, the veiner, and the gouge.

Caution! Linoleum carving tools are sharp. Handle them with care. Always push the cutting tool away from your body. Keep both hands out of the path of the blade when cutting.

Both the knife and veiner can be used to outline the image. If a knife is used, hold it at a slight angle to avoid cutting under the raised image. A slightly beveled edge is required around the raised image. The veiner, a V-shaped chisel, will automatically produce a beveled edge. When it is used correctly, the point of the V is the part of the tool that first contacts the linoleum.

After the image is outlined, remove all non-image areas with a gouge. A gouge is a U-shaped chisel. All non-printing areas must be cut at least 1/16 inch below the surface of the linoleum. Otherwise these sections may reproduce when the block is printed.

Linoleum blocks are made type high (0.918″) by gluing chipboard or paper to

A proof of the block is pulled so that you can see any errors or places where more linoleum has to be removed. Once you have made the necessary corrections, the linoleum block can be locked up and printed. Procedures for printing are described in Unit 27.

Multicolor Linoleum Block Printing. Multicolor images can be printed with linoleum block printing plates. A separate block must be carved for each color in the design. If a two-color image is to be printed, two blocks must be carved. A four-color design requires four linoleum blocks, one for each color.

PHOTOENGRAVINGS. Photoengravings are letterpress plates produced through a combination of photographic and etching techniques. They can print either line or halftone images. A photo engraved plate is shown in Figure 22-15.

the back of the block. A type high gage is used to measure the height of the block, Figure 22-14. Proofing is then done in a galley on the proof press. Procedures for proofing are described in Unit 16.

Figure 22-14. *Use a type high gage to check the height of the block. Type high is 0.918 inch.*

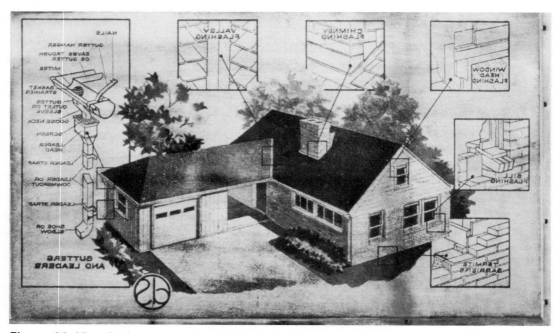

Figure 22-15. *A photoengraving is an original letterpress plate.*

Traditionally, photoengravings have been prepared on sheets of zinc, magnesium, or copper. Zinc and magnesium are generally used for line images. Halftone images are most often prepared on copper sheets. Today, many photoengravings are being made from plastic sheets rather than metal ones.

The first step in preparing a photoengraving is to sensitize the metal or plastic sheet by coating the sheet with a light-sensitive emulsion. Some brands of metal and plastic sheets can be purchased with the light-sensitive coating already applied. These are called presensitized plates.

After the sheet is sensitized, position it in an exposure frame. Place a line or halftone negative in contact with the light-sensitive emulsion. The wrong-reading side of the negative must face up. Then expose the plate through the negative to a strong source of light. Light passing through the transparent areas of the negative hardens the emulsion on the plate below. Because no light passes through the opaque areas of the negative, the emulsion below is not affected. After exposure, process the plate to make the image visible. Processing also removes the light-sensitive coating from the unexposed areas of the plate.

The emulsion remaining on the plate serves as a resist. Areas beneath the resist are not affected when the plate is immersed in an etching bath. The unprotected areas, however, are eaten or etched away. An acid solution is gener-

ally used to etch metal plates. An alkaline solution is used with plastic plates. One type of etching machine is pictured in Figure 22-16.

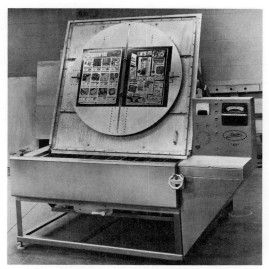

Figure 22-16. *A machine used to etch photoengravings. (Master Sales & Service Corp.)*

After the plate is etched, large non-image areas may be deepened mechanically with a router. The plate is then mounted type high and proofed on a proof press. Finally it is locked in a chase in preparation for printing.

STEREOTYPE PLATES. Stereotypes are duplicate plates. They are produced from paper molds or matrices, either flat or curved. Curved stereotypes are printed on rotary-type presses.

Stereotype plates cannot be used to reproduce fine detail. The quality of a stereotype image is relatively poor. Halftones must generally be limited to 85 lines and coarser. Stereotype plates are most often used for newspaper printing.

Figure 22-17. *A matrix press is used to produce a stereotype matrix.*

Making Stereotype Plates. Stereotypes are produced from original type forms and photoengravings that have been locked up in a chase. Matrix paper is placed over the original plates and pressure is applied. See Figure 22-17. A stereotype matrix or mat results.

The stereotype mat is next placed in a casting box. The mat may be used flat or it may be curved. Molten metal is then poured directly onto the matrix.

After the metal solidifies, the mat is stripped away and the stereotype plate is prepared for the press. Preparation includes cutting the plate to size, shaving it to uniform thickness, and routing excess metal away from the non-image areas. Flat plates must be mounted to make them type high.

ELECTROTYPE PLATES. Electrotypes are high-quality duplicate plates. They are made by depositing or plating metal on molds made from original type forms and photoengravings.

Electrotypes can be made flat or curved. Curved electrotypes are used on rotary type presses. Books and magazines produced by letterpress are generally printed from electrotype plates.

Making Electrotype Plates. A special sheet of matrix material is placed over the type and photoengravings locked up in a chase. Pressure is applied to the

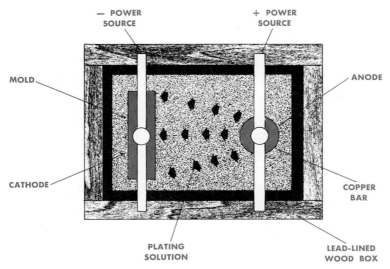

Figure 22-18. *The electroplating process.*

matrix material, and it is stripped away from the original plate. The mold is sprayed with silver paint or coated with graphite so that it will conduct electricity during the plating operation.

Figure 22-18 shows the electroplating process. The mold is connected to the negative terminal of a power source. A pure copper bar is attached to the positive terminal of the same power source. Both the mold and the copper bar are then suspended in a liquid plating solution. As current flows through the solution, copper atoms travel from the bar to the mold.

The electroplating process is allowed to continue until a thin shell of copper is formed on the mold. Once it is formed, the shell is removed from the mold and

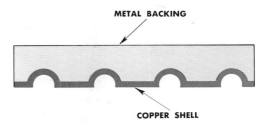

Figure 22-19. *The thin copper shell must be filled with metal to improve its strength and increase its thickness.*

filled with a molten metal, Figure 22-19. This increases the thickness and strength of the shell.

Once the metal solidifies, the electrotype may be prepared for printing. The plate is cut to size and shaved to uniform thickness. Excess metal is routed away from the non-image areas. Plates that are flat must be mounted to make them type high.

RUBBER PLATES. Rubber plates may also be made from molds. They are duplicate plates that can be printed on flat-bed or rotary type letterpresses.

Most printing on paper bags, cellophane, and plastic is done from rubber plates using special aniline inks. Printing with rubber plates is called *flexography*. A single flexible rubber plate is capable of a million or more printing impressions.

Rubber stamps are produced the same way as flexographic plates. First a mold is made from an original letterpress plate. Then the mold is used to create a relief image on the surface of a piece of rubber.

Rubber Stamp Making. A press used for making rubber stamps, Figure 22-20, basically consists of two heated platens. The distance between the two platens is controlled by a handwheel at the right. To make a rubber stamp, proceed as follows:

1. Prepare a type form. You may use hand-set foundry type or machine-set type. However, if available, type made specifically for rubber stamp making is best. Such type can better withstand the heat and pressure

Figure 22-20. Rubber stamp press. (Brodhead-Garrett Co.)

needed to produce a rubber stamp.

2. Lock the type form in the rubber stamp chase. Follow the lockup procedures described earlier in this unit. Metal furniture should be used in place of wood furniture.

3. Place the chase in the rubber stamp press and all w it to preheat for two minutes. The temperature of the platens should be 300°F.

4. Remove the preheated form from the press and cover it with a piece of matrix board. The board should be approximately ¼ inch larger than the type form on all sides. Place the red or Bakelite side of the matrix board against the type. Cover the back of the board with a piece of paper to keep the board from sticking to the upper platen.

5. Insert the chase, matrix board, and paper cover into the press. Turn the handwheel clockwise until the first resistance is felt. Allow the matrix to heat for one minute and become soft. After one minute raise the bottom platen to the limit stops on the chase.

6. After ten minutes remove the chase and matrix from the press. Carefully place it on a metal surface to cool. When cool, pry the matrix from the type form with a screwdriver, Figure 22-21.

7. Cut a piece of stamp rubber to the size of the matrix. Peel off the protective cloth and sprinkle powdered soapstone on the uncovered rubber surface. This prevents the rubber from sticking to the matrix. Also coat the matrix with soapstone. Brush excess powder from the matrix before proceeding.

8. Place the matrix, image side up, on the vulcanizing tray. Cover the matrix with the powdered side of the stamp rubber. Place a piece of paper over the back of the rubber to keep it from sticking to the platen.

9. Insert the tray, matrix, rubber, and paper cover into the press. Turn the handwheel clockwise until the lower plate cannot be raised any higher. Keep the stamp rubber in the press for approximately six minutes.

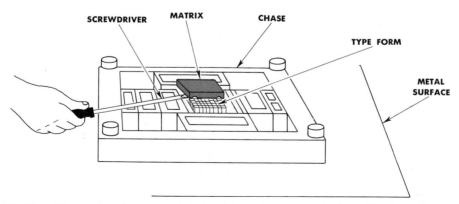

Figure 22-21. *Removing the completed rubber stamp matrix from the type form.*

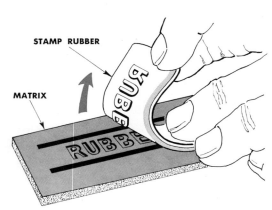

STAMP RUBBER

MATRIX

RUBBER

RUBBE

Figure 22-22. *Stripping the rubber stamp from the matrix.*

10. After six minutes, lower the bottom platen. Carefully remove the vulcanizing tray and place it on a metal surface to cool. Once it is cool, the rubber can be stripped from the matrix, Figure 22-22. All letters should be clear with sharp edges.

11. Trim the rubber to size and mount it on a wooden handle. Use a backsaw to cut the handle to size. Use rubber cement to attach the stamp rubber to the spongelike pad of the handle. To mount, coat the back of the rubber and the pad with rubber cement. Allow the cement on each surface to dry before pressing the surfaces together.

TEST YOUR KNOWLEDGE

1. Describe the major difference between original and duplicate letterpress plates.
2. List three types of original letterpress plates and three types of duplicate letterpress plates.
3. List the basic steps in locking up a type form.
4. Prepare a simple diagram of the chaser method of locking up a type form.
5. Describe what is meant by the term *imposition.*
6. List in proper sequence the basic steps in preparing a linoleum block.
7. Locate in this book three illustrations that are suitable for reproduction using a linoleum block plate.
8. Explain the safety precautions to be taken when cutting a linoleum block.
9. Describe what is meant by *photoengraving.*
10. Explain the major differences between stereotypes and electrotypes.
11. List in sequence the basic steps in making a rubber stamp.

UNIT 23

PLATES FOR GRAVURE PRINTING

Objectives

When you have completed this unit, you will be able to:
1. Identify the difference between engravings and etchings.
2. List the steps in preparing a drypoint plate.
3. Select designs suitable for reproduction using a drypoint plate.
4. List the steps in preparing a metal etching.
5. Explain the safety precautions to be followed when etching metal.
6. Tell how gravure cylinders create tones in the printed image.

Terms to Know

Here are some of the words you will need to understand before reading this unit. If the meaning of a word is not clear to you, look it up in the Glossary in the back of this book.

gravure printing	image carrier	drypoint engravings
intaglio printing	plates	metal etchings

TYPES OF GRAVURE PLATES

Printing from a lowered surface is called *gravure* or *intaglio* printing. There are two basic types of gravure plates: engravings and etchings. Engravings are made from designs cut mechanically into the surface of metal or plastic plates. The design may be cut with hand tools.

Acid may also be used for cutting designs into metal plates. Gravure plates prepared with acid are called *etchings*.

DRYPOINT ENGRAVINGS. The simplest type of engraving to produce is the drypoint. It is prepared by scratching a design into a clear plastic sheet with a pointed tool called a *scriber*.

Preparing a Drypoint Plate. The first step in drypoint plate preparation is creating or selecting a design. Designs suitable for drypoint engraving are composed of lines only. Solid areas of color cannot be reproduced by this technique. An appropriate design for an engraving is pictured in Figure 23-1.

To obtain a right-reading image when the plate is printed, you must prepare and transfer the design to the plate in reverse. Carbon paper placed carbon side up against the back side of the design can be used to reverse the

Figure 23-1. *Designs made from fine lines are appropriate for drypoint engraving.*

image. After the image is traced and the tracing is turned over, a reverse carbon image appears.

Tape the reversed design behind a piece of transparent plastic between 0.015 and 0.040 inch thick. The plastic should be approximately one inch larger all around than the design. You will then cut into the plastic guided by the design taped below.

Use a scriber to engrave the design. Deeply engraved lines will reproduce

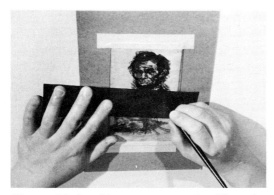

Figure 23-2. *Lines are scratched into the drypoint plate with a scriber. Place a piece of black paper between the plate and design to check for accuracy.*

darker than will shallow scratches. Crosshatching the engraved lines will produce shadow areas. Figure 23-2 shows a drypoint plate being engraved. Note the piece of black paper. It is used between the design and plate to better check for accuracy.

The completed drypoint plate is printed on an etching press. Procedures for printing a drypoint engraving are described in Unit 28.

METAL ETCHINGS. Prepare metal etchings by first coating the surface of a metal sheet with a *resist,* a material that does not let acid penetrate. Then scratch the design through the resist with a scriber.

When the design is complete, place the metal sheet into an acid bath. Areas of the sheet protected by the resist are not affected by the acid. Bare metal, however, is dissolved away, forming a gravure image on the etched plate.

Preparing the Metal Etching. Designs suitable for drypoint engraving are also

suitable for metal etching. Again, the design must be transferred to the plate in reverse.

Although almost any metal can be used, aluminum is recommended because it is easy to etch. Before you apply the resist, make sure the plate is clean and free from fingerprints. Be sure to apply resist to both sides of the plate so that the back side will not be etched away when it is placed in the acid bath.

After the resist is dry, transfer the design to the plate. Use a scriber to scratch through the resist. Make scratches deep enough to expose the metal without cutting into the aluminum.

Next place the plate in an aluminum etching solution. Use tongs. Also wear eye protection and rubber gloves when working with etching solutions.

Caution! Always add acid to water when mixing the etching solution. If you add water to acid, a violent reaction may occur.

Figure 23-3. *Etching the metal plate.*

Figure 23-3 shows a plate being etched. The longer the plate remains in the etching bath, the deeper will be the depressions formed in the surface of the plate.

Deeper depressions will reproduce darker than will shallow ones.

When the desired depth is reached, remove the plate from the etching bath and wash it under running water to remove all traces of the etching solution. Then remove the resist with a suitable solvent.

After the metal is etched, it is printed on an etching press. Procedures for printing a metal etching are further described in Unit 28.

GRAVURE CYLINDERS. Gravure cylinders are the image carriers (plates) used on the rotogravure press. A rotogravure press is described in Unit 28. A gravure cylinder is pictured in Figure 23-4. Because the image may wrap completely around the cylinder, continuous patterns can be printed on products such as wall coverings and textiles. Paper money, postage stamps, and many magazines and catalogs are also printed by gravure cylinders.

Preparing the Gravure Cylinder. The first step in rotogravure is to expose a sheet of carbon tissue through a special screen and through line and continuous tone film positives. Carbon tissue is a coating of a light-sensitive emulsion on a paper backing sheet. The exposure process is shown in Figure 23-5. Both type matter and illustrations are screened.

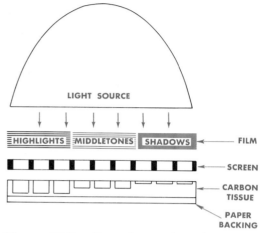

Figure 23-5. *Exposing carbon tissue.*

Light striking the emulsion of the carbon tissue causes it to harden. The degree of hardening depends upon the intensity of the light reaching the emulsion. The emulsion directly below the highlight areas becomes harder than the emulsion below middletone areas. Relatively

Figure 23-4. *A gravure cylinder. (Gravure Technical Association, Inc.)*

little light passes through the shadow areas of the film and, therefore, the carbon tissue emulsion in these areas is relatively soft.

After exposure, the carbon tissue is adhered to a copper-plated cylinder. A portion of a cylinder with carbon tissue attached is shown in Figure 23-6. After the tissue is adhered, the paper backing is removed and the unhardened gelatin emulsion areas are washed away with hot water.

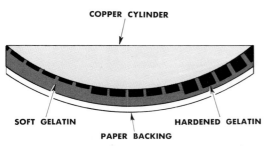

COPPER CYLINDER

SOFT GELATIN   HARDENED GELATIN
PAPER BACKING

Figure 23-6. After exposure the carbon tissue is adhered to a copper cylinder.

The cylinder is then placed in an etching bath. The acid must penetrate the gelatin before it can etch the cylinder. Because the gelatin is softest in the shadow areas, the acid penetrates to the surface of the cylinder in these areas rather quickly. Gelatin in the highlight areas is rather hard, however, and the acid penetrates the highlight areas much more slowly.

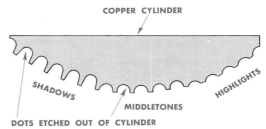

COPPER CYLINDER

SHADOWS   HIGHLIGHTS
MIDDLETONES
DOTS ETCHED OUT OF CYLINDER

Figure 23-7. An exaggerated view of a portion of a gravure cylinder after etching.

An etched cylinder is shown in Figure 23-7. The shadow areas are etched the deepest because they began to be etched first. Highlight areas are shallowest because they were etched last. Middletones are not as deep as the shadows, but they are deeper than the highlights.

The depth of the wells formed during etching determines the amount of ink each area of the plate can hold. It is the ink variation that creates different tones in the printed image.

1. Tell the major difference between engravings and etchings.
2. List in proper sequence the steps in preparing a drypoint plate.
3. Locate three illustrations in this book that are suitable for reproduction using a drypoint plate.
4. List in proper sequence the steps to prepare a metal etching.
5. Identify the safety precautions to be taken when etching a metal plate.
6. Describe how gravure cylinders can lay down varying amounts of ink to create tones in the printed image.

UNIT 24

PLATES FOR LITHOGRAPHIC PRINTING

Objectives

When you have completed this unit, you will be able to:

1. Identify the grease receptive and water receptive areas on a lithographic plate.
2. Explain three materials from which lithographic plates are made.
3. List the basic steps in preparing direct-image plates.
4. Outline the procedures for stripping a flat.
5. Explain how to opaque a negative.
6. Describe how to burn and process a presensitized plate.
7. List the basic steps in preparing diffusion-transfer plates.

Terms to Know

Here are some of the words you will need to understand before reading this unit. If the meaning of a word is not clear to you, look it up in the Glossary in the back of this book.

lithography	goldenrod	gray scale
planographic printing	burning	opaquing
image carriers	stripping	platemaker
direct-image plate	flat	developer
presensitized plate	light table	xerography
diffusion-transfer		

TYPES OF LITHOGRAPHIC PLATES

Printing from a flat surface is termed *lithography*. It is also called photo-offset printing. This method of printing is based on the principle that grease and water do not mix. Image carriers or plates used in lithography are called lithographic plates.

Lithographic plates may be made from thin sheets of paper, plastic, or metal. The image areas of these plates are grease receptive and water repellent. They attract oil-base inks and repel water. Non-image areas are water receptive and grease repellent. Non-image areas attract water and repel oil-base inks.

Images may be made on lithographic plates in several ways. They may be drawn or typed directly on the plate. Plates prepared in this way are called *direct-image plates*. Images may also be placed on the plate photographically by contact printing through a negative. These are called *presensitized plates*. A third technique produces plates directly from copy without first making a process negative. *Diffusion transfer* and *xerographic plates* are produced in this manner.

DIRECT-IMAGE PLATES. An image is drawn or typed directly on the surface of direct-image plates. Almost any greasy substance can be used to place the image on the plate. Grease pencils, crayons, and special typewriter ribbons are most often used for this purpose.

A direct-image plate is usually made from paper. The surface of the plate is specially treated to accept the grease image. This treatment also increases the printing life of the plate and makes the non-image areas more receptive to water.

Preparing Direct-Image Plates. Most direct-image plates contain preprinted guidelines to aid in typing. These guidelines do not reproduce when the plate is printed. A direct-image plate is pictured in Figure 24-1.

Either a manual or an electric typewriter may be used with a special ribbon for preparing direct-image plates. Handle the plate by its edges to avoid transferring fingerprints to its surface. Place the plate in the typewriter and begin to type. Use a low impression setting to avoid embossing (pressing into) the surface of the plate. You may use a soft eraser to remove errors on the direct-image plate.

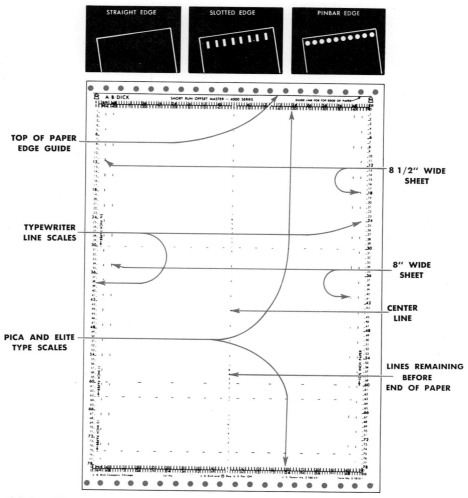

Figure 24-1. *The guidelines on this direct-image plate serve as an aid to the typist.*

Illustrations or signatures can be added to a direct-image plate with special reproducing pens and pencils. If necessary, nonreproducing pencils may be used to draw guidelines. Again, avoid touching the surface of the plate with your fingers. Keep the plate, typewriter, and work area free from dirt.

PRESENSITIZED PLATES. An image is placed on the surface of a presensitized plate photographically by contact printing through a negative. The base of

the plate can be made from paper, plastic, or metal. Either one or both sides of the base may be coated with light-sensitive emulsion.

The plate is exposed through one or more film negatives. Certain types of presensitized plates require film positives.

A special piece of paper called *goldenrod* holds the negative or negatives in position while *burning* (exposing) the plate. Goldenrod is a coated yellow paper that does not allow the light used during exposure to pass through it. Arranging (imposing) and mounting the negative or negatives on the goldenrod is called *stripping*. Goldenrod with negatives attached is called a *flat*.

Figure 24-2. *A light table is used for stripping a flat. (nuArc Company, Inc.)*

Stripping the Flat. A light table, Figure 24-2, is used in stripping. Align the piece of goldenrod with a T-square on the glass surface of the light table. The size of the goldenrod should equal the size of the plate. Fasten the corners of the goldenrod to the glass with tape.

Locate the line on the goldenrod sheet that corresponds to the top edge of the paper to be printed. Using this line as a starting point, locate and, with a pen or pencil, mark the left, right, and bottom dimensions of the paper. Now locate and mark the position of the image to be printed. See Figure 24-3.

Figure 24-3. *The dimensions of the paper and the location of the image to be printed have been marked on this piece of goldenrod.*

Place the negative, emulsion side up, on top of the goldenrod. Position the negative image within the marked area. Use a T-square and triangle to make sure that the image will be square with the edges of the goldenrod. After positioning the negative, tape its corners to the goldenrod paper, Figure 24-4.

Figure 24-4. *After positioning the negative, tape it by its corners to the goldenrod masking sheet.*

Detach the goldenrod from the glass top and turn it over so that the emulsion of the negative is against the glass. Using a sharp razor blade, cut a window into the goldenrod. *Cut only through the goldenrod. Do not cut into the negative.* The window should be 1/8 to 1/4 inch larger than the image on the negative.

After cutting, remove the piece of golden-rod from within the window area. Figure 24-5 shows a properly cut window.

Figure 24-5. *The size of the window should be ⅛" to ¼" larger than the image on the negative.*

You may also strip a platemaker's sensitivity guide, Figure 24-6, into the flat.

Figure 24-6. *A sensitivity guide used in platemaking.*

This guide is a film negative of a stepped gray scale. It serves as an aid in determining proper exposure. Place the sensitivity guide in an area of the goldenrod outside of the paper dimension markings.

Opaquing the Flat. Pinholes and other unwanted transparent areas in the negative must be blocked out or opaqued. Otherwise they develop on the plate and reproduce during the printing process.

A negative is opaqued on a light table. Place the flat with the emulsion side of the negative down on the glass top. With a fine brush and photographic opaquing solution, paint out pinholes and other unwanted areas on the negative. See Figure 24-7. If the opaquing solution becomes too thick, thin it with water. Be sure the opaque is thoroughly dry before burning the plate.

Figure 24-7. *Opaquing is done to cover pinholes and other unwanted transparent areas in the negative.*

Burning the Plate. A platemaker, Figure 24-8, is used to burn the plate. It has a vacuum frame to hold the flat and plate in tight contact, and it has a light source. The light source in the platemaker shown in Figure 24-8 is located in the base.

Figure 24-8. *A flip-top platemaker. (nuArc Company, Inc.)*

After you clean both sides of the glass cover, place the plate, emulsion side up, on the rubber blanket of the vacuum frame. Position the flat, emulsion side down, on top of the plate. The emulsion of the film negative should contact the emulsion on the plate. Be sure to align the edges of the flat with the edges of the plate.

Close the vacuum frame and turn on the vacuum pump. Once the air is evacuated, the flat and plate will be held tightly together. Flip the vacuum frame over so that the flat and plate face the light source. Set the timer for the correct exposure and burn the plate.

Caution! *The light source emits ultraviolet light. Do not look directly at the light source. Ultraviolet light can damage your eyes.*

Correct exposure depends upon the type of plate and light source being used, as well as the distance between the two. A correctly exposed plate will show a solid step 6 on the platemaker's sensitivity guide (gray scale) when the plate is developed. Step 6 should develop up as dark as step 1. If it doesn't, the exposure time was too short. If step 7 develops up as dark as step 1, the exposure time used was too long.

Processing the Plate. After the plate has been exposed, remove it from the vacuum frame and place it in a plate developing sink, Figure 24-9, or on a clean, flat surface. The plate is now

Figure 24-9. *A plate developing sink. (nuArc Company, Inc.)*

ready for processing. Be sure to follow the processing instructions supplied by the manufacturer of the plate you are using. Also, use processing solutions that are recommended for your plate. A typical procedure is explained here.

First remove the unexposed light-sensitive coating by pouring a small quantity of desensitizer onto the plate. Use a clean sponge or cotton pad to spread the desensitizer over the entire plate.

Next produce a visible image on the surface of the plate with developer (lacquer). While the desensitizer is still wet, pour a small amount of developer onto the plate. With a second clean sponge or cotton pad wipe the developer over the plate. Press lightly to avoid scratching the image.

After the plate has been developed, wash the excess developer from the plate with water. The plate is now ready to be placed on the offset press. If the plate will not be printed immediately, use a cotton pad to coat its surface with gum arabic. Gum arabic protects the plate from scratches and prevents it from oxidizing.

DIFFUSION-TRANSFER PLATES. To produce diffusion-transfer plates, process negatives are not needed. Instead, a paper negative is made by a contact printing technique directly from the copy. As the exposed silver crystals on the paper negative develop, the silver crystals that were not exposed to light are transferred to a flexible printing plate. These silver crystals then develop up to form the image on the plate.

Figure 24-10. *A machine for exposing and processing diffusion-transfer plates. (Scriptomatic, Inc.)*

Preparing Diffusion-Transfer Plates.
A platemaking machine that operates on the principle of diffusion-transfer is shown in Figure 24-10. It consists of two basic units: an exposure unit and a processing unit.

Place the paper negative, emulsion side up, on the glass plate of the exposure unit. Position the original copy, image side down, on top of the paper negative. The negative is now ready to be exposed. When the lid is closed, a vacuum is created and the exposure is made. Exposure results from light passing through the negative, striking the white areas surrounding the copy image, and reflecting back onto the emulsion of the negative.

After exposure, process the negative. Place the metal plate face up at the entrance to the processing unit. Position the paper negative, emulsion side down, on the plate. Then feed the plate and negative into the processing unit. As they enter the developing bath, the plate and negative are separated slightly. They come together, however, and when the plate and negative

Figure 24-11. *The image on the plate results when unexposed silver crystals are transferred from the negative and developed on the plate. (nuArc Company, Inc.)*

emerge from the processing unit, the plate will contain image areas that duplicate the original copy, Figure 24-11.

After about a minute, strip the negative from the plate. Desensitize and lacquer the plate according to the manufacturer's instructions. The plate is now ready for the offset press. If the plate will not be printed immediately, coat it with gum arabic.

XEROGRAPHIC PLATES. Xerographic plates are also made directly from copy without a process negative. The images on such paper or metal plates are produced electrostatically. The electrostatic process (xerography) is described in Unit 7.

TEST YOUR KNOWLEDGE

1. On a sheet of paper, draw a rectangle to represent an offset plate. Draw a simple picture on the plate to represent the image. Now identify and label each of the following areas: grease receptive, water receptive, grease repellent, and water repellent.
2. Name three materials from which lithographic plates are made.
3. List in sequence the basic steps in preparing a direct-image plate.
4. Prepare an outline of the procedures for stripping a flat.
5. Describe how to opaque a negative.
6. Identify the procedures for burning and processing a presensitized plate.
7. List in proper sequence the steps in preparing a diffusion-transfer plate.

UNIT 25

STENCILS FOR SCREEN-PROCESS PRINTING

Objectives

When you have completed this unit, you will be able to:

1. Select designs suitable for reproduction using hand-cut paper, hand-cut film, and photographic stencils.
2. List the basic steps in cutting and adhering a paper stencil.
3. Identify the solvents used to adhere lacquer-soluble and water-soluble films and the inks that can be used with each type of stencil.
4. List the basic steps in cutting and adhering a hand-cut film stencil.
5. Describe the major difference between an indirect and a direct photographic stencil.
6. List the basic steps in exposing, processing, and adhering an indirect photographic stencil.
7. Outline the procedures for preparing a direct photographic stencil.
8. Explain how to prepare a tusche and glue stencil.

Terms to Know

Here are some of the words you will need to understand before reading this unit. If the meaning of a word is not clear to you, look it up in the Glossary in the back of this book.

solvent   platemaker   emulsion
screen-process printing

TYPES OF STENCILS

Printing by forcing ink through openings in a stencil that has been adhered to a woven screen is referred to as screen-process printing. Other names for this method are stencil printing, screen printing, and silk screen printing.

The stencil serves as the plate in screen-process printing. Openings or holes in the stencil allow ink to pass through to the paper below. The shape of the stencil openings determines the shape of the image that is printed.

Stencils for screen-process printing may be hand-cut from paper or film, prepared photographically, or painted directly on the screen. Each type of stencil is described here.

Figure 25-1. *Silhouette designs can be converted into hand-cut paper stencils.*

HAND-CUT PAPER STENCILS. Paper stencils are generally used for short printing runs of less than 100 impres-

sions. Designs should be kept simple. Avoid designs that have loose centers such as the inside of the letter *O*. A silhouette design like the one in Figure 25-1 can readily be made into a paper stencil.

Cutting and Adhering the Paper Stencil. A stencil is made by cutting openings or holes in a piece of kraft wrapping paper. First cut the paper slightly smaller than the outside dimensions of the screen frame. You may draw the desired image directly on the kraft paper. To transfer an already prepared design, you may use carbon paper.

Place the kraft paper with the image drawn on a piece of smooth cardboard or a glass plate. Use a sharp stencil knife or single-edge razor blade to cut the design. Do not remove the cutout sections.

Carefully place the cut stencil on the base of a clean screen printing frame. Lower the screen almost to the base and position the stencil.

Next adhere the entire stencil to the screen by running a bead of ink across the screen with a squeegee. The ink serves as an adhesive. After you remove the cutouts from the bottom of the screen, the stencil can be printed. Procedures for screen-process printing are described in Unit 30.

HAND-CUT FILM STENCILS. Hand-cut film stencils are quite durable. Many thousands of impressions can be made from a single stencil. Appropriate designs include poster size lettering and illustrations that do not contain fine detail.

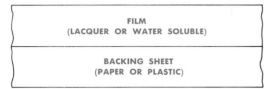

Figure 25-2. *The two layers of a piece of hand-cut stencil film.*

A cross section of a piece of hand-cut stencil film is shown in Figure 25-2. It consists of a thin layer of lacquer or water soluble gelatin material on a paper or plastic backing sheet.

Lacquer and water soluble films are prepared in much the same manner. The solvents used to adhere each type of film to the screen are different, however. Lacquer films, which are soluble in lacquer thinnner can be used with water-base and oil-base inks but not lacquer-base inks. Water soluble films are adhered with water. They can be used with oil and lacquer-base inks but not water base inks.

Cutting the Film Stencil. Cut a piece of stencil film approximately four inches wider and four inches longer than the design. Tape the design to a smooth, hard surface. Center the stencil film, film side up, over the design and tape it in

place. The design will be visible through the stencil film, Figure 25-3.

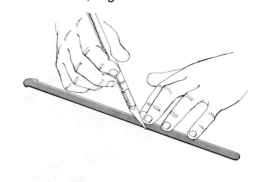

Figure 25-3. *A piece of stencil film has been taped to this design in preparation for cutting.*

The stencil is ready to be cut. Use a *sharp* stencil knife or single-edge razor blade to cut the design. Cut through the film layer only. *Do not cut through the backing sheet.*

After each open area of the design is outlined, use the point of your knife to lift a corner of the film to be removed. Slowly peel this unwanted film from the backing, Figure 25-4. Be careful to remove only those parts of the film that will form the image during printing.

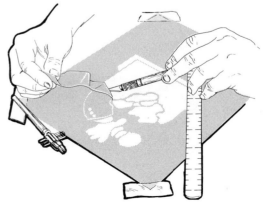

Figure 25-4. *Removing the unwanted film from the image areas of the stencil.*

Adhering the Film Stencil. Lacquer film is adhered to the bottom of the screen with lacquer thinner. Water soluble film is adhered with water. Some water soluble stencil films may be adhered with a mixture of water and alcohol. Be sure to use the adhering solution recommended by the manufacturer.

Place the stencil, film side up, on a pad of newspaper and position a clean screen over the stencil. Dampen an absorbent cloth pad with the required adherent. Starting at one corner of the stencil, press the dampened cloth pad against the film. Continue to do this until four to six square inches of the film's surface have been moistened. The adherent will soften the film and cause it to stick to the screen fabric. Be careful not to use too much adherent or the film will begin to dissolve. Now quickly wipe the area of the stencil that was just adhered with a dry cloth. Repeat the above procedure until the entire stencil is adhered.

A film stencil being adhered to a screen is pictured in Figure 25-5. Note that the adhered part of the stencil appears darker than the area that has not yet been adhered. A properly adhered stencil will have a uniform dark color. Light spots on the stencil indicate improper adhesion. Go back and adhere these spots, but be careful. Too much solvent will begin to dissolve the film, leaving a hole.

Allow the film stencil to dry before removing the stencil backing. A fan may be used to shorten drying time. When the stencil is completely dry, remove the backing sheet, Figure 25-6.

Figure 25-6. *Removing the backing sheet from the hand-cut stencil.*

INDIRECT PHOTOGRAPHIC STENCILS. Photographic stencils are used when it is necessary to reproduce fine detail. Halftones can also be printed with this type of stencil. An indirect photographic stencil is prepared by contact printing through a film positive onto a light-sensitive stencil material. After the stencil is processed, it is adhered to the screen with water.

Preparing the Positive. A positive transparency is required to produce a

Figure 25-5. *Adhering the stencil to the screen.*

Figure 25-7. *A platemaker is used to expose the indirect photographic stencil. (nuArc Company, Inc.)*

photographic stencil. The image areas must be completely opaque. Non-image areas may be transparent or translucent.

Positives are usually prepared in one of two ways. They may be made by drawing an india ink image on tracing paper or on a clear sheet of plastic. They may also be prepared by contact printing a negative on process film. Procedures for making film positives from photographic negatives are discussed further in Unit 21.

Exposing the Stencil. The stencil material described here is a light-sensitive emulsion on a plastic backing. Keep this material away from sunlight and fluorescent lights. It is a good idea to handle any photographic stencil material under subdued light only.

A platemaker, Figure 25-7, can be used to expose the stencil. A platemaker includes a vacuum frame for holding the film positive and stencil material in tight contact and a light source located in the base.

Place the photographic stencil material, emulsion side down, on the rubber blanket of the vacuum frame. Place the film positive, emulsion side down, on top of the stencil material. Figure 25-8 shows the correct relationship between the film positive and the stencil material during exposure.

Close the vacuum frame and turn on the vacuum pump. When the air is evacuated, the positive and stencil material will be held tightly together. Flip the

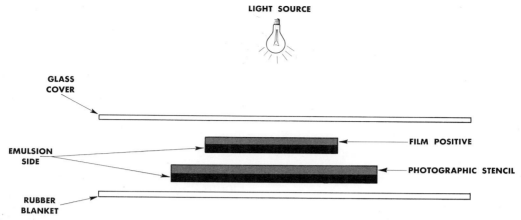

Figure 25-8. *Note the arrangement of the film positive and photographic stencil material during exposure. Exposure is made through the back of the positive and the back of the stencil.*

vacuum frame over, set the timer for correct exposure, and expose the stencil.

Light passing through the clear areas of the film positive will harden the stencil's emulsion. Because no light passes through the opaque areas of the positive, the emulsion behind these areas will remain soft.

Caution! *The light source emits ultraviolet light. Do not look directly at the light source. Ultraviolet light can damage your eyes.*

Correct exposure will depend upon the type of stencil material, the light source being used, and the distance between the light source and the stencil. A 35-amp carbon arc located 30 inches from the stencil should produce a good exposure on most stencil materials.

Processing the Stencil. The stencil is processed in a special developer. Prepare the developer according to the manufacturer's instructions and pour it

into a tray. Remove the exposed stencil from the vacuum frame and place it, emulsion side up, into the tray of developer. Develop the stencil material for the recommended time.

When you remove the stencil from the developer, the image is not yet visible. Washing under running water makes the image appear.

Set the water temperature according to the manufacturer's directions. Place the stencil, emulsion side up, in the sink. Wash the stencil until all of the unexposed (image) areas are dissolved away. After the image areas are clear, allow the stencil to sit in a bath of cold water for approximately one minute. This will harden the emulsion that remains.

Adhering the Stencil. Adhere the photographic stencil to the screen immediately after washing. Place the stencil, emulsion side up, on top of a pad of newspaper and position a clean screen over the stencil. The stencil is adhered by pressing the screen into the emulsion while it is moist and still soft.

Start at one corner of the screen and blot the stencil with a paper towel. Press the stencil while blotting. Repeat this procedure over the entire surface until all of the moisture has been absorbed from the stencil. Change paper towels when they become too damp.

Allow the emulsion to dry thoroughly before removing the stencil backing. A fan may be used to shorten the drying time.

DIRECT PHOTOGRAPHIC STENCILS. Direct photographic stencils are prepared directly on the screen fabric. The screen is coated with a light-sensitive emulsion; then it is exposed to a source of light through a film positive. Light passing through the clear areas of the film positive hardens the emulsion below. Because no light passes through the opaque areas of the positive, the emulsion behind these areas remains soft. After the stencil is exposed, the unhardened areas of the emulsion are washed away with hot water and form the openings in the stencil.

Coating the Screen. Follow the manufacturer's recommendations when you mix commercially prepared emulsions and sensitizers. The sensitizer is a light-sensitive ingredient added to the emulsion just before you coat the screen.

Coat the screen under safelight conditions as recommended by the manufacturer. Use a stiff piece of cardboard or a brush to spread a thin, even coating of emulsion across the underside of the

screen. After the emulsion dries, the screen is ready to be exposed.

Exposing the Screen. The sensitized screen is exposed through a film positive to a strong source of light. During exposure the film positive and screen must remain in tight contact. One method of maintaining contact between the positive and screen is illustrated in Figure 25-9.

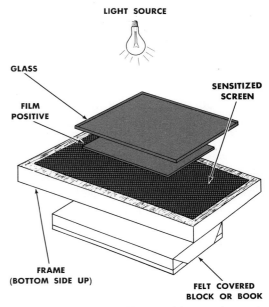

Figure 25-9. *The film positive and sensitized screen must remain in tight contact during exposure. The weight of the glass helps to maintain the required contact.*

Photoflood lamps, fluorescent tubes, carbon arc lights, or direct sunlight can be used to expose direct photographic emulsion. Follow the manufacturer's recommendations as to exposure time.

Washing Out the Image Areas. Remove the unhardened emulsion representing the area to be printed by washing the screen under a stream of moderately hot (approximately 110° F) water. When the image areas are clear, place the screen under cold water for about one minute.

A fan can be used to shorten the drying time. Once the screen is dry, the stencil may be printed.

TUSCHE AND GLUE STENCILS. Tusche and glue stencils are prepared by painting directly on the screen fabric with liquid tusche or with a lithographic crayon. Place the original design beneath the fabric and lightly trace over it with pencil. The pencil image serves as a guide when painting the screen with tusche. Painting should be done on the top surface of the screen.

After the tusche has dried, coat the top of the screen with a water soluble glue.

The glue fills the open weave of the fabric. It does not, however, fill the weave in the image areas that have been coated with tusche. Instead it merely covers the tusche image.

When the glue has dried, remove the tusche or lithographic crayon image from the screen. Saturate a cloth with benzine or lacquer thinner and rub it over the back of the screen. As the tusche dissolves, the glue coating over the image area will flake away.

The stencil is now ready for printing. Oil or lacquer-base inks may be used. Water-base inks cannot be used with this type of stencil because they would dissolve the water soluble glue. Procedures for printing screen process stencils are described in Unit 30.

TEST YOUR KNOWLEDGE

1. Locate two illustrations in this book that are suitable for reproduction using a hand-cut paper stencil, two that are suitable for reproduction using a hand-cut film stencil, and two that can be reproduced with a photographic stencil.
2. List in proper sequence the steps in cutting and adhering a paper stencil.
3. Prepare a chart showing the solvents used to adhere lacquer-soluble and water-soluble films. Also indicate the inks that can be used with each of these stencils.
4. List in proper sequence the basic steps in cutting and adhering a hand-cut film stencil.
5. Describe the major differences between an indirect and a direct photographic stencil.
6. List in proper sequence the basic steps in exposing, processing, and adhering an indirect photographic stencil.
7. Prepare an outline of the procedures for preparing a direct photographic stencil.
8. Describe how to prepare a tusche and glue stencil.

UNIT 26

PREPARING MASTERS FOR DUPLICATION

Objectives

When you have completed this unit, you will be able to:
1. List the steps in preparing a spirit master.
2. Describe how to produce a spirit master capable of printing several colors.
3. Explain three techniques for correcting a spirit master.
4. Outline the procedures for preparing a mimeograph stencil.
5. Explain how to correct a mimeograph stencil.

Terms to Know

Here are some of the words you will need to understand before reading this unit. If the meaning of a word is not clear to you, look it up in the Glossary in the back of this book.

spirit duplication	screen-process printing	stencil
planographic printing	electronic stencilmaker	electrostatic copying
mimeograph duplicating		

SPIRIT MASTERS

Spirit duplication is printing done from a flat sheet of paper called a master. The image area on the master is formed by the addition of an aniline dye.

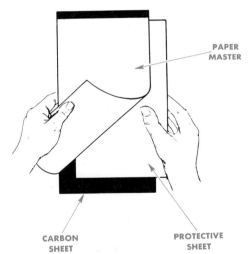

PAPER MASTER

CARBON SHEET

PROTECTIVE SHEET

Figure 26-1. *Parts of a spirit master.*

Spirit masters, Figure 26-1, consist of three sheets. Two of the sheets are attached to each other. These are the *paper master,* which receives the dye image, and the *aniline dye carbon sheet,* which contains the dye. A *protective tissue sheet* is placed between the master and carbon sheets to prevent the dye from transferring the paper master until desired.

Spirit masters are available in short-run, medium-run, and long-run grades. They can also be purchased in a variety of colors, such as purple, red, green, black and blue. The color of the master is determined by the color of the dye on the carbon sheet.

PREPARING THE MASTER. To prepare a spirit master, remove the protective sheet from between the paper master and carbon sheet, and apply pressure to the front side of the paper master by writing, drawing or typing. Write or draw with the spirit master resting on a hard, smooth surface. Use a ballpoint pen, hard lead pencil, or stylus to impress the image. If the master is typed, clean the typewriter keys first. Type with a uniform pressure. The pressure causes the back side of the paper master to pick up dye from the carbon sheet. The image formed on the back side of the paper master sheet is "wrong reading" or a mirror image.

Multiple Color Masters. Masters capable of reproducing more than one color are prepared by using two or more aniline-dye carbon sheets. All of the required colors are transferred to the back of a single paper master. This master will then print all of the colors at the same time.

Making Corrections. Corrections are made on a spirit master by removing the unwanted image and replacing it with the desired image. You can scrape away the unwanted carbon image from the back of the master with a sharp knife or razor blade. An ink eraser can also be used for this purpose. Another way to remove the unwanted image is to cover it with a piece of paper tape.

Replace the old, unwanted image with a new image. Back up the image area with a fresh piece of carbon paper. Be sure the aniline-dye side of carbon paper is against the back of the paper master during the correction process. Apply uniform pressure as you did for the original.

MIMEOGRAPH STENCILS

Mimeograph duplicating is based on the screen process of printing. Mimeograph duplicating uses a stencil which controls the placement of ink on paper.

A mimeograph stencil is made from a porous, tissue-like material that has been coated on both sides with wax. The wax does not permit ink to pass through. Wherever wax has been removed, however, ink can pass through the uncovered porous base.

Figure 26-2 shows the parts of a mimeograph stencil. A *stencil sheet* is a wax-coated, porous material used for printing. A *backing sheet* is a hard, smooth base that insures a uniform impression. When the stencil is typed, a *typing cushion* is inserted between the stencil and backing sheets to improve the image area. *Typing film* placed over the stencil sheet reduces the possibility of cutting completely through the stencil while typing.

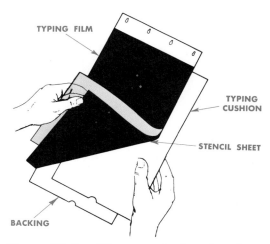

Figure 26-2. *Mimeograph stencil parts.*

PREPARING THE STENCIL. Form the image area of the stencil by pushing aside the wax coating on the stencil sheet to expose the porous tissue-like base. This can easily be done with a ballpoint pen, with a special stylus, or by typing directly on the stencil sheet. An enlarged mimeograph stencil image is shown in Figure 26-3.

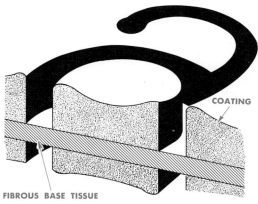

Figure 26-3. *Enlarged view of a mimeograph stencil. Pressure on the stencil causes the wax coating to be moved aside.*

Before you write or draw on a stencil, place a smooth, hard-surface paper or plastic sheet between the stencil sheet and the backing sheet.

If a stencil is to be typed, clean the typewriter keys. Set the typewriter ribbon selector to the "stencil" or "white" position. On this setting, the typewriter keys will contact the stencil sheet directly without first striking the ribbon. Place the typing cushion between the stencil and backing sheets and place the typing film over the stencil sheet.

Making Corrections. Correct mimeograph stencils by covering the unwanted image with correction fluid. When the fluid has dried completely, recut the stencil with a pen, stylus, or typewriter.

Electronic Stencilmakers. An electronic stencilmaker, Figure 26-4, is used to prepare mimeograph stencils electronically. The original copy is fastened to the left-hand side of the drum. A stencil is fastened to the right-hand side of the same drum. To make the stencil, the drum rotates rapidly while an electric eye scans the original copy. Variations in the color and density of the copy cause varying amounts of current to flow within the stencilmaker. The varying current heats a stylus which burns the image into the stencil.

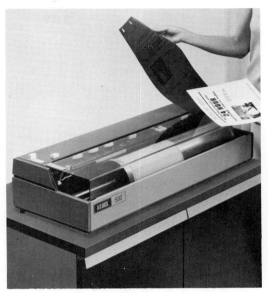

Figure 26-4. Electronic stencilmaker. Copy is placed on the left side of cylinder and stencil is produced on the right. (A. B. Dick Co.)

ELECTROSTATIC COPYING

Specially prepared plates, masters, and stencils are not required for electrostatic copying. Instead, duplicate copies are produced directly from just about any handwritten, typed, or printed original. Duplication procedures are described in Unit 31.

TEST YOUR KNOWLEDGE

1. List in proper sequence the basic steps in preparing a spirit master.
2. Tell how to produce a spirit master capable of printing multiple colors.
3. Identify three techniques that can be used to correct a spirit master.
4. Tell how to prepare a mimeograph stencil.
5. Explain how corrections may be made on a mimeograph stencil.

SECTION 9

PRINTING

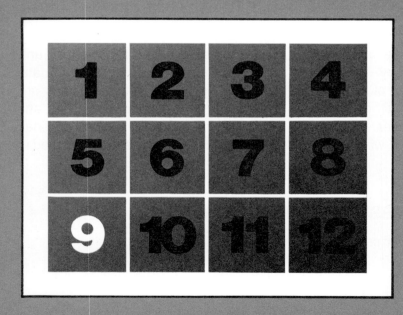

UNIT 27

PRINTING FROM RELIEF OR LETTERPRESS PLATES

Objectives

When you have completed this unit, you will be able to:

1. Illustrate the operating principles of platen, cylinder, and rotary presses.
2. List eight safety rules that must be followed when preparing, operating, and cleaning a platen press.
3. Outline the procedures for preparing a platen press for printing.
4. Define *makeready* and describe how it is done.
5. List the steps in printing with a platen press.

Terms to Know

Here are some of the words you will need to understand before reading this unit. If the meaning of a word is not clear to you, look it up in the Glossary in the back of this book.

platen press	chase	impression cylinder
cylinder press	quoins	electrotype
rotary press	gage pins	stereotype
type form	makeready	web-fed
plates	overlay	thermography
pilot press	delivery system	tympan

TYPES OF PRESSES

In letterpress or relief printing, ink is applied to raised plate surfaces with a roller. The inked surfaces are then pressed against the paper, transferring the image to the paper. The relief or letterpress process is illustrated in Figure 27-1.

Three types of presses are used to print letterpress plates: the platen press, the cylinder press, and the rotary press.

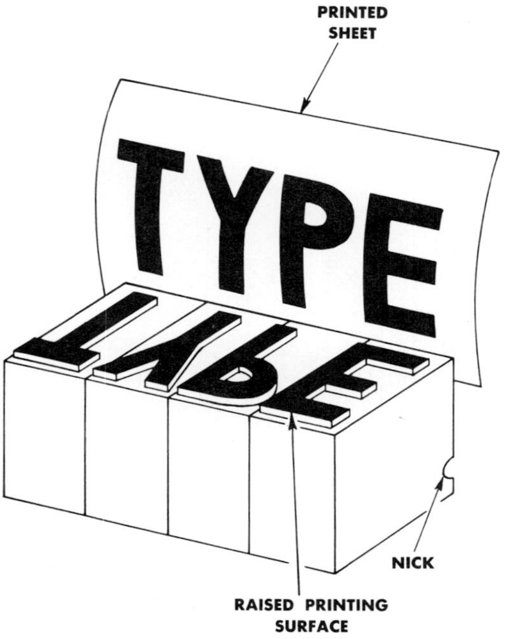

PLATEN PRESS. The operating principle of a platen press is shown in Figure 27-2. The paper to be printed is placed on a flat surface called a *platen*. A typeform or a plate rests on another flat surface called the *bed*. Rollers ink the typeform or plate each time the press is opened. When the press is closed, paper is pressed against the entire form and the image is transferred to the paper.

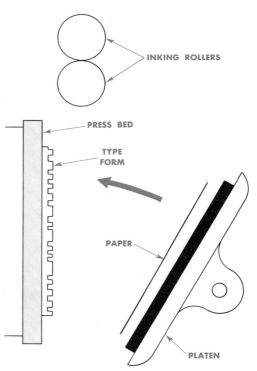

Figure 27-1. *Letterpress printing. Ink is transferred from the raised surface of the plate to the paper.*

Figure 27-2. *Operating principle of the platen press.*

Figures 27-3 through 27-5 illustrate the three basic kinds of platen presses. A hand-operated platen press, called a *pilot press,* is pictured in Figure 27-3. Figure 27-4 shows a *hand-fed, power-operated platen press.* A *power-operated platen press with automatic feed* is shown in Figure 27-5.

Figure 27-5. *A power-operated platen press with automatic feed. (Heidelberg Eastern, Inc.)*

Figure 27-3. *Hand-operated pilot press. (Brodhead-Garrett Co.)*

We will concentrate on procedures for printing with a hand-fed, power-operated platen press such as the one shown in Figure 27-6. Note the individual parts of the press. There are four general operating procedures: preparation, makeready, operation, and cleanup.

Safety Notes. Before you turn on the press, roll up your sleeves, remove your tie and make sure your shirttails or any loose clothing are tucked in. Remove rings, watches and all items that can be caught by press parts and cause you to be pulled into the machine.

Press Preparation. Several procedures must be followed to prepare a hand-fed, power-operated press for printing. These include:

1. *Lubricating the press.* Oil the press according to manufacturer's recommendations.
2. *Inking the press.* For short runs do not use the ink fountain. Instead

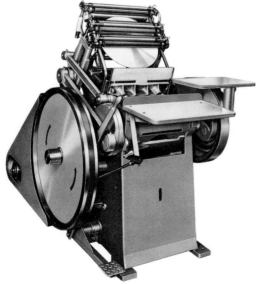

Figure 27-4. *A hand-fed, power-operated platen press. (Brandtjen and Kluge, Inc.)*

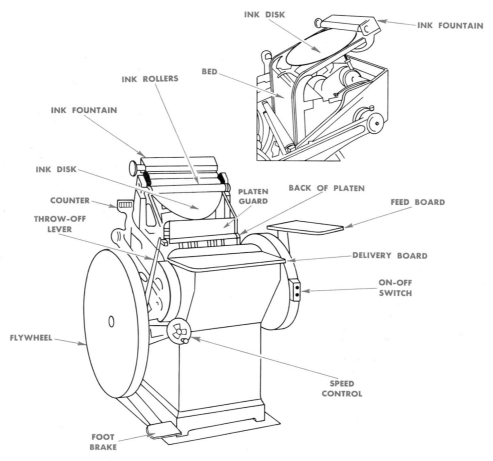

Figure 27-6. *Parts of a hand-fed, power-operated platen press.*

place a small quantity of ink on the lower left side of the ink disk, Figure

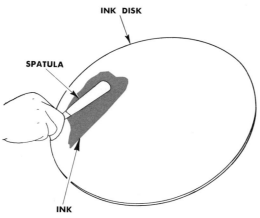

Figure 27-7. *Ink the press by putting a small amount of ink on the ink disk.*

27-7. Turn on the power and allow the press to run at slow speed to distribute the ink over the surface of the disk. After the ink is distributed, turn off the press.

3. *Dressing the press.* Cover the platen with *packing* and a *tympan* or *draw-sheet.* Packing is a piece of pressboard (smooth finished hardboard) and several hanger sheets (book paper). Check with your teacher to determine the proper amount of packing. Cut the packing slightly smaller than the platen. Use a single piece of oiled manila paper, called a tympan sheet, to hold the packing on

the platen. The tympan should be as wide as the platen and long enough to extend under the two bales located at the top and bottom of the platen, Figure 27-8.

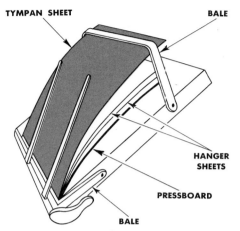

Figure 27-8.   *Dressing the press. The tympan sheet is held in position on the platen by the bales. Packing is placed under the tympan.*

4. *Installing the chase.* Turn the flywheel by hand to run the rollers down to their lowest position. Carefully place the chase in the bed of the press. Push the clamp at the top of the bed down over the edge of the chase to hold the chase securely in place. Quoins should be positioned at the top and the right sides of the press, Figure 27-9.

5. *Printing on the tympan.* Check the position of the grippers. If they are in front of the typeform when an impression is made, they will crush the type. If necessary, move the grippers to the outer edges of the platen. Tighten the gripper nuts before proceeding.

    Turn the press on and let it run slowly. The throw-off lever should be in the OFF position. Once the type-

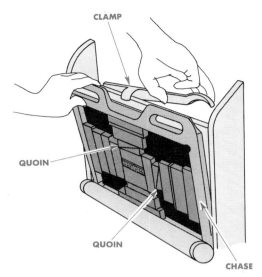

Figure 27-9.   *The chase is clamped in the bed of the press. Quoins are positioned to the top and right.*

form has been inked, pull the throw-off lever to the ON position. After printing on the tympan sheet, push the throw-off lever back to the OFF position and turn off the power.

6. *Positioning the paper.* The image on the tympan serves as a guide for positioning the paper. Draw center lines through the printed image as shown in Figure 27-10. Next draw perpendicular lines on the piece of paper on which printing is to be done. The location of the point at which the lines cross on the paper should correspond to the center point of the image that has been printed on the tympan. Now place the paper on top of the tympan. Align the two sets of center lines and outline the paper on the tympan.

7. *Positioning the gage pins. Gage pins* hold the paper in place on the platen. Usually two pins are placed at the bottom and one to the left of the image. Insert the point of each

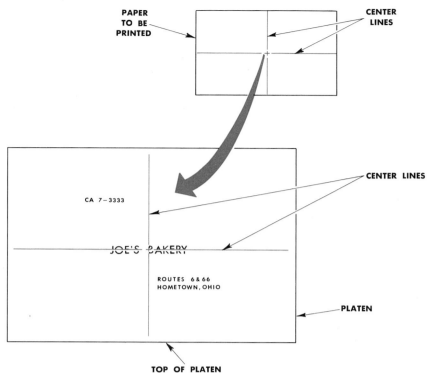

PAPER TO BE PRINTED

CENTER LINES

CENTER LINES

CA 7−3333

JOE'S BAKERY

ROUTES 6 & 66
HOMETOWN, OHIO

PLATEN

TOP OF PLATEN

Figure 27-10. Center lines drawn through the image on the tympan will guide in positioning the paper.

gage pin into the tympan about ⅛ inch outside of the outlined paper border. Slide the point under the tympan sheet only, and then bring it back through the top surface. *Do not allow the pin to penetrate the hanger sheets.* Then align the straight edge of each gage pin with the outlined border on the tympan. Properly positioned gage pins are illustrated in Figure 27-11.

8. *Setting the gage pins.* Be sure that the gage pins and gage pin tongues clear the typeform. If .they are between the typeform and the' paper when the press is closed, they will crush the type.

Place a sheet of paper against the gage pins. Turn on the press and let it run slowly. The throw-off lever should be in the OFF position. Once the typeform has been inked, pull the throw-off lever to the ON position. After printing on the paper, push the throw-off lever to the OFF position and turn off the power.

Check the position of the image on the paper. Use a ruler to insure accuracy. If necessary, move the gage pins and repeat the above process. When the pins are in position, hold them as shown in Figure 27-12. Tap each pin lightly with a quoin key to set it in place.

9. *Removing the tympan image.* Remove the ink from the tympan, so that it is not transferred to the back of the printed sheets. Use a cloth moistened with a solvent appropriate for this purpose. Then apply talcum

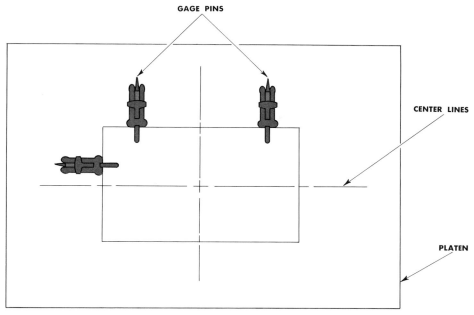

GAGE PINS

CENTER LINES

PLATEN

Figure 27-11. Gage pins are used to hold the paper in place on the platen. They are positioned at the bottom and left sides of the tympan image.

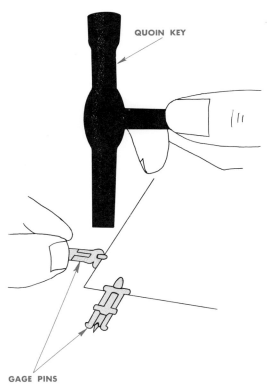

QUOIN KEY

GAGE PINS

Figure 27-12. Set the gage pins by tapping them with a quoin key.

powder or chalk dust to the tympan to completely absorb any moisture.

Press Makeready. *Makeready* means equalizing the impression made by all parts of the typeform on the printed sheet of paper. These procedures include:

1. *Checking the impression.* Place a sheet of paper against the gage pins. Turn the press on and let it run slowly. The throw-off lever should be in the OFF position. Once the type form has been inked, pull the throw-off lever to the ON position. After printing on the paper, turn off the press. The impression on the paper should be clear and uniform.

2. *Adjusting the ink supply.* If the image is not sharp and clear, adjust the ink supply. First rub your finger over the printed image. If there is too much ink, the image will smudge

easily. To correct this, remove some ink from the ink disk. If the image does not smudge at all, add ink to the ink disk.

3. *Reducing impression.* If the back of the printed sheet is embossed by the typeform, you have used too much packing. Remove one or more hanger sheets.

4. *Increasing the impression.* If the overall image is too light, increase the impression on the printed sheet by adding one or more hanger sheets to the packing. Be careful not to overpack the platen.

5. *Obtaining a uniform impression.* All parts of the typeform must print with a firm, even impression. For a uniform impression, paste small pieces of tissue paper in the light areas behind the tympan sheet image (overlay) or behind the low parts of the typeform (underlay).

6. *Positioning the Grippers.* The grippers hold the paper against the platen while printing. Position the grippers so that they will contact the paper and not the typeform. A rubberband stretched across the two grippers will also keep the paper in place on the platen.

Safety Notes. Do not reach into a moving press to remove sheets, to apply ink, or to make adjustments. Do not leave a press while it is running. Only one person should operate a press at a time. Avoid running a press at speeds higher than you can comfortably handle. When operating a press, stand erect, take your time, and concentrate on feeding and delivering the paper.

Press Operation. Fan out the stack of paper to be printed to separate the sheets and make them easy to pick up. Then place the paper on the feed board in preparation for printing. To operate a hand-fed, power-operated platen press:

1. Remove all tools and unnecessary materials from the press.
2. Set the impression counter at zero.
3. With the throw-off lever in the OFF position, turn on the power and let the press run at a slow speed.
4. Take a single sheet from the pile on the feed board with your right hand. Place the sheet in position on the platen by feeding it to the bottom gage pins first, then sliding it against the side pin, Figure 27-13.

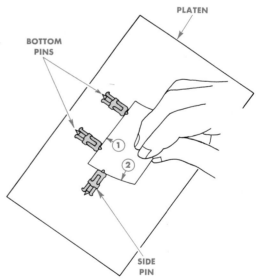

Figure 27-13. *Feeding a platen press. Feed to the bottom gage pins first. Then slide the paper to the left.*

5. With your left hand, pull the throw-off lever to the ON position. After the impression is made, remove the printed sheet with your left hand and place it on the delivery table. At the

same time, position a fresh sheet of paper on the platen. Another sheet of paper will be printed each time the platen closes. *Caution!* If a sheet is improperly positioned on the platen, you must return the throw-off lever to the OFF position to prevent printing on the tympan sheet. As the press opens, straighten the sheet, pull the throw-off lever to the ON position, and resume printing.

Press Cleanup. All printing ink must be removed from the typeform, ink disk, and rollers before it dries. Press cleanup procedures include:

1. Remove the chase from the press. Place it on a stone and wash the typeform with a suitable solvent.
2. Remove gage pins, tympan, and packing from the platen. Be sure to close the bales before proceeding.
3. Saturate a cloth with solvent and rub it over the ink disk. Use it to loosen the ink only. Wipe the loosened ink from the disk with a sheet of newspaper.
4. Cover the clean ink disk with a fresh sheet of newspaper. Raise the ink rollers onto the disk by turning the flywheel by hand. Now use a clean cloth saturated with solvent to loosen and remove the ink on the rollers. Repeat as required to remove all traces of ink from the press.

Do not leave the press with the rollers resting on the ink disk or flat spots may develop on the rollers.

Safety Note. Place cloths containing solvents and inks in a special metal safety can.

CYLINDER PRESS. The operating principle of a cylinder press is shown in Figure 27-14. A typeform is placed on a moving flat bed. A rotating cylinder provides the necessary printing pressure. The paper is held in place around the cylinder by grippers.

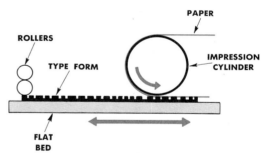

Figure 27-14. *Operating principle of the cylinder press.*

As the typeform passes under the impression cylinder, the image is transferred. Only a narrow portion of the form presses against the paper at any one time. The complete image is transferred only after the entire typeform passes under the impression cylinder. Then the printed sheet is delivered to a table, the bed is returned to its starting position, and the typeform re-inked for the next impression. One type of cylinder press is shown in Figure 27-15.

Figure 27-15. *Flat-bed cylinder press used for reproduction proofing. (Vandersons Corp.)*

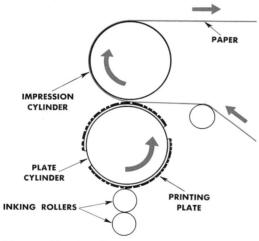

Figure 27-16. *Operating principle of the rotary press.*

ROTARY PRESS. The operating principle of a rotary press is illustrated in Figure 27-16. The printing plate is curved. Electrotypes, stereotypes, and rubber plates may be used. The plate is held on one (plate) cylinder, while a second (impression) cylinder provides the necessary printing pressure. As the plate cylinder rotates, the plate is inked.

Figure 27-17. *A sheet-fed rotary press. (Roberts & Porter, Inc.)*

Figure 27-18. *A web-fed, multicolor rotary press. (Rand McNally & Co.)*

The paper to be printed can be supplied to the press in sheets or in continuous rolls. A small sheet-fed rotary press is pictured in Figure 27-17. A roll-fed or web-fed, multicolor rotary press is shown in Figure 27-18. Large web-fed rotary presses can produce over 50,000 newspapers per hour.

THERMOGRAPHY

Thermography, also called imitation engraving, is a technique used to raise the image on a printed product. Raised images on business cards, announcements, and stationary are generally produced this way.

Thermography is simple to do. Immediately after the piece has been printed, sprinkle special thermography powder onto the wet ink. Then remove the excess powder by tapping the back of the sheet. Place the printed sheet under a heating element until the powder melts and fuses to the image. The fused powder creates a raised image on the printed product.

Powders used in thermography come in transparent, opaque, and metallic colors. Transparent powders allow the color of the base ink to show through. A machine used to heat the powder is pictured in Figure 27-19.

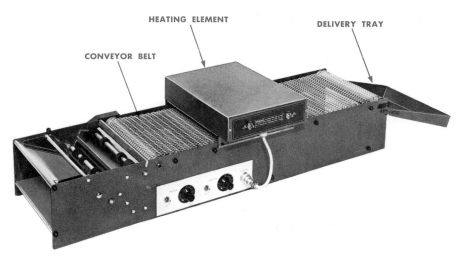

HEATING ELEMENT

DELIVERY TRAY

CONVEYOR BELT

Figure 27-19. *A thermography machine is used to raise the image on a printed product.* (MBM Corp.)

TEST YOUR KNOWLEDGE

1. Use simple diagrams to illustrate the operating principle of the platen press, the cylinder press, and the rotary press.
2. List eight safety rules that must be followed when preparing, operating, and cleaning a platen press.
3. Outline the basic procedures to be followed when preparing the platen press for printing.
4. Describe what is meant by the term *makeready* and explain how to reduce impression, increase impression, and obtain a uniform impression.
5. List in proper sequence the steps for printing with a platen press.

UNIT 28

PRINTING FROM GRAVURE PLATES

Objectives

When you have completed this unit, you will be able to:

1. Illustrate the operating principle of an engraving and etching press.
2. Describe how to prepare paper and ink used when printing engravings and etchings.
3. List the steps in printing with an engraving and etching press.
4. Illustrate the operating principle of the rotogravure press.

Terms to Know

Here are some of the words you will need to understand before reading this unit. If the meaning of a word is not clear to you, look it up in the Glossary in the back of this book.

rotogravure   metal etching   impression cylinder
drypoint engraving   doctor blade   web-fed
engraving and etching press

TYPES OF PRESSES

In gravure printing, ink is transferred to paper from a lowered surface. The image area of a gravure plate is cut below or into the surface of the plate. The entire surface of the plate is inked and then wiped clean. This leaves ink in the lowered areas of the plate. When paper is pressed against the plate, ink transfers to the paper. The gravure or intaglio process is shown in Figure 28-1.

Two basic types of presses are used to print gravure plates: the engraving and etching press and the rotogravure press.

ENGRAVING AND ETCHING PRESS.

A hand-operated engraving and etching press with major parts identified is pictured in Figure 28-2. This type of press is used to print the drypoint engravings and metal etchings discussed in Unit 23.

The plate to be printed is inked and placed on the bed of the press. The plate is then covered with a dampened sheet of paper and a felt blanket. Pressure, applied by the impression roller, causes the ink to transfer to the paper.

Printing Engravings and Etchings.
The procedures used to print drypoint engravings and metal etchings are:
1. *Preparing the paper.* Cut several pieces of soft, uncoated paper, such as mimeograph stock, to size. The paper should be at least two inches wider and two inches longer than the dimensions of the plate. Place the paper, one sheet at a time, into a tray of water.
2. *Preparing the ink.* Place a small amount of letterpress ink on a glass plate. Add a drop or two of linseed oil. With an ink knife thoroughly mix the ink and the linseed oil together.

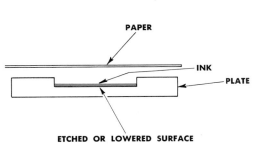

Figure 28-1. In the gravure process, printing ink is transferred to the paper from a lowered surface.

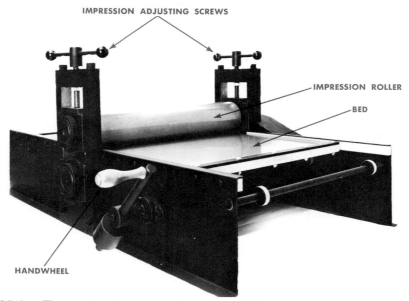

IMPRESSION ADJUSTING SCREWS

IMPRESSION ROLLER

BED

HANDWHEEL

Figure 28-2. *The parts of an engraving and etching press. (Rembrandt Graphic Arts)*

3. *Inking the plate.* Ink the plate with a dauber, a piece of folded cloth, or your fingertips. Force the ink into the lowered image areas. Completely fill these areas with ink. The inking process is shown in Figure 28-3.

4. *Cleaning the surface of the plate.* Fold a clean wiping cloth to form a

Figure 28-3. *Inking a drypoint plate. Force the ink into the lines with a dauber.*

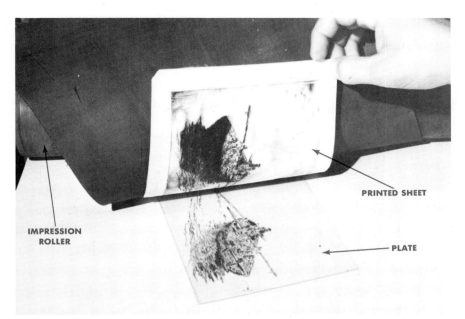

Figure 28-4. *Strip the printed sheet from the plate after it passes under the impression roller.*

pad. Use this pad to remove all of the ink from the surface of the plate. The heel of the hand may be used to further clean non-printing areas of the plate. Be careful not to remove ink from the lowered image areas.

5. *Preparing to print the plate.* Place the ink plate, face up, on the bed of the press. Remove a sheet of paper from the water tray and place it on a piece of blotter paper. Blot with a second piece of blotter paper to remove all excess moisture. Remove the blotters and cover the printing plate with the damp sheet of paper. Next place a felt blanket over the paper. The plate is now ready for printing.

6. *Printing the plate.* Turn the wheel of the press until the lead edge of the plate is just under the impression roller. Hand tighten the impression screws to increase the pressure on the paper and plate. Now continue to

turn the wheel until the plate emerges on the other side of the impression roller. Strip the printed sheet from the plate and place it on a rack to dry, Figure 28-4. Additional prints may be made by repeating steps 3 through 6.

7. *Cleaning the plate.* Use a suitable solvent to remove all ink from the plate. This is especially important if the plate is to be printed again at a later date.

ROTOGRAVURE PRESS. The operating principle of a rotogravure press is illustrated in Figure 28-5. The gravure cylinder discussed in Unit 23 is the image carrier or plate. Image cavities are filled with a thin ink as the gravure cylinder revolves in an ink bath. A fine steel squeegee, called a *doctor blade,* is used to remove excess ink from the surface of non-image areas of the cylinder. A rubber covered impression cylin-

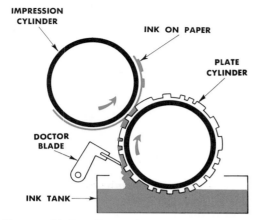

Figure 28-5. *Operating principle of the rotogravure press.*

der provides the necessary printing pressure during the printing operation.

The paper to be printed can be supplied to the press in sheets or in continuous rolls. A roll-fed or web-fed multicolor rotogravure press is shown in Figure 28-6. Large web-fed presses can print 100-inch wide rolls of paper at speeds of 1500 feet or more per minute.

Figure 28-6. *Web-fed, multicolor rotogravure press. (Gravure Technical Association Inc.)*

TEST YOUR KNOWLEDGE

1. Prepare a simple diagram showing how an engraving and etching press works. Label each of the major parts of this press.
2. Describe the procedures for preparing the paper and ink used in printing engravings and etchings.
3. Outline the basic steps to be followed when printing with an engraving and etching press.
4. Prepare a simple diagram to illustrate how a rotogravure press operates. Label each of the major parts of this press.

UNIT 29

PRINTING FROM LITHOGRAPHIC PLATES

Objectives

When you have completed this unit, you will be able to:

1. Describe the difference between a duplicator and a press.
2. List five operating systems that comprise an offset duplicator or press.
3. Illustrate two techniques to dampen a plate.
4. Describe the characteristics of the fountain solution and inks used in lithographic printing.
5. Illustrate two techniques to ink a plate.
6. Diagram both friction-feeding and vacuum-feeding techniques.
7. Describe the differences between a two-cylinder and a three-cylinder printing system.
8. Explain the difference between chute and chain delivery.

Terms to Know

Here are some of the words you will need to understand before reading this unit. If the meaning of a word is not clear to you, look it up in the Glossary in the back of this book.

lithography	dampening system	plate cylinder
offset duplicator	fountain solution	blanket cylinder
offset press	inking system	impression cylinder
sheet-fed	printing system	delivery system
web-fed	feeding and registering system	

OFFSET DUPLICATORS AND PRESSES

Lithographic or photo-offset printing is printing from a greasy image applied to a flat surface. Unit 24 describes the procedures for placing greasy images on flat surfaces.

The photo-offset printing process is diagrammed in Figure 29-1. First water is

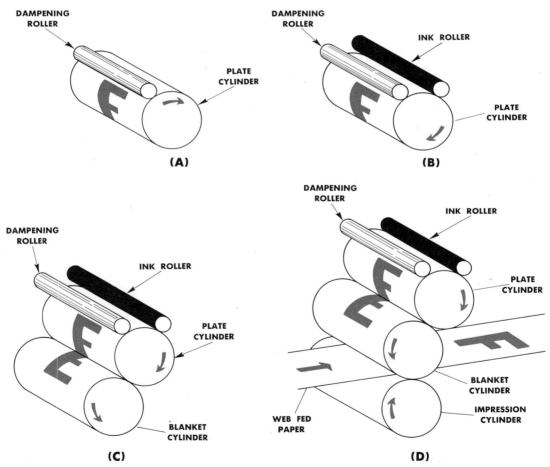

Figure 29-1. *Photo-offset printing. (A) The plate is made wet. (B) The plate is inked. (C) The image is transferred to a rubber blanket. (D) Paper receives the image from the blanket.*

applied to the plate with the greasy image, Figure 29-1A. Water covers only the non-image area of the plate. The greasy image repels water because water and grease do not mix.

Next the entire plate is coated with ink, Figure 29-1B. Because the ink is greasy, it adheres to the greasy image but not to the wet portions of the plate. Wherever water covers the non-image area of the plate, it repels the greasy ink.

After the plate is wet and inked, the image is transferred to a rubber blanket, Figure 29-1C. To print, the paper is pressed against the surface of the blanket, Figure 29-1D.

Figure 29-3. *A floor model offset duplicator. (A. B. Dick Co.)*

Figure 29-2. *A table-top offset duplicator. (A. B. Dick Co.)*

Figure 29-4. *This duplicator can print on sheets of paper that measure 12" × 18". (Heidelberg Eastern, Inc.)*

Duplicators and presses are used to print lithographic plates. Offset duplicators are used for relatively small printing jobs. There are approximately a dozen different brands of duplicators that print on paper sizes up to 14" × 20". A table-top offset duplicator is shown in Figure 29-2. A small, floor model offset duplicator is shown in Figure 29-3. Figure 29-4

illustrates a duplicator capable of handling 12" × 18" paper.

Offset presses contain more precise controls and systems than duplicators.

Figure 29-5. *A sheet-fed offset press. (Heidelberg Eastern, Inc.)*

Offset presses are used to print magazines, books, and newspapers from sheets or from rolls of paper. A sheet-fed offset press is shown in Figure 29-5. Figure 29-6 shows an offset lithography press used to print high-quality multicolored materials.

Although a wide variety of machines is used to print lithographic plates, they all contain the same operating systems: the dampening system, the inking system, the feeding and registering system, the printing system, and the delivery system.

DAMPENING SYSTEM. The dampening system coats the non-image area of the plate with water. There are two basic

techniques employed: *conventional* and *combined,* Figure 29-7. In the conventional technique (Figure 29-7A), water is carried from the fountain to the plate by a series of dampening rollers. A separate set of rollers is used to ink the plate. In the combined technique (Figure 29-7B), however, some of the same rollers are used to transfer both the water and the ink to the plate. These rollers are first covered with ink, then with water. The water rides on top of the ink and is transferred to the non-image area of the plate at the same time the ink coats the image area.

Fountain Solution. The solution transferred to the plate by the dampening system is basically water. Generally a

Figure 29-6. *A four-color, sheet-fed offset press. A different color ink is laid down on the sheet as it passes from each printing unit to the next. (Heidelberg Eastern, Inc.)*

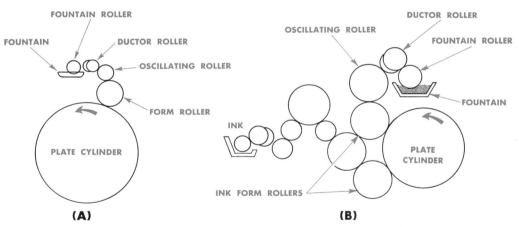

(A)   **(B)**

Figure 29-7. *A dampening system is needed to coat the non-image area of the plate with water.* (A) *Conventional technique.* (B) *Combined technique.*

small amount of fountain concentrate is added to produce a mildly acidic solution.

INKING SYSTEM. The inking system coats the image area of the plate with ink. Again *conventional* and *combined* techniques are used. Schematic drawings of both are shown in Figure 29-8. Both techniques use a trough which serves as an ink fountain and a series of rollers.

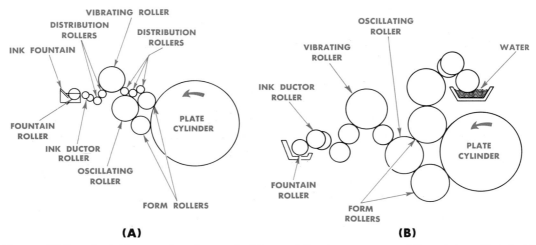

Figure 29-8. *An inking system is needed to coat the image area of the plate with ink. (A) Conventional technique. (B) Combined technique.*

A *fountain roller* transfers ink from the ink fountain to the ink ductor roller. The *ductor* moves back and forth between the fountain roller and a train of ink *distribution rollers*. *Vibrator* and *oscillating rollers* insure that the ink will uniformly coat the ink form rollers. The *form rollers* actually coat the image area of the plate with ink.

Lithographic Ink. Inks used in offset lithography are prepared especially for offset presses. Lithographic inks must not combine with or absorb any fountain solution. They must also be able to provide sufficient coverage even though the blanket picks up only a portion of the ink on the plate.

FEEDING AND REGISTERING SYSTEM. The feeding and registering system is used to transfer individual sheets of paper from a paper pile to a predetermined position. From this position the paper is fed into the printing system.

Both friction and air-and-vacuum mechanisms are used to feed individual

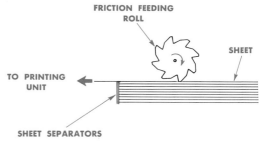

Figure 29-9. *Friction feeding system for an offset duplicator.*

sheets. Friction feeding is shown in Figure 29-9.

The feed system on most presses is air-and-vacuum operated, Figure 29-10. An air blast lifts the top sheets from the paper pile. A suction foot (sucker) picks up the top sheet by vacuum and transfers it to a set of pullout rolls. The pullout rolls then pass the sheet, by means of friction, to the register table.

On the register table, the paper first passes through a multiple-sheet detector to insure that only one sheet of paper will be printed at a time. The single sheet is then conveyed down the regis-

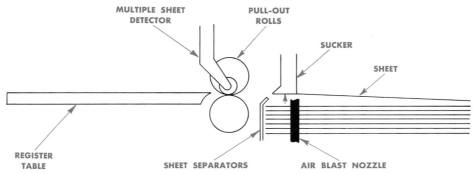

Figure 29-10. *Air and vacuum feeding system for an offset duplicator.*

ter table to a front stop. Here, it is jogged into a predetermined position before being fed into the printing system.

PRINTING SYSTEM. Most press manufacturers use a three-cylinder printing system, Figure 29-11. The plate on the plate cylinder transfers the image to the blanket. This image is then offset onto the paper as it passes between the blanket and impression cylinders. Cylinder grippers carry the paper through the printing system.

A two-cylinder printing system is diagrammed in Figure 29-12. Here a large, upper cylinder contains a plate and an impression segment. A small, lower cylinder holds the blanket. The plate segment on the large cylinder first comes in contact with the blanket and transfers the image to it. Paper is not traveling through the printing system at this point. However, when the impression seg-

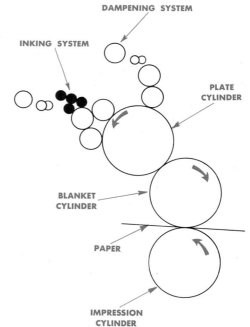

Figure 29-11. *A three-cylinder printing system.*

ment of the large cylinder is opposite the blanket, paper will pass between the two cylinders and the image will offset from the blanket onto the sheet.

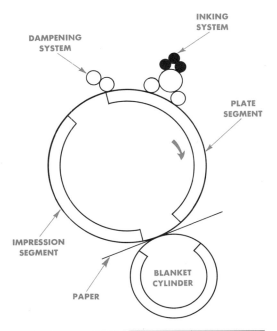

Figure 29-12. *A two-cylinder printing system. The Davidson duplicator is a two-cylinder machine.* (Bottom, *ATF Davidson Co.*)

DELIVERY SYSTEM. After receiving the image, the sheet is transferred from the printing system to a tray or table. Two basic delivery techniques are used.

Figure 29-13 illustrates the *chute delivery* technique. Note that the printed sheet is simply ejected into a delivery tray. The ejector rolls help to propel the sheet into the tray.

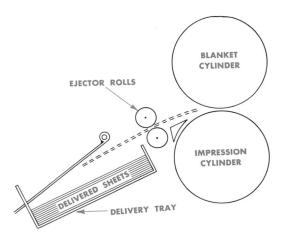

Figure 29-13. *Chute delivery.*

The *chain delivery* technique is illustrated in Figure 29-14. Here gripper bars mounted between two endless chains are used to convey the printed sheets from the printing system to a delivery table. The table is automatically lowered as the printed sheets pile up. This type of delivery table is called a *receding stacker.*

PROCEDURES FOR OPERATING AN OFFSET DUPLICATOR

Different makes and models of offset duplicators are available. Operating controls and procedures differ somewhat from one model to the next. For this reason you should consult the instruction manual supplied by the manufacturer of your machine for specific operating instructions.

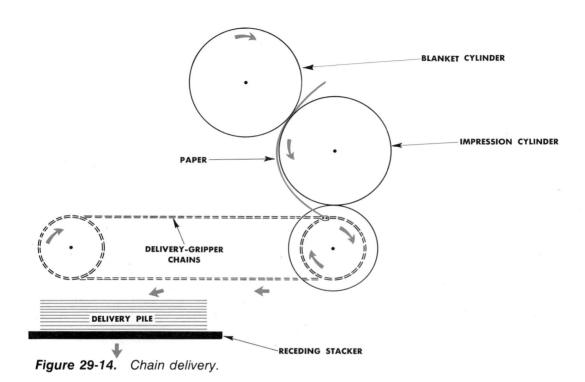

BLANKET CYLINDER

IMPRESSION CYLINDER

PAPER

DELIVERY-GRIPPER
CHAINS

DELIVERY PILE

RECEDING STACKER

Figure 29-14. *Chain delivery.*

Figure 29-15 illustrates the inking, dampening, and printing systems of an A. B. Dick Model 360 offset duplicator. The rest of this unit will explain how to operate this machine.

Figure 29-16 identifies the major parts and controls of the A. B. Dick 360. Although the names and locations of parts and controls vary with different duplicators, their operation is basically the same.

PREPARING THE INKING SYSTEM.
The inking system is prepared first, in the following manner:

Night Latches. Lift the safety cover over the ink rollers and lower the ink oscillating roller. Also place the Aquamatic oscillating roller in its operating position. Move the Aquamatic night latch handle (13) to its operating position and the operation control lever (15) to neutral. Turn the form roller control knobs (9) to the ON position.

Inking. Place ink in the ink fountain. Rotate the ink fountain roller knob (10) counterclockwise to coat the ink fountain roller. Then turn the handwheel (7) counterclockwise until the ink ductor roller is touching the ink fountain roller. Next raise the Aquamatic lockout latch (11). Finally, set the ink fountain control to the No. 4 position and the Aquamatic control (12) to the No. 45 position. The ink is now ready to be distributed.

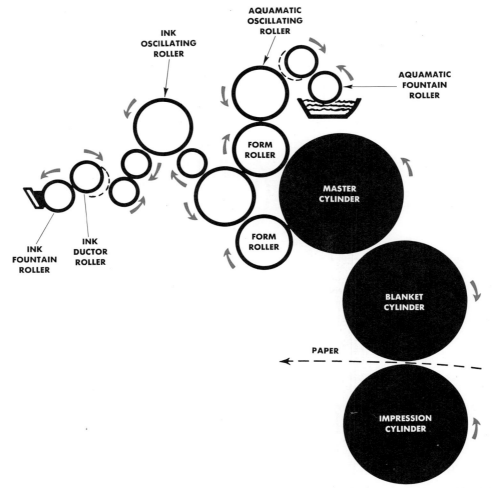

Figure 29-15. *The inking, dampening, and printing systems of an A. B. Dick Model 360 offset duplicator. (A. B. Dick Co.)*

Close all safety covers and turn the motor drive switch (8) to the ON position. Set the speed control (5) at medium speed. Now adjust the screws located along the ink fountain until all rollers are evenly covered with a thin film of ink. Turning the screws to the right decreases the ink supply. Turning them to the left increases the amount of ink on the rollers.

When all of the rollers are evenly coated, move the ink fountain control to the No. 1 position and the Aquamatic control to the No. 20 position. Then lower the Aquamatic lockout latch (11) and turn the motor drive switch (8) off.

PREPARING THE DAMPENING SYSTEM. Fill the fountain solution bottle with fountain solution. Cap the bottle and place it in position over the fountain solution trough (14). Allow the fountain solution to fill the trough.

PREPARING THE FEEDING SYSTEM. After the inking and dampening systems

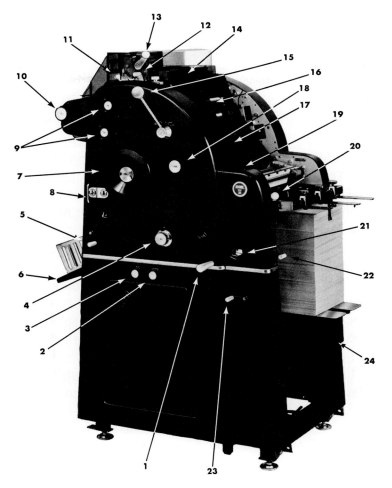

Figure 29-16. *An A. B. Dick Model 360 offset duplicator. (A. B. Dick Co.)*

1. PAPER ELEVATOR CRANK
2. VACUUM CONTROL
3. AIR CONTROL
4. BUCKLE CONTROL
5. SPEED CONTROL
6. RECEIVING TRAY
7. HAND WHEEL
8. MOTOR DRIVE AND VACUUM PUMP SWITCHES
9. FORM ROLLER CONTROL KNOBS
10. INK FOUNTAIN ROLLER KNOB
11. AQUAMATIC LOCK-OUT LATCH
12. AQUAMATIC CONTROL
13. AQUAMATIC NIGHT LATCH HANDLE
14. FOUNTAIN SOLUTION TROUGH
15. OPERATION CONTROL LEVER
16. MASTER CYLINDER
17. BLANKET CYLINDER
18. VERTICAL COPY ADJUSTING LOCK
19. COPY COUNTER
20. PAPER FEED LEVER
21. TABLE RELEASE
22. PAPER STACK HEIGHT ADJUSTMENT
23. PAPER GUIDE CRANK
24. FEED TABLE

have been prepared, adjust the various controls of the feeding system.

Loading the Feed Table. Using the paper guide cranks (23) on both sides of the machine, set the paper guides to the width of the paper being used. Refer to the scale at the front of the machine.

Lower the feed table (24) by pressing the table release (21) down and turning the paper elevator crank (1) counterclockwise. Now position the paper stack supports on the feed table (24). Place a paper stack support board on the paper stack supports. The support board should be slightly smaller than the paper. Next fan out the paper to be printed and load it on the support board.

Raising the Paper Pile. Turn the handwheel (7) counterclockwise until the four paper height regulators located above the scale at the front of the machine are in their lowest position. Next raise the table release (21) and turn the paper elevator crank (1) until the top of the paper pile contacts the paper height regulators.

Positioning Feet and Levelers. The suction feet and paper levelers are located above the lead edge of the paper pile in the suction foot bar. Position the suction feet and paper levelers according to the width of the paper being printed.

To reposition a suction foot or paper leveler simply unscrew the foot or leveler and screw it into the new position. Seal any open positions with the plugs provided for this purpose. With most papers, the lowest point of the levelers should be set slightly lower than the lowest point of the suction feet.

Positioning the Guides and Paper Weight. Position the side and back guides at the tail end of the paper pile.

The guides should just touch the paper pile. Now position the paper weight wire, which is located above the paper pile. The paper weight should be placed in a forward notch for lightweight papers and farther back for heavier papers.

Adjusting the Paper Height. The height of the paper pile is controlled by raising or lowering the paper height control lever (22). Set the control to a low number for lightweight papers and a high number for heavier papers.

Adjusting Air and Vacuum. Make sure that all safety covers are closed. Turn the motor drive switch (8) on. Allow the machine to run until the paper pile reaches its maximum height. Then turn the motor drive switch off.

Turn the paper feed lever (20) to the OFF position. Rotate the air (3) and vacuum (2) control knobs clockwise as far as they will go. Then turn each knob counterclockwise one and a half turns.

Check the blowing action by turning the motor and vacuum pump switches (8) on. The top sheets on the paper pile should fluff up and follow the four height regulators. Readjust the air control (3) as required.

To check the suction, turn the motor drive off. Lift the paper feed lever (20) and turn the handwheel (7) counterclockwise to manually feed one sheet of paper through the machine. Adjust the vacuum control (2) when required. Then turn the vacuum pump switch (8) and paper feed lever (20) off.

Buckle Control. The buckle control dial (4) is used to insure that every sheet of paper is delivered to the printing unit in proper position. Set the control to a high number when feeding lightweight papers and a lower number for heavy stock.

PREPARING THE DELIVERY SYSTEM. Prepare the delivery system by positioning the receiving tray and ejector wheels and rings.

Positioning the Receiving Tray. Set the guide on the left-hand side of the receiving tray (6) according to the size of the paper being used. A scale is provided for this purpose. Now place a sheet of paper on the receiving tray and position the back guide. The top edge of the paper should be even with the top edge of the receiving tray.

The guide on the right-hand side of the tray jogs the paper against the left guide during delivery. Set the right-hand guide when it is in its extreme inward position. This can be determined by turning the handwheel (7) counterclockwise.

Setting Ejector Wheels and Rings. Turn on the vacuum pump switch (8) and paper feed lever (20). Turn the handwheel (7) counterclockwise to manually feed one sheet of paper through the machine. Stop turning when the sheet emerges from the printing unit on the delivery side of the machine. Turn the vacuum pump switch (8) and paper feed lever (20) off.

Position the ejector wheels to ride the extreme right and left margins of the sheet. After the ejector wheels are set, position the ejector rings either inside or outside the lower ejector wheels. When the paper tends to curl down, place the rings outside the ejector wheels. For paper that curls up, set the rings inside the wheels.

PREPARING THE PRINTING SYSTEM. Finally the printing system is prepared.

Attaching and Etching the Plate. Lower the safety cover and attach the lead edge of the plate to the head clamp on the master cylinder (16). Crease the plate at the head clamp. Now, hold the tail end of the plate taut with the right hand and turn the handwheel (7) counterclockwise with your left hand. Then attach the tail end of the plate to the master cylinder with the tail clamp.

After the plate is attached, it must be etched. Coat the surface of the plate with an etch solution as recommended by the manufacturer of the plate.

**PRINTING WITH THE OFFSET DUPLI-
CATOR.** Close all safety covers and
turn the motor drive and vacuum pump
switches (8) on. Move the operation
control lever (15) to the INK position to
ink the plate. Then move the operation
control lever to the IMAGE position and
hold it there for three or four revolutions.
This causes the plate image to transfer
to the blanket. Next, move the operation
control lever to the FEED position and
allow sheets to pass through the press.
Lower the paper feed lever (20) to turn
off the paper feed.

Inspect the printed sheets. If accept-
able, set the copy counter (19) to 0 and
lift the paper feed lever (20) to the ON
position. Use the Aquamatic control (12)
and the ink fountain control to adjust the
amounts of water and ink as needed
throughout the run.

When the required number of copies
has been printed, lower the paper feed
lever (20) and move the operation lever
(15) to the NEUTRAL position. Turn off
the vacuum pump and motor drive
switches (8). Then lower the safety
cover and remove the plate. Finally
clean the blanket with a cloth dampened
with blanket wash.

TEST YOUR KNOWLEDGE

1. Explain the difference between an offset duplicator and an offset press.
2. List five operating systems of an offset duplicator or press.
3. Prepare simple diagrams to illustrate the conventional and combined techniques for dampening a lithographic plate.
4. Describe the special characteristics of the fountain solution and inks used in lithographic printing.
5. Prepare simple diagrams to illustrate the conventional and combined techniques for inking a lithographic plate.
6. Prepare simple diagrams to illustrate the friction and air-and-vacuum feeding techniques used on offset duplicators.
7. Using simple diagrams, illustrate the differences between a two-cylinder and a three-cylinder printing system. Label each of the parts shown.
8. Describe the difference between chute delivery and chain delivery.

UNIT 30

SCREEN-PROCESS PRINTING

Objectives

When you have completed this unit, you will be able to:

1. Illustrate the basic parts of a hand-operated screen printing press.
2. Describe two methods of stretching screen fabric.
3. Give two reasons for taping and sealing a screen.
4. List the basic steps in screen-process printing.
5. Identify the proper solvents to use with water-base, lacquer-base, and oil-base inks; water-base and lacquer-base blockouts; and the various kinds of stencils.
6. Describe the procedures for removing a lacquer film stencil from the screen fabric.

Terms to Know

Here are some of the words you will need to understand before reading this unit. If the meaning of a word is not clear to you, look it up in the Glossary in the back of this book.

stencil	squeegee	cylinder press
screen fabric	solvent	

TYPES OF PRESSES

Screen-process printing forces ink through openings or holes in a stencil that is attached to a screen. The stencil may be hand cut from paper or film, prepared photographically, or painted directly on the screen.

The screen consists of a piece of woven material stretched tightly across a wooden or metal frame. Silk, nylon, dacron, and stainless steel mesh are most often used.

The paper to be printed is placed under the printing frame, and ink, with a paint-like consistency, is applied to the top of the screen. Printing takes place when the ink is spread and forced through the stencil with a rubber squeegee. The screen process of printing is shown in Figure 30-1.

Hand-operated presses are most often used for short runs. Power-operated flatbed and cylinder presses are used to print large quantities of material by the screen-process technique. Many specially designed screen-printing presses have also been developed to print on a variety of shapes and materials.

HAND-OPERATED SCREEN PRINTING PRESS. A hand-operated screen printing press is pictured in Figure 30-2. The basic parts of this press are

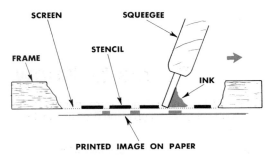

Figure 30-1. Screen-process printing. Ink is forced through the openings in the screen formed by the stencil and deposited on the paper below.

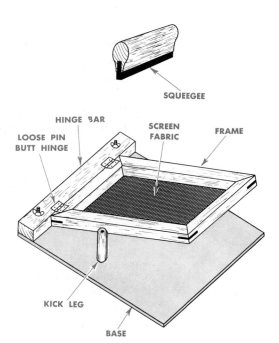

Figure 30-2. A hand-operated screen printing press with its major parts labeled.

the frame, screen fabric, base, and squeegee.

Frame. The frame is usually made from a softwood such as pine or fir. Miter, end lap, or spline joints may be used, Figure 30-3. The corners of the frame are secured with glue and nails or corrugated fasteners.

Screen Fabric. Silk, nylon, dacron, and stainless steel mesh are the fabrics most often used to make a screen. Silk is the most popular fabric for screen-process printing.

The mesh count or weave opening of silk is indicated by a number ranging from 0000 to 25. The mesh count indicates the number of openings per inch of fabric. Mesh counts for numbers 6

NUMBER	MESH COUNT
6 xx	74
8 xx	86
10 xx	109
12 xx	125
14 xx	139
16 xx	157
18 xx	166
20 xx	173
25 xx	200

Figure 30-4. *Mesh count indicates the coarseness or fineness of the weave.*

through 18 silk are shown in Figure 30-4. Number 12XX silk is used for most general purpose screen-process work. A closely woven silk, such as number 18XX, is employed when printing extremely fine detail. For coarse work, a number 6 or 8XX silk can be used.

The strength of the silk fiber is indicated by one or more X's after the silk number. The more X's, the stronger the fiber. Fibers rated XXXX are more durable than fibers rated XX.

Base. The base of the screen printing press is usually made from a sheet of plywood or masonite. It is fastened to the frame with loose-pin butt hinges. The base is the surface on which paper is positioned and held during printing.

Squeegee. The squeegee is used to spread ink across the screen and force it through the stencil. It is a hard rubber blade projecting from a wooden handle. Generally the blade is from 3/16 to 1/2 inch thick. The shape of the squeegee blade depends on the type of printing being done. Figure 30-5 shows several blade shapes. Use a square-edged blade (A) for general printing on flat surfaces. A square-edged blade with rounded corners (B) leaves extra heavy thick ink deposits. For textile printing, a blade with a rounded edge (C) should be

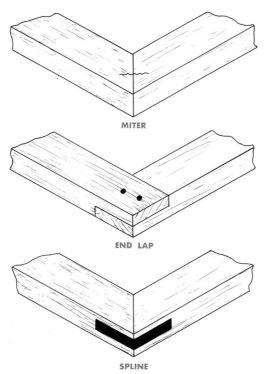

MITER

END LAP

SPLINE

Figure 30-3. *Miter, end lap, or spline joints can be used to hold the sides of the frame together.*

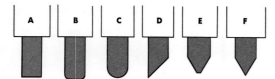

Figure 30-5. *The shape of the edge of the squeegee is chosen according to the type of printing to be done.*

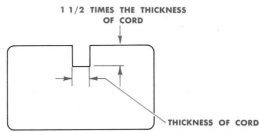

Figure 30-6. *The relationship between the depth and width of the groove that must be cut into each side of the frame when you use cord to hold the screen fabric in place.*

used. The bevel-edged blade *(D)* is used for printing on glass. A flat point bevel-edged blade *(E)* may be used for printing on ceramic materials. The V-shaped blade *(F)* is ideal for printing on bottles and other containers.

Stretching the Screen Fabric. The screen fabric is attached to the frame with staples or with strips of heavy cord. If staples are used, insert them approximately one inch apart. Use a staple gun loaded with heavy duty staples. First staple the center of each side of the fabric to the center of each side of the frame. Stretch the silk before stapling. Continue stapling the silk along the long sides of the frame from center to ends. Now repeat the procedure along the short sides of the frame. The frame is now ready for taping and sealing.

To attach the fabric to the frame with cord, cut a groove down the center of each side of the frame, Figure 30-6, with a table saw. Now cut a piece of fabric approximately four inches wider and four inches longer than the frame. Next place the frame, groove side up, on a workbench and cover it with the screen fabric. Make sure that the frame is in the center and that the fabric extends the same amount on all sides.

Fasten the fabric by pressing a length of cord into each groove in the frame.

Press the cords all the way down into the grooves with a thin piece of wood or bookbinder's folding bone. Be sure that the fabric is stretched tightly. Trim away the excess fabric. The screen is now ready to be taped and sealed.

Taping and Sealing. Taping and sealing simplifies cleanup and extends the life of the screen. Cover the stapled or grooved side of the frame with gummed tape. The tape should extend onto the screen approximately ½ inch.

Now turn the frame over and tape the four inside edges of the frame. Use four lengths of tape that have been folded lengthwise in half, adhesive side out. Each length of tape should contact the inside of the frame and the top surface of the silk.

After the gummed tape has dried, paint the tape and frame with shellac. Allow the shellac sealer to extend onto the fabric about ⅛ inch. When the shellac is dry, the hand-operated screen printing press is ready for use.

PRINTING WITH A HAND-OPERATED SCREEN PRINTING PRESS. Techniques for preparing several types of stencils and adhering these stencils to the screen are discussed in Unit 25. Although stencil preparation and adhering techniques vary, printing procedures do not. All types of stencils are printed in much the same way.

Setting the Guides. Place a sheet of paper to be printed on the base of the printing frame. Position the paper according to the location of the stencil image. After the paper is in position, raise the screen slowly and mark the location of the paper on the base. Short leads or strips of chipboard may be used as registration guides. Fasten these guides to the base with masking tape. Generally use two guides along the long edge of the paper and one guide along the short edge. Figure 30-7 shows how to locate and fasten registration guides.

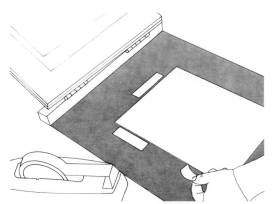

Figure 30-7. *Registration guides are used to position the paper before printing.*

Masking the Screen. Nonprinting areas around the perimeter of the stencil must be *masked* or blocked out before printing. Masking tape may be used for this purpose. Apply the tape to the underside of the screen. Tape strips of paper

to the screen with masking tape in order to block out the larger nonprinting areas.

The screen may be masked with water-base or lacquer-base liquid masking material. Water-base blockout is needed when the job is to be printed with an oil-base or lacquer-base ink. Use lacquer-base blockout when a water-base ink is used.

Apply blockout to the screen with a brush or with a piece of cardboard. Cover the nonprinting areas only. Masking is shown in Figure 30-8. Allow the blockout to dry completely.

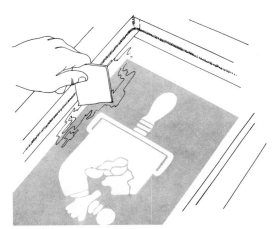

Figure 30-8. *Use a cardboard squeegee to cover the nonprinting areas of the screen with a thin layer of blockout.*

Inking the Screen. Use a spatula to run a bead of ink along one edge of the stencil. Apply enough ink to produce several prints. Add more ink when needed.

Printing. Raise the frame and place a sheet of paper against the registration guides. Now lower the frame and pull the ink across the image area of the

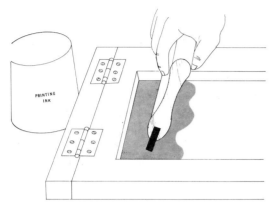

Figure 30-9. *Hold the squeegee firmly. Keep it at a sixty degree angle with the screen.*

Figure 30-10. *A rack used for drying screen-process prints. (Advance Process Supply Co.)*

stencil with the edge of the squeegee. Hold the squeegee as shown in Figure 30-9. Apply downward pressure as you pull the squeegee across the stencil. Pull the squeegee once for each print.

After printing, raise the frame and remove the print from the baseboard. Place the print on a rack to dry, Figure 30-10. Print additional copies by repeating the procedures. After all required copies have been made, clean the screen.

Cleanup. Before it dries, all ink must be removed from the screen, squeegee, and spatula. The blockout and stencil must also be removed unless the stencil is to be used again.

Removing the Ink. Cover the baseboard with several sheets of newspaper. Scoop up the excess ink on the screen with a piece of cardboard and return it to the ink can. Also use cardboard to scrape excess ink from the squeegee and spatula. After returning the ink to the can, discard the cardboard.

Pour a small quantity of ink solvent on the screen. Use water to remove water-base ink, lacquer thinner for a lacquer-base ink, and mineral spirits for removing oil-base ink. Wipe the screen with clean paper towels or a cloth moistened with solvent to remove the ink. Repeat until the screen is clean. Remove ink from the squeegee and spatula the same way.

Removing the Blockout. Separate the frame from its base by removing the pins from the hinges. With a suitable solvent dissolve the blockout. Use water to remove water-base masking material and lacquer thinner to remove lacquer-base blockout.

Removing the Stencil. Hand-cut water soluble stencils, tusche stencils, and indirect photographic stencils may be removed by holding the screen under hot running water.

Photographic direct stencils are re-moved from the screen with a special solvent. Follow the emulsion manufac-turer's recommendations for removing the stencil.

Remove lacquer film stencils with lac-quer thinner. Place a pad of several newspaper sheets beneath the frame. Then pour a small amount of lacquer thinner on the screen. Allow the lacquer thinner to soften the stencil. After the stencil has had a chance to soak, rub

the top of the screen with a clean cloth. As the stencil dissolves, it will stick to the newspaper. Remove one or two newspaper sheets and repeat the above process until all traces of the stencil have been removed.

POWER-OPERATED FLATBED SCREEN PRINTING PRESS. A power-operated flatbed screen printing press is pictured in Figure 30-11. The raising and lowering of the screen on this press

Figure 30-11. *Power-operated flatbed screen printing press. (Jos. E. Podgor Com-pany, Inc.)*

Figure 30-12. *Automatic screen-process cylinder press with automatic feeding unit. (General Research, Inc.)*

is mechanized. So too is the action of the squeegee. Some power-operated presses are also equipped with automatic feed and delivery systems.

POWER-OPERATED CYLINDER PRESS.

A cylinder screen-printing press is shown in Figure 30-12. Figure 30-13 shows the operating principle of this machine. The screen containing the

stencil moves over a cylinder that carries the material to be printed. A vacuum holds the printed material against the cylinder. The squeegee is held stationary during printing, while the material to be printed moves forward at the same speed as the screen. At the completion of the printing cycle, the squeegee rises, and the cylinder and frame are returned to their starting positions.

PRINTING ON CYLINDRICAL-SHAPED OBJECTS.

A hand-operated screen-printing press designed for use with cylindrical objects is shown in Figure 30-14. An image can be transferred to any round object such as bottle or can with a machine of this type. The squeegee is held stationary, while the screen moves back and forth during the printing. The round object is rotated by the movement of the screen during the printing operation.

Figure 30-13. *Operating principle of a cylinder press used in screen printing.*

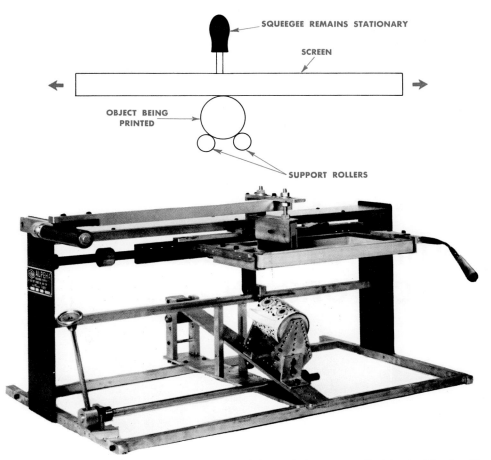

Figure 30-14. *A screen-process press used for printing on cylindrical objects.* (Bottom, Naz-Dar *Co.)*

TEST YOUR KNOWLEDGE

1. Sketch a hand-operated screen printing press. Label each of its major parts.
2. Describe two methods that can be used to stretch and attach screen fabric to the frame.
3. Tell two important reasons why screens should be taped and sealed prior to their use.
4. List in proper sequence the basic steps to be followed when printing with a hand-operated screen printing press.
5. Prepare a chart which illustrates the proper solvent to be used with water-base ink, lacquer-base ink, oil-base ink, water-base blockout, lacquer-base blockout, hand-cut stencils, tusche stencils, and photographic stencils.
6. Outline the procedures to be followed when removing a lacquer film stencil from the screen fabric.

UNIT 31

PRINTING WITH OFFICE DUPLICATORS AND COPIERS

Objectives

When you have completed this unit, you will be able to:
1. Outline the procedures for printing with a spirit duplicator.
2. List the basic steps used in printing with a mimeograph duplicator.
3. Describe general operating procedures for an electrostatic copier.

Terms to Know

Here are some of the words you will need to understand before reading this unit. If the meaning of a word is not clear to you, look it up in the Glossary in the back of this book.

spirit duplicating	mimeograph duplicating
solvent	electrostatic copying

SPIRIT DUPLICATOR

Spirit duplicating is a planographic process. Printing is done from a flat sheet of paper called a spirit master. Techniques for preparing spirit masters are described in Unit 26.

A master containing an aniline-dye image is attached to the master cylinder of a spirit duplicator. Each sheet of paper is moistened with solvent capable of dissolving aniline dye. As the moistened paper contacts the spirit master, the solvent dissolves some of the dye.

The loosened dye is transferred to the paper as it passes between the spirit master and impression rolls. The printed sheet of paper is then delivered to a receiving tray.

PRINTING WITH A SPIRIT DUPLICATOR. Many different models of duplicators are available. Figure 31-1 shows a typical spirit duplicator with major parts labeled. Some duplicators are hand-operated. Others are power-driven. Because operating controls and procedures may differ slightly from one model

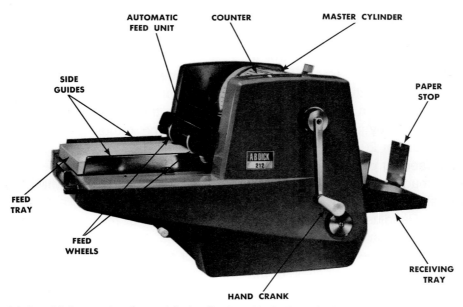

Figure 31-1. *Major parts of a spirit duplicator. (A. B. Dick Co.)*

to the next, consult the manufacturer's instruction manual for specific operating instructions. Only general printing procedures will be discussed here.

1. Clamp the master to the cylinder with the master clamp. Make sure the master lies flat on the cylinder.
2. Load the paper in the feed tray. The automatic feed unit should be in the OFF (UP) position. Side guides must be set to the width of the paper. The separator fingers should rest on the corners of the lead edge of the paper pile.
3. Adjust the automatic feed unit. Feed wheels should be positioned about ¾ inch from each edge of the paper. Set the feed pressure according to the weight of the paper used. Use a low-pressure setting for lightweight papers and a high-pressure setting for heavy stock.
4. Set the receiving tray by feeding one sheet through the press or by sighting along the edge of the master. Set the guides and paper stop as required.
5. Turn the duplicator fluid control to the ON position. Regulate the amount of fluid. If the duplicator has not been used for a while, it will have to be primed by allowing the machine to run for 20 to 30 revolutions without feeding paper.
6. Check image placement by feeding a few sheets of paper through the machine. Readjust the feed tray side guides to obtain the desired side margins. Reset the receiving tray as required. The vertical position of the image on the sheet may also have to be adjusted.

7. Set the counter to zero. Turn on the duplicator and lower the automatic feed unit. Use the impression control to regulate the amount of dye that is transferred to the paper.
8. After the required number of copies have been printed, turn the machine off. Also set the fluid control to the OFF position.
9. Remove the master and discard or store it. If the master is to be used again, place a clean sheet of paper against the carbon side to protect the image.

MIMEOGRAPH DUPLICATOR

Mimeograph duplicating is based on the screen process of printing. A stencil is used to control the placement of ink on the paper. Techniques for preparing mimeograph stencils are described in Unit 26.

The cut stencil is attached to the cylinder of a mimeograph duplicator. During printing, ink passes through holes in the cylinder and onto an absorbent pad located behind the stencil.

As paper passes between the stencil and impression roller, ink is forced through the stencil openings onto the paper. The printed sheet of paper is then delivered to a receiving tray.

PRINTING WITH A MIMEOGRAPH DUPLICATOR. There are many different models of mimeograph duplicators available. A mimeograph duplicator with major parts labeled is pictured in Figure 31-2. Mimeograph duplicators may be hand-operated or power-driven. Operating controls and procedures differ

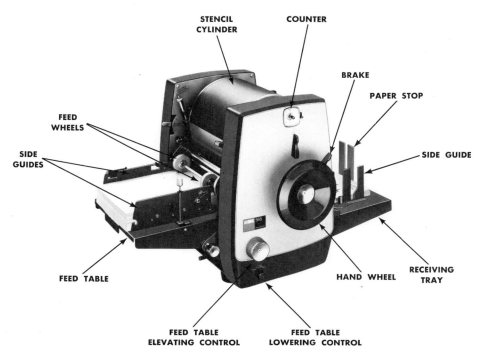

STENCIL CYLINDER

COUNTER

BRAKE

PAPER STOP

FEED WHEELS

SIDE GUIDES

SIDE GUIDE

FEED TABLE

HAND WHEEL

RECEIVING TRAY

FEED TABLE ELEVATING CONTROL

FEED TABLE LOWERING CONTROL

Figure 31-2. *Major parts of a mimeograph duplicator. (A. B. Dick Co.)*

slightly from one model to the next. Consult the instruction manual supplied by the manufacturer of your machine for specific operating instructions. General printing procedures are discussed here.

1. Attach the head of the stencil, backing sheet up, to the stencil cylinder with the head clamp. Separate and tear the backing sheet from the stencil. Now, holding the tail end of the stencil in your right hand while turning the handwheel with your left, place the stencil so that it rests smoothly on the ink pad. Finally, attach the tail end of the stencil to the cylinder with the tail clamp.

2. Lower the feed table and insert the paper. Set the side guides to the width of the paper. Separator fingers should rest on the corners of the lead edge of the paper pile.

3. Position the feed wheels between ¼ and ¾ inch from each edge of the paper. Set the feed pressure according to the weight of the paper used, light pressure for light paper.

4. Prepare the receiving tray by feeding one sheet through the press or by using the scale markings provided. Then set the side guides and paper stop.

5. Ink the duplicator by pouring or squeezing ink into the cylinder. Do not overfill.

6. Check the placement of the image on the paper by feeding a few sheets through the machine. Readjust the feed table side guides to obtain the desired side margins. If necessary, reset the receiving tray. Also adjust the vertical position of the image if required.

7. Set the counter to zero. Turn on the duplicator and engage the feed unit. After the desired number of copies have been printed, turn the machine off.
8. Remove the stencil. If it is to be used again, place it in an absorbent folder or between two absorbent pieces of paper.
9. Protect the ink pad by attaching a protective cover sheet as if it were a stencil. Cover the duplicator to keep it clean.

ELECTROSTATIC COPIERS
An electrostatic copier that produces duplicate color copies on plain paper by the transfer process is shown in Figure 31-3. A copier that makes black and white copies on specially treated paper is shown in Figure 31-4. It uses a direct electrostatic process. Both the transfer process and the direct process of electrostatic copying are described in more detail in Unit 7.

Figure 31-4. *This electrostatic copier produces black and white copies on a specially treated paper. (Apēco Corp.)*

Specially prepared plates, masters, and stencils are not required for electrostatic copying. Instead, duplicate copies are produced directly from just about any handwritten, typed, or printed original.

Figure 31-3. *A plain-paper, electrostatic color copier. (Xerox Corp.)*

OPERATING AN ELECTROSTATIC COPIER. Operating controls and procedures may differ slightly from one model copier to the next. For this reason it is best to consult the instruction manual for your machine. Only general operating procedures are included here.

1. Check that there is enough paper. Add paper when necessary.
2. Check the toner supply tank. Replenish when needed.
3. Turn on the power.
4. Set the counter for the desired number of copies.
5. Feed the original into the machine or place it on the glass plate. The image side of the original must face the lens.
6. After the desired number of copies are complete, turn off the power. Be sure to remove the original along with the copies.

TEST YOUR KNOWLEDGE

1. Prepare an outline of the procedures to follow when printing with a spirit duplicator.
2. List in proper sequence the basic steps involved in printing with a mimeograph duplicator.
3. List the general procedures for operating an electrostatic copier.

UNIT 32

COLOR PRINTING

Objectives

When you have completed this unit, you will be able to:

1. Describe the difference between flat-color and process-color printing.
2. Illustrate how red, blue, and green light can be used to produce magenta, cyan, yellow, and white light.
3. List the three additive and three subtractive primary colors.
4. Define *filter.*
5. Define *color separation, color correction,* and *color reproduction.*
6. Illustrate how additive primary colors are created by over-printing pairs of subtactive primary color inks.
7. Explain the reason for adding black ink during color reproduction.

Terms to Know

Here are some of the words you will need to understand before reading this unit. If the meaning of a word is not clear to you, look it up in the Glossary in the back of this book.

flat-color printing	subtractive primary colors	halftone screen
color separation	filter	color correction
additive primary colors		

PROCESS-COLOR PRINTING

Products may be printed in two or more colors by any of the processes described in Section 9. The simplest method of color reproduction, *flat-color printing,* is illustrated in Figure 32-1. A separate plate is prepared for each color desired. Plates are then printed in sequence on a single sheet of paper. Each plate is covered with the desired color ink and then printed in register with all of the other color images.

The *process-color printing* method is used to reproduce full-color pictures such as the continuous tone photograph shown in Figure 32-2. Process-color activities include: color separation, color correction, and color reproduction.

COLOR SEPARATION. A beam of white light passed through a glass prism results in a rainbow of color. This is because white light is really a mixture of all the colors of light. Each color refracts or bends differently as it enters and leaves the prism, Figure 32-3.

Three colors of light—red, blue, and green—can be used to reproduce white light, Figure 32-4. Where all three colors of light overlap, white is produced. Red, blue, and green are called *additive primary colors* because added together they form white light.

Figure 32-1. *Flat-color printing. A separate plate is needed to lay down each color of ink.*

Figure 32-2. *Color photographs such as this one are reproduced using process-color printing techniques.*

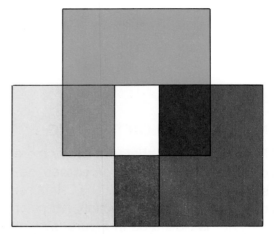

Figure 32-4. *Red, blue, and green light can be added together to produce white light. Red, blue, and green are called additive primary colors.*

Where any two additive primary colors of light overlap, a third color is formed. Red and blue combine to form *magenta*. Blue and green form *cyan*. Red and green combine to produce *yellow*. Magenta, cyan, and yellow are called *subtractive primary colors* because they

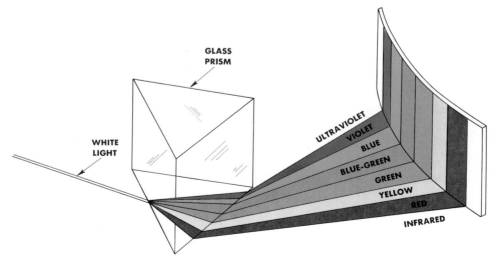

Figure 32-3. *White light is made up of many different colors of light.*

subtract colors from white light to form black. The subtractive process is shown in Figure 32-5.

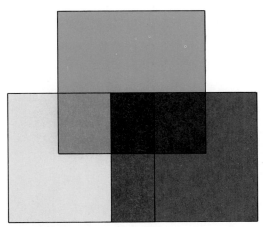

Figure 32-5. *Magenta, cyan, and yellow subtract colors from white light to produce black. Magenta, cyan, and yellow are called subtractive primary colors.*

Color separation is done by photographing the original color copy three times. The procedure for doing this is similar to producing a halftone negative. There are two important differences, however; the use of filters and the position of the halftone screen.

Filters. A *filter* is a piece of colored glass or gelatin material which allows only light of its own color to pass through. Other colors are absorbed by the filter. Filters are used to record, on three separate pieces of photographic film, the amounts of red, blue, and green contained in a color illustration.

Each of the three negatives is produced through a different color filter. Because

different amounts of light are absorbed by each filter, exposure times for each negative will be different.

Photographing through a red filter produces a negative recording of the red in the original. Red light passes through the filter and exposes the process film. Blues and greens (cyan light) cannot pass through the red filter. They are not recorded and are represented by clear areas in the negative. The resulting negative is known as a *red separation negative.*

Photographing through a blue filter produces a negative recording of the blue in the original. Blue light passes through the filter and exposes the process film. Reds and greens (yellow light) are not recorded and become clear areas in the negative. The negative that results is called a *blue separation negative.*

Photographing through a green filter produces a negative recording of the green in the original. Only green light passes through the green filter. Blues and reds (magenta light) are not recorded on the film. Blues and reds are represented by clear areas in this negative which is called a *green separation negative.*

Halftone Screen. Each separation negative is also a halftone negative. Each negative must be exposed through a halftone screen and will contain a halftone dot pattern. Dots must not interfere with each other when the job is printed. If they do interfere, an objectional pattern, called a *moiré* (pronounced mwä' ray), will result. A moiré pattern is shown in Figure 32-6.

Figure 32-6. *Moiré patterns are formed when halftone dots interfere with one another.*

Moiré patterns are avoided by changing the angle of the halftone screen for each separation negative. Revolve the screen 30° after each exposure to reduce the possibility of a moiré pattern developing.

Figure 32-7. *Color correction. (A) A print that has not been color corrected. (B) The same print after correcting for the deficiencies of process inks.*

COLOR CORRECTION. Color correction can compensate for color deficiencies of process inks. Manual etching, photographic masking, and electronic scanning are techniques that can be used. Color correction allows less ink of certain colors to be printed in selected areas of the reproduction. Uncorrected and corrected color prints may be compared in Figure 32-7.

COLOR REPRODUCTION. Subtractive primary color inks are transferred to the paper when the plates made from the separation negatives are printed. Magenta (blue + red) ink is printed by the plate made from the green separation negative. Cyan (blue + green) ink is printed by the plate made from the red separation negative. Yellow (red + green) ink is printed by a plate made from the blue separation negative.

Process-color prints are made by printing yellow, magenta, and cyan plates in perfect register on a single sheet of paper. Figure 32-8 shows how additive primary colors are created by overprinting pairs of subtractive primary color inks. By controlling the amounts of yellow, magenta, and cyan inks, you can

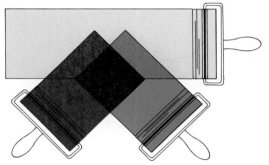

Figure 32-8. *Where two subtractive colors overlap, an additive-primary color is formed. Cyan and magenta form blue. Magenta and yellow form red. Cyan and yellow form green.*

produce all other colors of the visible spectrum.

In theory, only the three subtractive primary colors of ink are necessary to reproduce all colors of the spectrum. This is not true in actual practice, however. A fourth ink, black is needed to improve the grays and shadows in the print.

Prints made from yellow, magenta, cyan, and black printing plates are pictured in Figure 32-9. Progressive proofs are also shown. Note the difference between the yellow + magenta + cyan proof and the final proof which has the black ink added.

Figure 32-9. *Yellow, magenta, cyan, and black plates are used for process-color printing. Proofs of each of these plates are shown. Progressive proofs illustrating the steps in reproducing full color are also shown.*

TEST YOUR KNOWLEDGE

1. Explain the difference between flat-color printing and process-color printing.
2. Draw a simple diagram to illustrate how red, blue, and green light can be used to produce magenta, cyan, yellow, and white light. Label each of these colors in your diagram.
3. List the three additive and three subtractive primary colors of light.
4. Describe what is meant by the term *filter*.
5. Define the terms *color separation, color correction,* and *color reproduction*.
6. Prepare a simple diagram to illustrate how each of the additive primary colors are created by overprinting pairs of subtractive primary color inks. Label each color in your diagram.
7. Explain why black ink is added as a fourth color during process-color printing.

SECTION 10

PAPERS AND INKS

UNIT 33

PAPER AND PAPERMAKING

Objectives

When you have completed this unit, you will be able to:
1. Trace the development and spread of papermaking throughout the world.
2. List the steps in making paper by hand.
3. Illustrate the paper manufacturing process.
4. Define basic size and basis weight.
5. List the names of seven kinds of paper and uses for each.

Terms to Know

Here are some of the words you will need to understand before reading this unit. If the meaning of a word is not clear to you, look it up in the Glossary in the back of this book.

paper	mimeograph duplicating	basis weight
Fourdrinier	basic size	ream

PAPER

Many types of materials can be printed. Plastic, glass, and fabric are just some. However, by far the most important printed material is paper. Paper is needed for letterheads, envelopes, invoices, checks, travel brochures, calendars, advertising pieces and catalogs. And, of course, paper is an essential ingredient in newspapers, books, and magazines.

Ts'ai Lun, a Chinese court official, is credited with the invention of paper. He did this nearly 1900 years ago in the year 105 A.D.

Prior to the invention of paper, writing was done on a variety of materials. For example, animal skins called *parchment* and *vellum* were used by ancient Greeks. *Papyrus,* a writing surface made by pounding a woven mat of papyrus reed into a thin, hard sheet, was used by ancient Egyptians. In fact, the word *paper* is derived from the word *papyrus.*

Papermaking techniques were introduced to the Western world in the tenth century A.D. These techniques were brought to Spain by the conquering Moors of North Africa who discovered the art while trading with the East.

Basically paper was prepared by dipping a screen into a vat containing water and rag fibers. Openings in the screen were large enough to allow the water to drain but small enough to keep the fibers from passing through. The screen was withdrawn, and the matted fibers that remained dried and formed paper. Making paper by hand was a slow and tedious process.

With the invention of movable type in the fifteenth century the need for paper increased dramatically. However, the urgent demand for inexpensive paper could not be met until the middle of the nineteenth century, when papermaking machines were put into general use. Today, the average amount of paper used each year by every person in America is well over 400 pounds.

MAKING PAPER BY HAND. Making paper by hand is an excellent way to become familiar with the basic procedures of papermaking. Extensive equipment and materials are not required.

Equipment includes a tub or large pail, a mold, and a deckle. These three items

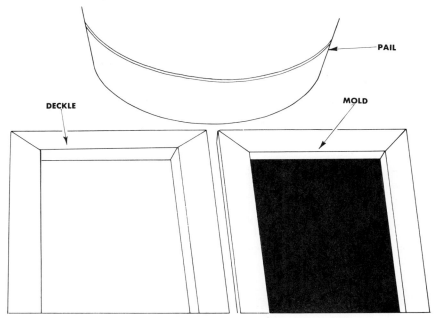

Figure 33-1. *A tub or large pail and a mold and deckle are needed when making paper by hand.*

are shown in Figure 33-1. The *mold* is a wooden frame covered with a metal screen. The *deckle* is another frame the same size as the mold. Other items needed are an egg beater, a rolling pin, an electric iron, blotting paper, instant laundry starch, and a box of soft facial tissues.

Papermaking is a rather simple process. Fill the tub with warm water. If wood pulp is available, it can be used. If not, shred about thirty tissues into the water. Do not use the "wet strength" kind. The tissues substitute for the wood pulp.

Now add one tablespoon of instant laundry starch to two cups of water. Pour this mixture into the tub. The starch serves to *size* or fill the pores of the paper that will be made.

Figure 33-2. *Beating the pulp mixture.*

Now beat the pulp mixture with an egg beater until it is free from lumps. See Figure 33-2.

You are now ready to form the sheet of paper. Place the deckle over the mold and slide both into the pulp mixture as shown in Figure 33-3. After leveling the deckle and mold assembly, lift it carefully from the mixture.

281

Figure 33-3. *Slide the deckle and mold, deckle side up, into the pulp mixture. Then level the deckle and mold and lift it from the mixture.*

Figure 33-4. *Transfer the newly made sheet of paper from the mold to a sheet of blotting paper.*

Remove the deckle from the mold and transfer the newly made sheet of paper to a piece of blotting paper, Figure 33-4. Now cover the newly made paper with a second blotter and press out the excess water with a rolling pin. Complete the drying process by pressing the paper with an electric iron. Do this while the sheet is still between the blotting papers. You have just made a sheet of paper by hand.

PAPER MANUFACTURING. Modern paper manufacturing techniques are similar to making paper by hand. The key steps in the processing of wood pulp and the making of paper are illustrated in Figure 33-5. Major differences lie in the preparation of the pulp, the mechanization of the papermaking process, and the tremendous quantities and types of papers that are produced. A typical papermaking plant is pictured in Figure 33-6.

Pulp Preparation. Figures 33-7 through 33-9 show how logs are converted into wooden chips that are fed into the digester. The logs are floated

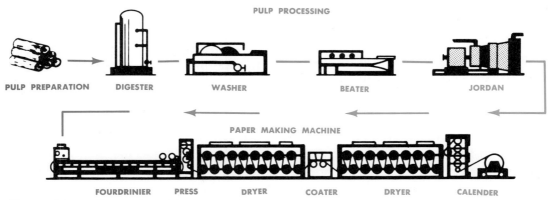

Figure 33-5. *Steps in making paper from wood pulp.*

Figure 33-6. *Hammermill Paper Company's main mill and general offices occupy a 225 acre tract of land. Approximately 2,000 persons are employed here. The mill produces over 280,000,000 pounds of paper each year. (Hammermill Paper Co.)*

Figure 33-7. *This 450-foot long flume is used to float the logs to the barking machine. (Hammermill Paper Co.)*

Figure 33-8. *Giant barking machines are used to strip the bark from the logs. (Hammermill Paper Co.)*

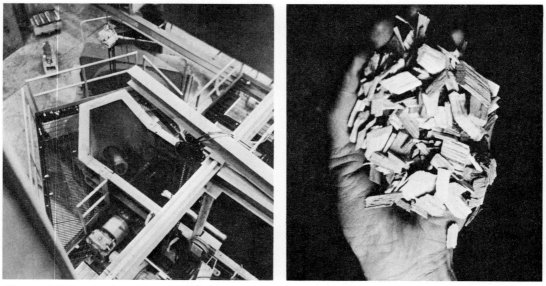

Figure 33-9. *In the chipper, rotating steel blades chew each log into wood chips. (Hammermill Paper Co.)*

along a flume to giant *barking machines,* Figure 33-7, which strip the bark from the logs, Figure 33-8. All bark must be removed from the logs before chipping. Figure 33-9 shows the *chipper* used to chew each log into chips to be fed into the digester.

Processing. A chemical *digester* is pictured in Figure 33-10. Wood chips are placed into this digester along with an acid solution. Here the chips are cooked under pressure and reduced to fiber form.

The fibrous pulp is then washed and bleached. A *washer,* Figure 33-11,

Figure 33-10. *Wood chips are fed into this 23-story high digester. Here the chips are cooked under pressure and reduced to fiber form. (Hammermill Paper Co.)*

Figure 33-11. *The pulp is washed and bleached in this machine called a washer. (Hammermill Paper Co.)*

sprays the pulp with water as it revolves on large drums. From the washer, the pulp is transferred to a *beater.* Here other papermaking materials such as dyes, sizing, and fillers are blended in with the pulp, Figure 33-12.

where the wood fibers are cut to a uniform size. The fibers are also treated to improve their adhesive qualities.

Figure 33-13. *Final processing of the wood pulp is done in a jordan. (Hammermill Paper Co.)*

Figure 33-12. *Dyestuffs, sizing, and fillers are added to the beater and blended in with the pulp. (Hammermill Paper Co.)*

The pulp is then piped to a refining machine called a *jordan,* Figure 33-13,

Papermaking Machine. A huge *papermaking machine* is shown in Figure 33-14. The pulp mixture containing more than 99 percent water is poured onto a wire screen called a *Fourdrinier.* As the

Figure 33-14. *Papermaking machine. Note the direction of the Fourdrinier wire screen. (Hammermill Paper Co.)*

Figure 33-15. *Calender rollers are used to place a smooth finish on the paper. (Hammermill Paper Co.)*

Fourdrinier screen moves forward, it also shakes sideways to weave and mat the fibers together as the water drains off.

A continuous sheet of paper is then pressed between rollers and passed through a dryer before coating or sizing. *Sizing* is done to seal the surface of the paper.

After further drying, the web of paper is given a smooth finish as it passes between heavy, polished rollers called *calendars*. Calendar rollers are shown in Figure 33-15.

The finished paper is then wound onto huge reels. These reels of paper are slit into narrow rolls and sometimes cut into sheets before being shipped to customers throughout the world.

KINDS, SIZES, AND WEIGHTS OF PAPER. Some of the most common printing papers are bond, book, cover, bristol, newsprint, duplicator, and mimeograph. Uses for each of these kinds of paper and information about their basic sizes and basis weight is included in Figure 33-16.

Basic size is the standard sheet size in inches. This size is used by the paper mill to compute the weight of each kind of paper. Note that the basic size is not the same for all kinds of paper. Also,

COMMON KINDS OF PAPER			
KIND OF PAPER	SOME GENERAL USES	BASIC SIZE (INCHES)	BASIS WEIGHTS (POUNDS)
BOND	STATIONARY, BUSINESS FORMS, DIRECT-MAIL ADVERTISING	17 x 22	9, 13, 16, 20, 24
BOOK	BOOKS, PAMPHLETS, BROCHURES, DIRECT-MAIL ADVERTISING	25 x 38	50, 60, 70, 80, 90, 100
COVER	COVERS FOR BOOKLETS, BINDERS, ANNOUNCEMENTS	20 x 26	50, 60, 65, 80, 90, 100
BRISTOL	INDEX CARDS, POSTCARDS, TICKETS, BOOKLET COVERS	25 1/2 x 30 1/2	90, 110, 140, 170
NEWSPRINT	NEWSPAPERS, DIRECT-MAIL ADVERTISING	24 x 36	32, 34
DUPLICATOR	SPIRIT-DUPLICATED MATERIALS	17 x 22	16, 20, 24
MIMEOGRAPH	MIMEOGRAPHED MATERIALS	17 x 22	16, 20, 24

Figure 33-16. *Common kinds of paper.*

paper in sizes other than the basic size given is usually available from the mill.

Basis weight is the weight in pounds of a *ream* (500 sheets) of paper cut into its basic size. Paper is often referred to in terms of its basis or ream weight: 20-pound bond, 50-pound book, etc. Each kind of paper will usually be available in several different basis weights.

TEST YOUR KNOWLEDGE

1. Prepare a chart which highlights the development and spread of papermaking throughout the world.
2. List in proper sequence the basic steps for making paper by hand.
3. Use simple diagrams to illustrate the key steps in paper manufacturing.
4. Describe what is meant by the terms *basic size* and *basis weight*.
5. List the names of several kinds of paper and some general uses for each.

UNIT 34

INK AND INK MANUFACTURING

Objectives

When you have completed this unit, you will be able to:

1. Define *pigment* and list five sources from which pigments are obtained.
2. Define *vehicle* and list four types of vehicles.
3. Illustrate the ink manufacturing process.
4. Describe the difference among letterpress, gravure, lithographic, and screen-process inks.
5. Explain why it is important to consider the eventual use of a printed item when selecting the ink to be used in printing the item.

Terms to Know

Here are some of the words you will need to understand before reading this unit. If the meaning of a word is not clear to you, look it up in the Glossary in the back of this book.

pigment   modifier

PRINTING INKS

Ink is transferred from a plate or stencil to paper or some other material during the printing process. The ink forms the image on the printed product. Over two thousand years ago, the Chinese made and used inks to print from wood blocks.

Most printing inks consist of pigments, vehicles, and modifiers. *Pigment* is the ingredient that provides the color of the ink. Many pigment colors are produced from rocks and clays. Others can be traced to plants, sea life, or even insects. Several pigments may be blended together to obtain a desired color ink.

The *vehicle* is the fluid that carries the pigment. Oil, lacquer, alcohol, and water are all used as ink vehicles.

Modifiers may be added to ink for certain desired characteristics. For example, *driers* are added to speed up the drying process. *Waxes* are used to minimize setoff. Setoff refers to the transfer of ink from a freshly printed sheet to the back of the sheet above.

INK MANUFACTURING. Figure 34-1 shows the key steps in the manufacture of printing inks. Ingredient preparation includes selecting and processing the required pigments, modifiers, and vehicle prior to mixing.

Ink is usually mixed in batches. The required quantities of all ingredients are blended in an *ink mixer,* Figure 34-2.

The blended ink mixture is then transferred to a *mill* or grinder, Figure 34-3. Here the size of the solid particles in the

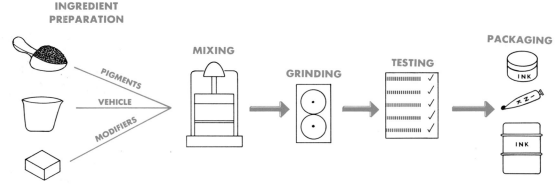

Figure 34-1. *Steps in manufacturing printing inks.*

Figure 34-2. An ink mixer is used to blend the pigments, modifiers, and vehicle together. (National Association of Printing Ink Manufacturers, Inc.)

Figure 34-3. A mill is used to grind the solid particles in the ink mixture and distribute them throughout the vehicle. (National Association of Printing Ink Manufacturers, Inc.)

mixture is reduced for better distribution throughout the vehicle.

Testing follows grinding. The ink is tested to insure that the batch of ink will behave as it is supposed to under actual printing conditions. One laboratory test is pictured in Figure 34-4.

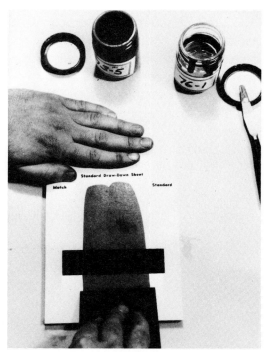

Figure 34-4. Testing an ink batch. (National Association of Printing Ink Manufacturers, Inc.)

Packing is the final step in the manufacture of printing inks. Inks may be packaged in tubes, cans, or drums. Where a large quantity of ink is required, such as in newspaper production, tank trucks may be used to deliver the ink to the customer.

MIXING INKS IN THE SHOP. Two or more inks can be mixed together to obtain a desired shade or color of printing ink. Mixing is generally done on a slab of glass with an ink knife or spatula.

Several manufacturers now offer a kit containing six to eight different colors of ink, a color chart, and instructions. With such a kit it is possible to mix more than 400 different colors of printing ink.

SELECTING THE RIGHT INK FOR THE JOB. Each printing process requires the use of an ink developed specifically for that process. Letterpress, gravure, lithographic, and screen-process inks are specially formulated to match the requirements of the printing process. For example, letterpress inks are designed to distribute evenly over and adhere well to raised plate surfaces. Gravure inks are quite fluid and dry rapidly. Lithographic inks are formulated so as not to absorb or combine with the fountain solution in the press. And inks used for screen-process printing will have the consistency of thick paint, which is usually required in this process.

Another consideration when selecting an ink is the eventual use of the printed item. For example, ink on items used outdoors must be able to withstand the weather. Ink printed on fabrics should hold up under repeated washings. Food packages should be printed with an odorless ink. And products that will be handled by young children must be printed with non-toxic inks.

TEST YOUR KNOWLEDGE

1. Define the term *pigment* and list five sources from which pigments are obtained.
2. Describe what is meant by the term *vehicle* and list four types of vehicles.
3. Use simple diagrams to illustrate the key steps in the manufacture of printing inks.
4. Prepare a description of the ink used in each of the four major printing processes.
5. Explain why you should consider the eventual use of a printed item before selecting the ink to be used in printing that item.

SECTION 11

BINDING AND FINISHING

UNIT 35

WAYS OF FINISHING AND BINDING PRINTED MATERIALS

Objectives

When you have completed this unit, you will be able to:
1. Define *finishing* and list eight finishing operations.
2. Outline the procedures for cutting paper with a guillotine paper cutter.
3. Describe the differences among scoring, perforating, embossing, and die cutting with a platen press.
4. Define *binding*.
5. Illustrate and describe seven methods of binding.

Terms to Know

Here are some of the words you will need to understand before reading this unit. If the meaning of a word is not clear to you, look it up in the Glossary in the back of this book.

finishing	perforating	saddle-wire binding
signature	drilling	side-wire binding
gathering	embossing	perfect binding
collator	die cutting	mechanical binding
scoring	bind	loose-leaf binding

FINISHING PRINTED MATERIALS

Finishing refers to any of several operations that may be performed on printed material after it has left the press. The most common finishing operations are cutting, folding, and gathering. Other finishing techniques include scoring, perforating, drilling, embossing, and die cutting.

CUTTING. A hand-lever "guillotine" paper cutter is shown in Figure 35-1. The paper to be cut is held in position on the bed of the machine by the paper clamp. Depth of cut is controlled by adjusting the distance between the back fence and the blade. As the operator pulls down on the hand lever, the paper is cut.

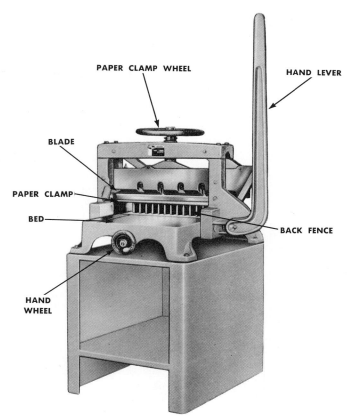

PAPER CLAMP WHEEL

HAND LEVER

BLADE

PAPER CLAMP

BED

BACK FENCE

HAND WHEEL

Figure 35-1. *Hand-lever "guillotine" paper cutter with major parts labeled. (The Challenge Machinery Co.)*

Another type of guillotine cutter is shown in Figure 35-2. It is a large hydraulic, power-driven model. The size of a paper cutter is the maximum width of the paper it can cut.

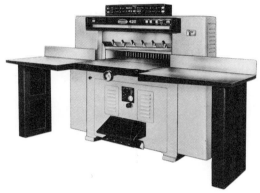

Figure 35-2. *Hydraulic power-driven paper cutter. (The Challenge Machinery Co.)*

Operating a Paper Cutter. The operation of hand-operated and power-operated cutters is essentially the same.

Safety Notes. Secure permission before using the paper cutter. Only one person should operate this machine at a time. Keep both hands away from the blade and out of the blade path.

Begin by moving the back fence to obtain the desired depth of cut. The front handwheel is used to move the back fence. The distance between the blade and fence on most cutters is shown on a measuring tape or a scale built into the bed of the machine.

Jog (straighten) the paper and place it on the bed of the cutter. Set the paper pile against the back fence and along the left side of the paper cutter.

Now place a strip of chipboard under the paper pile in the area directly below the blade. The chipboard extends the life of the wooden or plastic cutting stick which it covers. Place another strip of chipboard on top of the paper, directly below the paper clamp. This strip will protect the top sheets of paper from being damaged by the clamp.

Lower the paper clamp by turning the paper clamp wheel to the right. The clamp should press the paper tightly against the bed of the cutter.

Modern machines require an operator to use both hands to activate the cutter blade. Some hand-lever cutters contain a safety pin which must be held with the left hand while the right hand pulls on the lever. Others require the operator to grasp the lever with two hands in order to activate the blade. Power cutters are usually equipped with dual controls that must be operated with both hands.

When the cut is complete, raise the blade. Check to be sure the blade is locked in its uppermost position. Then raise the paper clamp and remove the pile of paper. If the other dimension needs to be trimmed, turn the paper and repeat the above process.

Safety Note. Always adjust the paper clamp to its lowest position before you leave the cutter area. Be sure to turn off the power on hydraulic machines.

FOLDING. A small folding machine, Figure 35-3, can fold a small sheet of

Figure 35-5. *This folder is capable of producing book and magazine signatures. (Heidelberg Eastern, Inc.)*

Figure 35-3. *A table-top folder is used to fold small sheets of paper. (MBM Corp.)*

paper such as a letter or brochure. Common paper folds are shown in Figure 35-4. A large, heavy-duty folder capable of folding book and magazine signatures is shown in Figure 35-5. A *signature* is a sheet of paper that has been folded a number of times, then trimmed with a paper cutter to form pages.

GATHERING. Assembling single sheets of paper or signatures in sequence before binding is called *gathering.* Gathering may be done by hand or by machine. Machines used for gathering are called *collators.* A small desktop collator is shown in Figure 35-6.

Figure 35-6. *A collator is used to assemble single sheets of paper or signatures in their proper sequence for binding. (The Challenge Machinery Co.)*

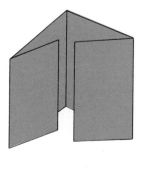

SINGLE FOLD   **SINGLE GATEFOLD**   **DOUBLE GATEFOLD**   **ACCORDION FOLD**

Figure 35-4. *Several of the common paper folds.*

SCORING. The scoring operation is used to crease heavy paper or cardboard so that it can be easily and smoothly folded. A platen press can be used for this purpose. Lock a piece of steel scoring rule in the chase. Scoring rule has a rounded face and is type high. Place the chase in the press and remove the ink rollers. Pack the platen and position the gage pins. Then feed the paper into the press as if it were being printed. Each sheet will be creased when the scoring rule strikes it.

Scoring can also be done by attaching scoring rollers to the delivery side of an offset duplicator, Figure 35-7. The rollers crease each sheet of paper as it is transferred from the printing unit to the delivery table.

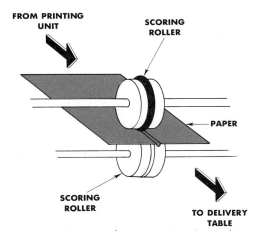

Figure 35-7. *Scoring paper on an offset duplicator.*

PERFORATING. Perforating is similar to scoring. The difference is that in perforating, a series of slits or holes are punched into the paper or cardstock to facilitate tearing. An offset duplicator can be used to perforate the sheet by a perforating wheel attached to the delivery end of the machine.

To perforate on a platen press, lock up a steel perforating rule in the chase. Remove the rollers to prevent the rule from cutting into them. Also protect the platen by covering it with a metal plate. Place a piece of tympan paper over this metal plate, and position the gage pins as required. Then feed the paper into the press as if it were being printed. Each sheet will be perforated when the rule strikes it.

DRILLING. A drill, Figure 35-8, is used for drilling round holes through paper. Several hundred sheets can be drilled at one time.

Paper drill bits come in various sizes and are hollow. As the bit cuts into the paper, round chips are fed up through the drill bit and into a waste compartment at the back of the machine. Loose-leaf pages are prepared in this way.

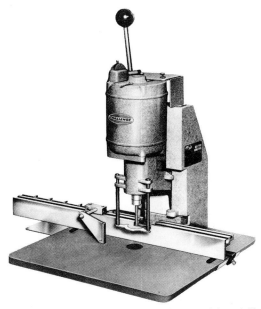

Figure 35-8. *A paper drill is used for drilling holes through paper. (The Challenge Machinery Co.)*

EMBOSSING. Embossing is generally done on a platen press. An embossing die is locked up in the bed of the press and a counter die of the embossed image is attached to the platen. When the paper is pressed between the embossing and counter dies, Figure 35-9, a raised or embossed image results on the paper.

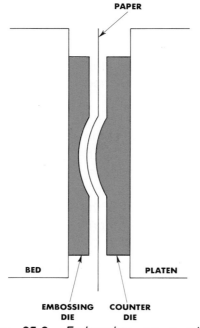

Figure 35-9. *Embossing on a platen press.*

The embossing die is usually made of brass. Its intaglio image is etched or engraved. The counter die for the platen is made by impressing the embossing die into soft paper maché forming a relief image. When dry, the paper maché die is glued to the platen where the embossing die will strike.

DIE CUTTING. Die cutting is cutting out various shapes in paper or cardboard. It includes punching regular and irregular shaped holes. Die cutting is usually done on a platen press.

A die consists of one or more pieces of steel cutting rule bent to form the desired shape. The die is set into a plywood saw kerf (cut) in the same shape. A band or jig saw can be used to make the cut. Several small pieces of sponge rubber or cork are then glued to the plywood base. These force the paper out of the die after it is cut. A die used to cut a small box blank is shown in Figure 35-10.

Die cutting on the platen press is done by locking up the die in the chase. Remove the rollers to prevent the die from cutting into them. Also protect the platen by covering it with a metal plate. Place a piece of tympan paper over this metal plate and position gage pins as required. Then feed the paper into the press as if it were being printed. Each sheet will be cut when the die strikes.

BINDING PRINTED MATERIALS
Sheets of paper may be bound together in several different ways. The most common methods include: saddle-wire, side-wire, sewn soft-cover, sewn case-bound, adhesive, mechanical, and loose-leaf binding.

SADDLE-WIRE BINDING. The saddle-wire method of binding, Figure 35-11, uses wire staples as the fastening device. These staples pass through the back of several pages that have been assembled and folded. A cover may or may not be included. Thin booklets and magazines are often bound by the saddle-wire method. Materials bound in this manner will lie flat when open.

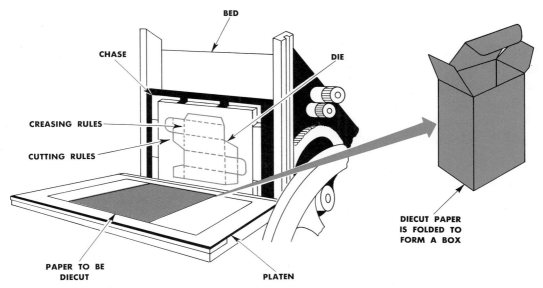

Figure 35-10. *This die is used to cut heavy paper, which is then folded to form a box.*

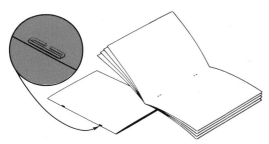

Figure 35-11. *Saddle-wire binding. Materials bound in this manner lie flat when open.*

SIDE-WIRE BINDING. The side-wire method of binding, Figure 35-12, can be used to bind thicker booklets and magazines. Wire staples are the fastening device. This time, however, the staples pass through one edge of the assembled pile of pages. Materials bound in this manner will not lie flat and will have to be held open.

SEWN SOFT-COVER BINDING. The sewn soft-cover binding method is illustrated in Figure 35-13. Binding thread is the fastening device. The thread is sewn through holes punched in the center fold of a signature or through one edge of an assembled pile of pages. Several signatures may be sewn together using this binding technique.

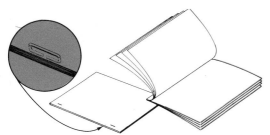

Figure 35-12. *Side-wire binding. Materials bound in this manner do not lie flat and have to be held open.*

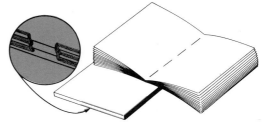

Figure 35-13. *Sewn soft-cover binding. Binding thread is used to hold the pages or signatures together.*

SEWN CASE-BOUND BOOKS. Sewn case-bound books will stand up under hard use. This method of binding is illustrated in Figure 35-14. Individual signatures are first sewn together with binding thread then encased between hard covers made from binder's board and cloth or other durable material.

Figure 35-14. Case binding. Books bound in this manner will stand up under hard use.

ADHESIVE BINDING. Adhesive binding is also referred to as *perfect binding,* Figure 35-15. An adhesive or padding compound is used to hold the assembled sheets of paper together. Notepads, telephone books, and pocketbooks are some products bound with adhesive.

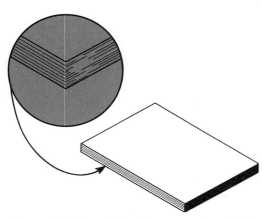

Figure 35-15. Adhesive or perfect binding. Sheets of paper are held together by a flexible adhesive.

MECHANICAL (SPIRAL) BINDING. Plastic combs and wire can also be used to fasten individual sheets together. The plastic comb or wire is inserted through holes that have been punched along one edge of the assembled pile of paper, Figure 35-16. A machine used for punching paper and inserting plastic combs is shown in Figure 35-17.

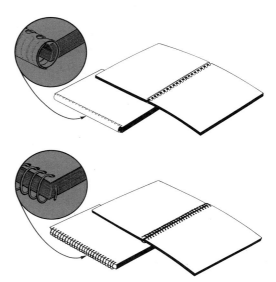

Figure 35-16. Mechanical binding is accomplished with plastic combs and with wire.

Figure 35-17. A mechanical binding machine is used to punch the paper and insert the plastic combs. (General Binding Corp.)

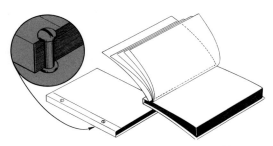

LOOSE-LEAF BINDING. Loose-leaf binding methods allow for the addition or removal of pages from the bound material. Post binders, Figure 35-18, and ring binders, Figure 35-19, are generally used for this purpose.

Figure 35-18. *Binding post type of loose-leaf binding.*

Figure 35-19. *A ring binder is also used for loose sheet binding.*

TEST YOUR KNOWLEDGE

1. Define the term *finishing* and list the names of eight finishing operations.
2. List the procedures to follow when cutting paper with a guillotine paper cutter.
3. Describe the differences among scoring, perforating, embossing, and die cutting with a platen press.
4. Explain what is meant by the term *binding* and list seven methods used to bind paper together.
5. Prepare a chart which illustrates and describes the seven binding methods discussed in this unit. Include simple diagrams to illustrate these methods and a brief description of the characteristics possessed by each.

UNIT 36

HAND AND MACHINE BOOKBINDING

Objectives

When you have completed this unit, you will be able to:
1. Outline the basic procedures for center sewing signatures together.
2. Describe how to side-sew loose sheets of paper together.
3. Define *forwarding* and list the names of the operations that comprise it.
4. Describe how to determine the size of the heavy paper, binder's board, and binding cloth used in casemaking.
5. List the steps in casemaking.
6. Outline the procedures for hanging a book in its case.

Terms to Know

Here are some of the words you will need to understand before reading this unit. If the meaning of a word is not clear to you, look it up in the Glossary in the back of this book.

casebound	endsheets	casing in
signatures	bone folder	

PRODUCING CASEBOUND BOOKS

The sequence of steps in binding hardcover books is shown in Figure 36-1.

These steps remain the same whether books are bound by hand or by machine.

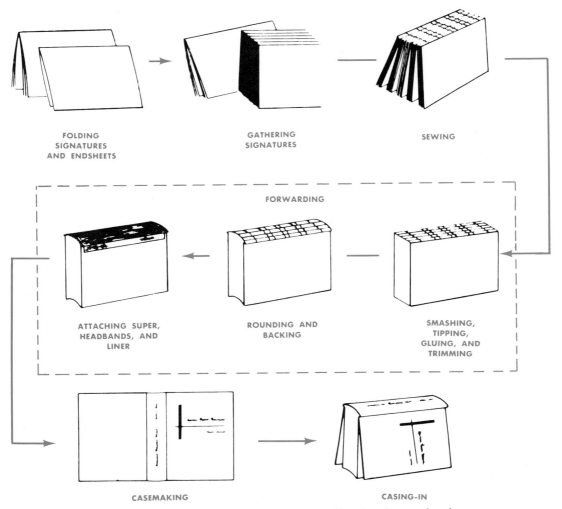

FOLDING
SIGNATURES
AND ENDSHEETS

GATHERING
SIGNATURES

SEWING

FORWARDING

ATTACHING SUPER,
HEADBANDS, AND
LINER

ROUNDING AND
BACKING

SMASHING,
TIPPING,
GLUING, AND
TRIMMING

CASEMAKING

CASING-IN

Figure 36-1. *The sequence of steps followed in binding hardcover books.*

FOLDING SIGNATURES AND END-SHEETS.

Large printed sheets are first folded to form signatures. A *signature* is a single sheet of paper folded to a certain number of pages. For example, one signature may yield 8, 16, or 32 individual pages when it is trimmed on three sides later in the binding process. Folding signatures by hand is shown in Figure 36-2. A folding machine set up to produce 16-page signatures is pictured in Figure 36-3.

Figure 36-2. *A bone folder should be used to fold signatures by hand.*

Two endsheets must also be folded for each book. An *endsheet* is a strong piece of paper that has been folded in half to make four pages. The size of each folded endsheet is the same as the book's signatures.

Endsheets are glued to the front of the first signature and to the back of the last signature. This process is called *tipping* and should be done after the signatures have been gathered and sewn.

GATHERING SIGNATURES.

Assembling signatures in proper sequence for binding is called *gathering*. Gathering signatures can be done by hand or with a gathering machine. A swing arm gathering machine is shown in Figure 36-4. The basic operation of this machine is illustrated in Figure 36-5.

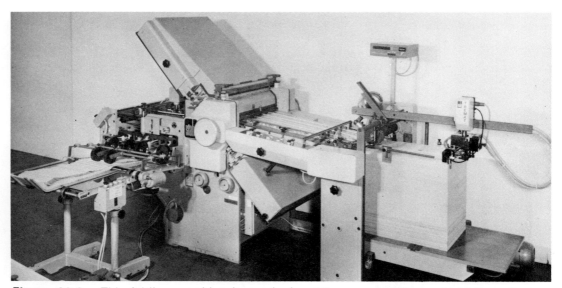

Figure 36-3. *This folding machine is producing 16-page signatures. (Heidelberg Eastern, Inc.)*

Figure 36-4. *Swing arm gathering machine. (Rand McNally & Co.)*

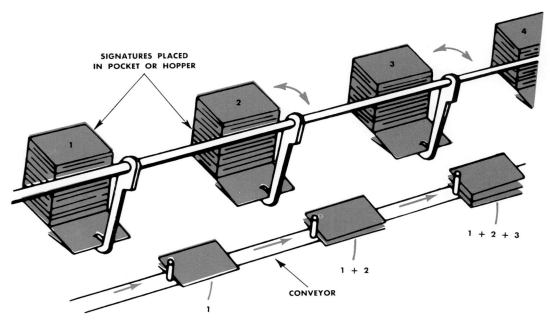

SIGNATURES PLACED
IN POCKET OR HOPPER

1 + 2 + 3

1 + 2

CONVEYOR

Figure 36-5. *The basic operation of a swing arm gathering machine.*

SEWING. Fastening the assembled signatures together with thread is the next step in binding. Two basic sewing techniques are center (Smythe) sewing and side-sewing. The center-sewing technique is used to saddle sew individual signatures and fasten these signatures together. Loose sheets of paper are generally bound together by side-sewing.

Center Sewing. Signatures can be center-sewn by hand or by machine. An automatic center-sewing machine is shown in Figure 36-6. To center-sew by hand place a piece of plywood on each side of the gathered signatures. Jog the assembly so that the center folds of all signatures are at the same level and flush with the top edges of the plywood sheets. Insert the assembly into a vise.

Figure 36-6. *Automatically fed center-sewing machine. (Kingsport Press)*

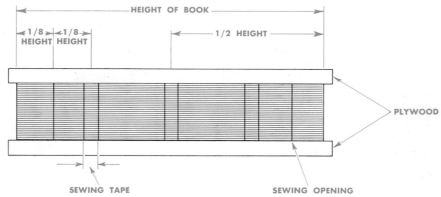

Figure 36-7. *A square is used to mark the back of the signatures. Sewing thread will later pass through holes cut along each of these lines.*

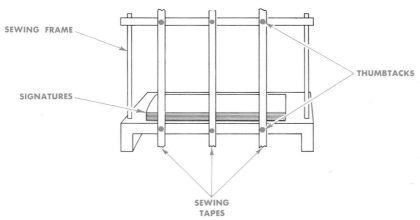

Figure 36-8. *Signatures are sewn in a sewing frame. Thumbtacks are used to hold the sewing tapes in position.*

The center folds should protrude about one-half inch above the jaws of the vise.

Measure and mark lines for positioning three sewing tapes on the back of the signatures, Figure 36-7. Make each pair of lines the same width as the sewing tape to be used.

With a backsaw or a dovetail saw, cut into the back of the book. Carefully follow along the marked lines until the saw just begins to enter the inner part of each signature. Do not cut too deeply.

Remove the signatures from the vise and position them on a sewing frame. Then fasten three pieces of sewing tape to the frame with thumbtacks as shown in Figure 36-8.

Now remove all but the last signature from the frame and begin sewing the last signature. The movement of the needle in and out of the signature is shown in Figure 36-9. Pass the needle through the back of the signature and into the center fold at hole 1. Exit at hole 2 and enter again at hole 3. Exit at hole 4 and enter at hole 5. Repeat this again at holes 6 and 7. The needle and thread finally exit the signature at hole 8.

Place the next-to-last signature on top of the signature already on the frame. Reverse the sewing procedure to pass the needle and thread back to the right side of the frame. This time, however, when the needle exits alongside a tape, loop the thread around the thread of the previous signature before re-entering the signature being sewn. *Looping* fas-

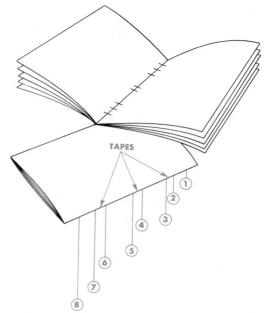

Figure 36-9. *The sewing needle enters the signature at hole 1 and exits at hole 8 after passing over the tapes that are positioned between holes 2 and 3, 4 and 5, and 6 and 7.*

tens each signature to the previous one, Figure 36-10. Tie the two signatures together at the right end.

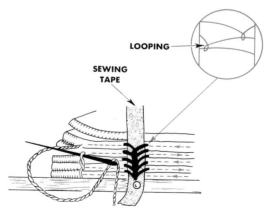

Figure 36-10. *Loop the thread around the thread of the previous signature each time the needle passes over a tape. This is done to fasten all of the signatures together.*

Repeat the procedure until all signatures are fastened together. Additional thread may be tied to the original length of thread if required. Each time your thread exits at the right, be sure to tie the end of the thread securely to the previous signature.

Finally, remove the sewn signatures from the sewing frame. Cut both ends of each tape so that they extend approximately one inch on each side of the bound signatures.

Side-Sewing. Loose sheets of paper may be bound together by side sewing. Again, either hand or machine methods can be used.

For hand side-sewing, drill holes through the side of the assembled and jogged pages as shown in Figure 36-11. Use a 1/16″ drill. Drill the holes as close to the back edge of the paper as possible and at least 1/2″ from the top and bottom edge of the paper pile.

Once drilled, the paper pile can be sewn. Starting at one edge, pass the needle in and out through the drilled holes. Sew from one edge of the book to the other. Then return the needle and thread back through the holes to the starting point. Complete the process by tying the two ends of the thread together.

FORWARDING. The term *forwarding* describes a number of things to be done to a book before it can be enclosed in its cover. These operations include smashing, tipping, gluing, trimming, rounding and backing, and attaching super, headbands, and liner.

Smashing. Compressing the back edge of the book is called *smashing*. Smashing is done with a book press or vise.

Tipping. Endsheets are attached to the front of the first signature and to the back of the last signature by *tipping*, Figure 36-12. A narrow band of glue is applied along the folded edge of each endsheet. The endsheets are then adhered to the first and last signatures. Tight contact is required.

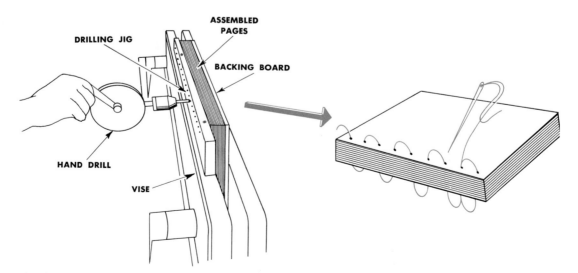

Figure 36-11. Holes are drilled along one edge of the assembled and jogged pages prior to side sewing.

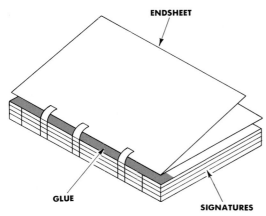

Figure 36-12. *Endsheets are glued to the first and last signatures of the book by tipping.*

Gluing. Apply glue to the back of the book to help keep the individual signatures from shifting. Keep the signatures under pressure until the glue is completely dry.

Trimming. Use a paper cutter to trim a book to size. Trim the front edge of the book first. Then trim the top and bottom edges. *Do not trim the back of the book.*

Rounding and Backing. Rounding is done to give the back of the book a slightly convex shape, Figure 36-13.

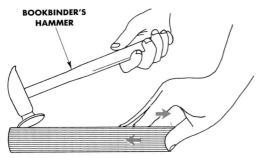

Figure 36-13. *The back of the book should be rounded slightly with a bookbinder's hammer.*

Place the book on a workbench and hold it as shown. Push on the front edge

of the book with your thumb while pulling the outside pages in the opposite direction with your other four fingers. Gently tap the back edge into shape with a bookbinder's hammer. Turn the book over and repeat this process. Be sure to round the back of the book evenly. Only a slight curve is needed.

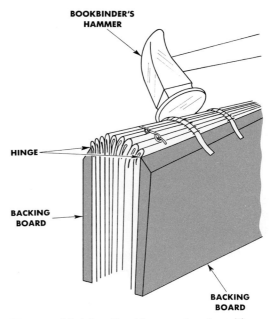

Figure 36-14. *Backing a book with a bookbinder's hammer.*

Backing forms a hinge along the front and back sides of the book about 1/8 inch to 1/4 inch in from the bound edge, Figure 36-14. Place the book between backing boards, the rounded edge of the book extending above the top edge of the boards. The actual distance will depend upon the size of the book and on the thickness of its cover. Gently tap the back edge of the book with a bookbinder's hammer. Form the two hinges gradually by striking from the center of the back toward the outer edges of the book.

Attaching Super, Headbands, and Liner. A bound book with super, headbands, and liner attached is shown in Figure 36-15. *Super* is a gauze-like material glued to the back of the book. It provides added strength to the finished

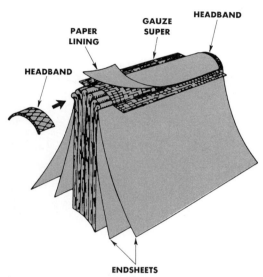

Figure 36-15. *The parts of a book minus its cover.*

book. The super should be cut approximately ½ inch shorter than the book and about 3 inches wider than its back.

Headbands may also be glued to the back of the book. They are used to decorate rather than add strength to the bound material. Each piece of headband should equal the thickness of the back. Position the headbands so that the decorative portion faces the front edge of the book.

Kraft paper is glued over the super and headbands to finish off the back of the book. This piece of paper is called a *liner.*

CASEMAKING. The case is the cover of a hardbound book. It consists of two pieces of binder's board and strip of heavy paper that have been glued to a piece of binding cloth.

Casemaking, making the case, can be done by machine or by hand. Casemaking by hand involves cutting the materials to size, gluing the binder's board and paper to the binding cloth, and folding the cloth to cover the edges of the binder's board.

Cutting Materials to Size. Two pieces of binder's board are required. The length of each should equal the height of the book plus the desired cover overhang. Generally, the cover will overhang each edge of the book by ⅛ inch.

The width of the binder's board is measured from the hinge that was formed along the back edge of the book, by backing, to its front edge. Be sure to add ⅛ inch to this measurement to provide the needed overhang.

The size of the heavy paper used to line the back of the case is equal to the measurements across the back of the book.

Book cloth dimensions are determined by measuring. The height of the cloth should equal the height of the binder's board plus two inches. The width of the cloth is equal to the combined widths of the two pieces of binder's board, plus two inches, plus the width around the back of the book from hinge to hinge.

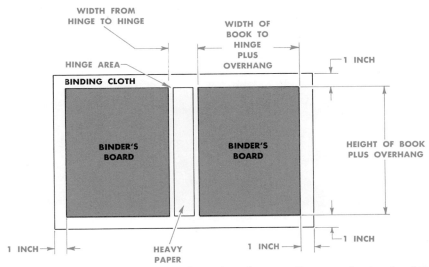

Figure 36-16. Positioning the binder's board and paper liner on the back of the binding cloth.

Gluing Materials in Position. Place the binder's boards and paper liner on the back of the binding cloth as shown in Figure 36-16. Outline the binder's boards and paper liner with a pencil to mark their exact locations. Then remove the binder's boards and paper liner from the book cloth.

With a brush and bookbinding paste, coat the back of the book cloth. Cover the entire surface evenly. Do not leave any lumps of paste. Now carefully position the boards and paper liner on the book cloth. Then turn the book cloth over and squeeze out any excess paste from between the cloth and binder's boards. With a bone folder, press from the center to the outer edges of the boards.

Folding the Book Cloth. Fold the binding cloth up over the edges of the binder's board to complete the case. First fold a corner of the book cloth up over one corner of the binder's board. Then fold the two adjacent sides of the

cloth over the board. Use a bone folder to stretch the cloth tightly over the edge of the binder's board. Repeat this procedure at each of the other corners to complete the case.

The corners you have just made are called *library corners.* Although capable of withstanding considerable abuse, library corners are bulky. *Nicked corners* are less bulky than library corners. They are formed by cutting away the corners of the book cloth before folding, Figure 36-17. Leave approximately 3/8" of cloth

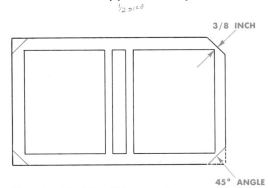

Figure 36-17. Trim each corner of the binding cloth at a 45-degree angle when making a nicked corner.

Figure 36-18. *A casing-in machine used to automatically hang books in their cases.* (Kingsport Press)

opposite each corner of the binder's board. Continue folding as for library corners.

CASING-IN. Hanging the book in the case is called casing-in. Casing-in can be done by hand or by machine. A casing-in machine is shown in Figure 36-18.

To hang a book by hand, insert a piece of waxed paper between each of the endsheets. The waxed paper should extend beyond the edges of the book. Waxed paper prevents the endsheets from sticking together when the book is pasted into its case.

Apply paste to the super, tapes, and endsheet located at the front of the book. Position the book within the case, pasted side up, and close the front cover. Then turn the book over, open the back cover and apply paste to the super, tapes, and back endsheet. Now close the back cover. Be sure the book is pressed up against the back of the case and in its proper position. Readjust the position of the book if necessary.

After hanging the book, place it between two pressing boards. The metal strip on each board should be fitted into the book's hinge.

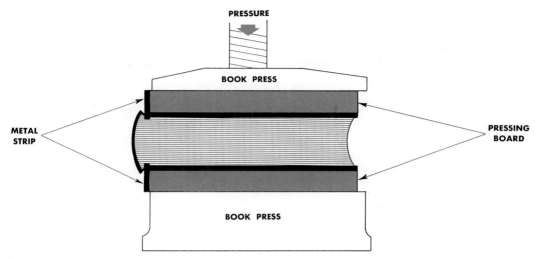

Figure 36-19. *Pressing a book between pressing boards in a book press.*

Place the pressing boards and book assembly into a book press until the paste is completely dry. The pressing operation is shown in Figure 36-19.

When dry, the book can be removed from between the pressing boards. Clean off the excess glue as required. The book is now complete.

TEST YOUR KNOWLEDGE

1. Briefly outline the procedures to be followed when center-sewing signatures together.
2. Describe how to side-sew loose sheets of paper together.
3. Define the term *forwarding* and list the names of each of the operations involved in forwarding.
4. Explain how to determine the dimensions of the heavy paper, binder's board, and binding cloth used in casemaking.
5. List in proper sequence the steps in making a case for a book.
6. Outline the procedures for hanging a book in its case.

SECTION 12

CAREERS IN THE GRAPHIC ARTS

UNIT 37

KINDS OF JOBS AVAILABLE AND HOW TO PREPARE FOR THEM

Objectives

When you have completed this unit you will be able to:

1. Describe the employment outlook within the graphic arts industry.
2. List and define eight general job categories in the graphic arts.
3. Identify three jobs in the graphic arts that you might consider training for and undertaking as a career.
4. Describe how you could learn more about the jobs that interest you as a possible career.

Terms to Know

Here are some of the words you will need to understand before reading this unit. If the meaning of a word is not clear to you, look it up in the Glossary in the back of this book.

artist/designer	compositor	process photography
stripping	platemaker	

CHOOSING A CAREER

The dictionary defines *career* as "a profession for which one trains and which is undertaken as a permanent calling." Choosing a career is one of the most important decisions you will have to make in your lifetime. What do you want to do with your future? Perhaps there is a career for you in the graphic arts.

The graphic arts industry includes over 40,000 commercial establishments, located throughout the country. Today, more than one million men and women earn their living in the graphic arts.

Career opportunities are available in the industry now. But what about the future? Is the industry expanding or is it stagnant? Will additional personnel be needed when you are ready to enter the job market? Yes, career opportunities for talented young men and women will expand as the industry grows.

THE JOB FOR YOU. The industry needs and will continue to need competent young women and men to fill a variety of jobs. Hundreds of different jobs exist. So how do you decide which one is for you?

Begin by looking at yourself as you are now. What are your interests? What do you like to do or dislike doing? What are your talents? Can you draw well? Are you a writer? Do you prefer working with people or with machines?

Look to the future. How do you see yourself five, ten, or even fifteen years from now? What are your goals? What do you want to do with your future?

Knowing yourself—your interests, your abilities, your desires—is the first step in choosing a career. The second step is to explore the job opportunities that are open to you.

JOB OPPORTUNITIES

Job opportunities in the graphic arts are in eight general categories. The categories and some of the jobs that comprise each are described on the following pages.

CREATIVE PROFESSIONALS. Artist/designer, photographer, writer, reporter, and editor are some creative professionals. People in these occupations create messages that are communicated graphically.

Artist/Designer. The artist/designer is involved in a number of graphic arts activities. He or she may be employed by a graphic arts firm or provide services on a freelance basis. Artist/designers work with writers and customers to design and lay out a job. Besides establishing a basic design, they select typefaces, create illustrations, and arrange various elements of the printed product.

Photographer. A photographer photographs, processes, and prints pictures for the final product. The photographer may be asked to produce color or black and white photographs for graphic reproduction. Some photographers work independently and freelance their services, Figure 37-1. Others are employed directly by newspapers, book and magazine publishers, or advertising agencies.

Figure 37-1. *A commercial photographer preparing to shoot an assignment.*

Writer. The writer writes a message that is transmitted by the printed product.

Writers must identify and outline the topics to be included, draft the copy, and rewrite as required. Some writers are employed by publishers and advertising agencies to write specific types of materials. Others do freelance work or submit manuscripts to publishers.

Reporter. Most reporters are employed by newspaper or magazine publishers. Reporters are responsible for gathering and writing the news. Some reporters cover a particular "beat" such as the police department. Others are assigned to any area where news is being made. Some reporters specialize in fields such as sports, business, or medicine.

Editor. Editors work with writing and illustrations created by other people. Editing involves correcting and polishing the text and illustrations that will make up the message. Editors may also select content and format for the printed product. Editors are generally employed by book, newspaper, and magazine publishers, but some edit on a freelance basis.

CRAFTSPEOPLE. A craft is an occupation or trade requiring manual dexterity or specialized skills, Figure 37-2. Workers who possess these skills are called craftspeople. Compositors, strippers, platemakers, process photographers, press operators, proofreaders, bookbinders, and papermaking machine tenders are some craftspeople employed by the graphic arts industry, Figure 37-3. Their jobs and the jobs of other craftspeople are discussed in the preceding units.

Figure 37-2. *Specialized skills are needed to operate this Comp/Set 500 photocomposing machine. (Addressograph Multigraph Corp.)*

Figure 37-3. *The man operating this offset duplicator is a craftsman. (A. B. Dick Co.)*

TECHNOLOGISTS. Technologists, such as scientists and engineers, are needed to supply ideas and inventions that result in advancements in printing technology. Scientists and engineers may be employed directly by the industry or by suppliers such as press manufacturers and chemical companies.

Scientists. A scientist conducts investigations to develop new products and new processes, Figure 37-4. Most scientists possess an advanced degree in chemistry, physics, or some other natural science.

Figure 37-4. *A scientist at work. He is employed by a paper company to develop new products and new processes. (Hammermill Paper Co.)*

Much research in the graphic arts industry is *applied* research. Its purpose is to discover new designs and processes that will have immediate value. Examples of projects that may be undertaken by a scientist are refinements in papermaking and improvements in the drying abilities of inks.

Engineer. Many different engineers serve the industry in a variety of ways. For example, the industrial engineer is concerned with improving production efficiency by eliminating waste, preventing delays, and reducing cost. Mechanical, chemical, and electrical engineers design and develop the industry's sophisticated production equipment. A college degree in engineering is required for these positions.

TECHNICIANS. Technicians include quality control technician, estimator, and computer specialist. Each of these jobs requires advanced technical training.

Quality Control Technician. The quality control technician establishes standards for the printed product. Responsibilities also include developing inspection and testing procedures.

Estimator. The estimator figures the cost of producing a printed product. To do this, the estimator must know the cost of materials, labor and equipment that will be needed. Company overhead expenses must also be considered when estimating product cost.

Computer Specialist. The computer has become an important tool in graphic arts. The computer specialist is responsible for maintaining and programming computers.

MARKETING. Many salespeople are needed to demonstrate and sell equipment and supplies used by the graphic arts industry. Others are needed to sell the products that the industry produces. Salespeople also sell advertising space in newspapers and magazines.

OFFICE AND CLERICAL WORKERS. Secretaries, typists, and file clerks play an important role in the day-to-day operation of graphic arts establishments. Secretaries take dictation, type letters, and answer phone calls. Typists may prepare letters, reports, or other typewritten materials, Figure 37-5. It is the job of the file clerk to file and maintain the correspondence and other paperwork produced and received by a company.

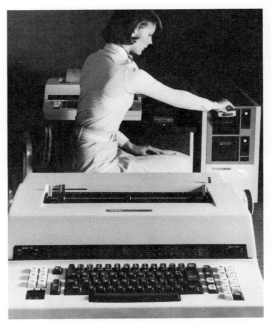

Figure 37-5. This woman is operating a Xerox 800 Electronic Typing System. The machine operates from magnetic tape or cards at speeds of up to 330 words a minute. (Xerox Corp.)

MANAGERS AND OWNERS. Managers and owners are the policy- and decision-makers in the industry.

Personnel Managers. Personnel managers recruit, select, orient, and train people to work in the company. When necessary they will advertise for workers and interview job applicants. Personnel managers may also be responsible for training new workers and providing in-service programs for current workers.

Production Managers. Production managers guide work through the production process. They establish schedules to insure the efficient use of labor, tools, equipment, and materials. The production manager must coordinate production operations to meet a delivery date.

Owners. It is still possible to establish a graphic arts company with a relatively small amount of money. Small business loans have helped many people start their own companies. The owner of a small graphic arts business is usually a craftsperson such as a compositor or press operator. If the company is small, the owner may do all the work alone. As business increases, others may be hired to take on some of the production responsibility.

TEACHERS AND TRAINERS. Education is essential to the continued progress of the graphic arts industry, Figure 37-6. Graphic arts courses are offered in over 4000 schools in the United States, in junior and senior high schools, vocational schools, and two- and four-year colleges.

Figure 37-6. *These students are receiving instruction on a Heidelberg 18" × 25¼" single-color offset press. (Heidelberg Eastern, Inc.)*

Graphic arts teachers are needed for courses in industrial arts, vocational, and technical education. Instructors and trainers are also needed to teach courses and seminars within the industry itself.

HOW TO PREPARE FOR A JOB IN THE GRAPHIC ARTS

Are you interested in a career in the graphic arts? Talk it over with your parents. Discuss your plans with your guidance counselor and graphic arts teacher.

Also talk to people who work in the graphic arts field. You can contact them through your local Printing Industries of America trade association, your local club of Printing House Craftsmen, and your local Litho Club. These are listed in the yellow pages of the telephone directory under *Associations.*

Remember, choosing a career may be one of the most important decisions you will have to make in your lifetime.

Choose it wisely!

TEST YOUR KNOWLEDGE

1. Describe the projected outlook for employment within the graphic arts industry.
2. Identify eight general categories of jobs that exist in the graphic arts.
3. List three jobs in the graphic arts that you might consider training for and undertaking as a career.
4. Describe how you could learn more about jobs in the graphic arts industry that you might consider training for and undertaking as a career.

GLOSSARY
OF
GRAPHIC ARTS
TERMS

additive primary colors: The colors used to reproduce white light. Red, blue, and green are the additive primary colors of light.

aperture: The opening in a lens through which light passes.

apprentice: An employee who receives formal training in a craft occupation in order to become a journeyman. On-the-job training, as well as classroom instruction, is normally provided.

artist: A person who creates pictorial and technical illustrations for graphic reproduction.

ASA number: A numbering system used to indicate a film's sensitivity to light.

ascender: The portion of a lowercase letter extending above the body. The letters b, d, f, h, k, l, and t are ascender letters.

balance: Arranging type and illustration elements so that a feeling of stability or equilibrium is conveyed to the viewer.

basic size: The standard sheet size in inches used to compute the weight of each kind of paper.

basis weight: The weight in pounds of a ream of paper cut to its basic size.

bellows: Accordian-like device used to keep light from entering between the lens and film in a camera or enlarger.

bind: To fasten pages of a book, etc., together with wire staples, thread, adhesive or other means.

blackletter: Typefaces that connote a feeling of age, reverence, and formality. These faces are also referred to as text type and Old English.

blanket: A reinforced rubber covering on the blanket cylinder of an offset press. It receives the inked image from the plate cylinder.

blanket cylinder: The cylinder on an offset press which receives the inked image from the plate cylinder and transfers it to the paper.

body: The portion of a piece of foundry type on which the typeface rests.

bone folder: A piece of flat, smooth plastic with rounded ends used to fold sheets of paper by hand.

borders: Decorative materials placed around type or illustrations.

brayer: A handled roller used to ink type forms prior to proofing.

burning: Process of exposing an offset plate through a flat to a source of light.

California job case: A storage case which contains a complete font of foundry type.

camera: A lightproof box fitted with a lens through which the image of an object is recorded on a light-sensitive material.

casebound: A book containing a stiff cardboard cover.

casing-in: Hanging a book within a stiff cardboard cover.

centering: Setting type so that all lines are ragged left and ragged right and have a common center line.

changing bag: A lightproof bag in which film can be loaded into a developing tank. Access to the film and tank is through two sleevelike openings.

chase: A steel frame in which type forms are locked prior to printing.

chaser method: A method of locking up a type form within a chase. The furniture surrounds the form in a pinwheel fashion.

clip art: Preprinted illustrations in sheet and book form. These illustrations are used to add clarity or interest to a visual message.

cold type composition: Setting type by photographic or mechanical means other than hot metal.

collator: A machine used to gather sheets or signatures in their proper sequence prior to binding.

color correction: Techniques used to compensate for the color deficiencies of process inks. Manual etching, photographic masking, and electronic scanning are the techniques employed.

color separation: Recording the colors of a continuous tone, full color original on sheets of black and white film.

communication: The process of conveying a message from one person or group of people to another.

composing stick: A tool for holding handset type while it is being assembled and justified.

compositor: A person who sets type.

comprehensive layout: A prototype of a product to be printed. It contains more detail than does the rough layout.

contact printing: The process of making a photographic print from either a negative or positive. The print is the same size as the negative or positive and may be made on sensitized paper, film, or a printing plate.

contact screen: Screen containing dots with fuzzy edges used to form dot pattern on negatives made from continuous tone prints.

continuous tone copy: Copy containing blacks, whites, and shades of grey. A black and white photograph is an example.

contrast: The tonal range from white to black in a photograph.

copy: Any material to be reproduced by printing including typewritten manuscript, photographs, and artwork.

copyboard: The portion of a process camera that holds the mechanical while it is photographed.

copyfitting: A technique for determining before typesetting if copy will fit into a given area.

cropping: Indicating the portion of a photograph or illustration to be reproduced.

cylinder press: A letterpress machine which prints as its cylinder passes over a flat type form.

dampening system: The portion of an offset press used to coat the non-image area of a lithographic plate with water.

darkroom: A room in which film is developed and printed. Safelights may be used with certain types of light-sensitive materials.

delivery system: The portion of an offset press that transports the paper from the printing system to a tray or table.

demons: Foundry type characters that are difficult to distinguish.

descender: The portion of a lowercase letter extending below the body. The letters g, j, p, and y are descender letters.

design: A plan for selecting and arranging type and illustration elements included in a printed product.

developer: A chemical solution that reduces silver bromide crystals to metallic silver.

developing tank: A light-tight tank used to hold film while it is being processed. Chemicals can be added and removed without exposing the film to light.

diagonal-line method: A technique for scaling photographs and illustrations.

diaphragm: A device used to control the amount of light that can pass through the lens of a camera.

die cutting: A finishing technique used to score and cut paper to shape.

diffusion transfer: The process of transferring the unexposed and undeveloped light-sensitive emulsion from a negative to a paper or metal plate.

diphthong: Two vowels, such as ae or oe, joined on a single piece of type.

direct-image plate: An offset plate that is prepared by typing or drawing directly on its surface.

display type: Type that is larger than fourteen points.

distribution: Returning type and other materials to their proper compartments.

doctor blade: The knife used in gravure printing to wipe away excess ink from the surface of the rotogravure cylinder.

drilling: A finishing operation used to form holes in piles of paper.

drypoint engraving: A gravure printing plate that is produced by scratching lines into a sheet of plastic.

dry-transfer type: Preprinted type characters attached to the back of a transparent plastic or paper carrier. Type is set by rubbing the carrier with a blunt tool.

dummy: A layout showing the general design and content of booklets, pamphlets, and other products containing multiple pages.

dumping: Transferring a type form from a composing stick to a galley.

duplicate plates: Plates that are made from original letterpress plates. Stereotypes, electrotypes, and rubber plates are duplicate letterpress plates.

easel: The device used to hold photographic paper while projection printing with an enlarger.

electronic stencilmaker: Machine for preparing mimeograph stencils electronically. Both copy and stencil are attached to a drum. As the drum revolves, the copy is scanned and the stencil cut.

electrostatic copying: Copying by the direct or transfer process of xerography.

electrotype: Duplicate letterpress plate that is formed by electroplating a matrix made from an original letterpress plate.

em: A spacing unit equal to the square of the type size being used.

embossing: A finishing operation in which a relief image is formed on the paper by pressing it between special dies.

emulsion: The light-sensitive coating on a piece of film or paper.

end sheet: A folded sheet of paper that is placed between the cover and the body of a book.

engraving and etching press: A machine used to print engraved and etched plates.

enlarger: A device used to produce projection prints from film negatives.

exposure: The time during which a light-sensitive surface is struck by light while in a camera or printing frame.

family: A group of related typefaces.

feeding and registering system: The portion of an offset press used to transport the paper to the printing system.

film positive: A piece of transparent film that contains a positive image of the subject that was originally photographed. Film positives are generally made by contact printing from a film negative.

film processing: Developing, stopping, fixing, and washing photographic film.

film speed: A measure of a film's sensitivity to light. Generally, the larger the silver crystals on the film, the more sensitive it will be to the action of light.

filter: A thin sheet of colored glass or gelatin which will allow light only of its own color to pass.

finishing: Several types of operations that may be performed on a printed material after it has left the press. Cutting, folding, gathering, scoring, perforating, drilling, embossing, and die cutting are all finishing operations.

fixer: A chemical solution that removes the unexposed light-sensitive crystals from film or paper after it is developed.

flash exposure: A second exposure in halftone photography used to strengthen the tiny dots in the shadow areas of a negative.

flat: An assembly of photographic negatives or positives in position on a goldenrod support. Presensitized lithographic plates are exposed through the flat.

flat-color printing: Preparing and using separate plates to print each of the colors required to reproduce a multi-color image.

flexography: Letterpress printing from rubber plates.

flush left: All lines of type are aligned with the left margin and are ragged right.

flush right: All lines of type are aligned with the right margin and are ragged left.

focusing: Adjusting the distance between the lens and film in a camera so that the image formed on the photographic film will be sharp and clear.

font: An assortment of type of one size and style including upper and lowercase letters, figures, and punctuation marks.

foundry type: Type cast in individual pieces and stored in California job cases. A composing stick is used to set foundry type.

fountain solution: A water-acid mixture used to cover the non-image area of an offset plate during printing.

four-color process: Reproducing full color by overprinting yellow, magenta, cyan, and black inks in perfect register. The plates used in this process are made from separation negatives.

fourdrinier: A continuous fine wire screen used in papermaking.

f/stops: The fixed openings in a camera's lens through which light passes. The size of each f/stop is indicated by an f number.

furniture: Wood or metal blocks used when locking type forms in a chase.

galley: A three-sided metal tray.

gathering: Assembling sheets of paper or signatures in their proper order for binding.

gage pin: A metal pin used to hold sheets in position on the tympan of a platen press.

goldenrod: Yellow or orange masking paper used to prepare flats.

graphic communication: Using symbols, photographs, and drawings to transmit a visual message.

gray scale: A strip of standard gray tones ranging from white to black used as a control device during photography.

gravure printing: Printing from a recessed surface. Also called intaglio printing.

halftone: A reproduction of continuous tone copy formed by printed dots of various sizes.

halftone screen: Screen containing dots with fuzzy edges used to form dot patterns on negatives made from continuous tone prints.

hand miterer: Machine used to cut the corners of borders and rule to be placed around type or illustrations.

head: The top of a type form.

highlight areas: The lightest areas of a photograph.

hot type composition: Setting type with metal characters cast from a mold. Foundry type, Monotype, and Linotype are examples of hot type.

image carriers: The plates used in the various printing processes to transfer the image to the paper.

imposing stone: A metal-topped table on which type forms are locked in chases.

imposition: The proper arrangement of type forms within a chase and proper placement of negatives on a flat.

impression cylinder: The cylinder on an offset press that impresses the paper against the blanket cylinder.

ink: The material that forms the image on the paper that is printed. Ink usually consists of a pigment, a vehicle, and modifiers.

inking system: The portion of an offset press used to coat the image area of a lithographic plate with ink.

intaglio printing: Printing from a recessed surface. Also called gravure printing.

justification: The spacing out of a line of type so that it fills the full measure to which the type is being set. All lines begin at the left margin and end at the right margin.

keyboarding: Setting type on a composing machine with a typewriter-like keyboard.

latent image: The invisible image that is formed on a piece of film after it is exposed but before it is developed.

layout: The plan for arranging type and illustration elements included in a printed product.

lead and slug cutter: Machine used to cut leads and slugs to length.

leading: Spacing used between lines of type.

leads: Thin strips of metal used to provide space between lines of hot type.

lens: Specially shaped pieces of glass used to focus light rays.

letterpress printing: Printing from a raised surface. Also called relief printing.

ligature: Two or more letters, such as fi, fl, ff, ffi, and ffl, cast on a single body.

light table: A glass-topped table lighted from below on which negatives are stripped into a flat.

line copy: Copy containing only blacks and whites. There are no gray tones.

line gage: Measuring instrument used by printers.

linoleum block: A sheet of battleship linoleum that has been mounted type high. Linoleum blocks are cut with veiners and gouges to form relief printing plates.

linotype: A machine which casts slugs or lines of type from assembled matrices.

lithography: Printing from a flat surface. Lithography is based on the principle that oil and water do not mix.

loose-leaf binding: Fastening pages together with binding posts or by placing them in a ring binder.

lowercase: Small letters as distinguished from capital or uppercase letters.

Ludlow: A machine used to cast lines of type from hand-set matrices.

main exposure: Exposure in halftone photography used to create different sizes of dots in the negative. Varying dot size is needed to reproduce a halftone.

makeready: Using overlays and underlays to produce a uniform impression in letterpress printing.

manuscript: Text copy that will be set into type.

matrix: A mold used in casting letters on a typesetting machine. Also a mold used to produce rubber stamps and stereotypes.

measure: The length to which a line of type is set.

mechanical: The pasteup used as camera-ready copy in line and halftone photography.

mechanical binding: Fastening pages together with plastic combs or wire rings.

mechanical drawing: Preparing illustrations with the aid of drawing instruments such as compasses, dividers, and triangles.

message: The product of the communication process. It is the information that is transmitted graphically.

metal etching: A gravure plate prepared by coating a metal plate with a resist, scribing the desired design through the resist, and etching the plate in an acid bath.

middletones: The gray tones between highlights and shadows in a continuous tone photograph.

mimeograph duplicating: Printing from a porous tissue-like stencil that is attached to a drum containing ink. Mimeograph duplicating is a form of screen-process printing.

modifiers: Various ingredients that are added to ink to provide it with desired characteristics.

monotype: Individual letters cast from machine-set matrices. Keyboard and casting machines are required.

negative: Film having an image that is black where the original image was white and clear where it was black. Light grays in the original are dark, and dark grays are light in the negative.

nick: A notch in the body of a piece of type which serves as a guide to the compositor.

novelty type: Specially designed typefaces used to get attention and to establish a mood. These are also called decorative typefaces.

offset duplicator: A small version of an offset press used for relatively small printing jobs on paper up to 14″ × 20″.

offset press: A machine used for lithographic printing. Offset presses contain more precise controls and systems than do offset duplicators.

Old English: Typefaces that connote a feeling of age, reverence, and formality. These faces are also referred to as text type and blackletter.

opaquing: Covering a portion of a negative with an opaque liquid so that light cannot pass through that portion of the negative.

optical center: A point on a page which is located slightly above the true center of the page.

original plates: Letterpress plates such as photoengravings, type forms, and wood and linoleum cuts.

orthochromatic: A light-sensitive emulsion that is not affected by red light.

overlay: A sheet of tracing paper or acetate placed over a mechanical to protect it, provide information, or hold copy that will appear in another color.

paper: A substance on which copy is either written or printed. Paper is normally made from wood or rag fibers.

pasteup: The mechanical used as camera-ready copy in line and halftone photography.

perfect binding: Fastening pages or signatures together with an adhesive. Also called adhesive binding.

perforating: A finishing operation in which holes or slits are cut into a piece of paper so that a portion of the sheet can be torn away.

photoengraving: A relief printing plate made by a photomechanical process. Non-image areas are etched below the surface of the plate.

phototypesetter: A cold type composing machine used to set type by contact or projection printing on film or paper.

pica: Printer's unit of measurement equal to one-sixth of an inch.

pictorial drawings: Illustrations that are prepared without the aid of drawing instruments.

pigment: The ingredient in ink that gives the ink its color.

pilot press: A small, hand-operated platen press.

planer: A hardwood block used to insure that all characters in a type form are resting squarely on the imposing stone during lockup.

planographic printing: Printing from a flat surface.

plates: Image carriers used in the various printing processes to transfer ink to the paper.

plate cylinder: The cylinder on an offset press which holds the plate.

platemaker: A machine used to burn a presensitized plate.

platen press: A type of letterpress in which the type form is pressed against a flat surface called a platen. The paper to be printed rests on the platen.

point: Printer's unit of measurement equal to $1/72$ of an inch.

point system: Printer's system of measurement based on the point. There are 72 points in an inch and 12 points in a pica.

presensitized plate: A printing plate that has been coated with a light-sensitive emulsion.

printing: The process of transferring an image from a plate onto paper or some other material.

printing system: The portion of an offset press which transfers the plate image to the paper. The plate, blanket, and impression cylinders comprise the printing system.

process camera: A camera used to expose line and halftone negatives.

process film: Film used to produce line and halftone negatives.

process photography: Photographing line and continuous tone copy to produce high contrast line and halftone negatives.

projection printing: The process of making a photographic print that is either larger or smaller than the negative used to produce the print.

proof press: A machine used to pull proofs of type forms and other letterpress plates.

proofreader's marks: Symbols used in proofreading to indicate changes to be made in the copy.

proportional scale: A device for scaling photographs and illustrations.

publisher: A firm that produces and sells newspapers, books, magazines, and other printed materials.

quads: Spacing material used in setting type by hand.

quoins: Wedge-shaped devices used to lock a type form in a chase.

ream: Five hundred sheets of paper.

register: Causing images to be placed in their proper position during printing.

reglets: Wooden strips 6 and 12 points thick used in locking up a type form.

relief printing: Printing from a raised surface. Also called letterpress printing.

reproduction (repro) proof: A proof made from a type form that is suitable for use as camera copy.

reverses: Prints made from copy in which blacks in the original are reproduced in white and whites are printed in black.

Roman type: A style of type characterized by their thick and thin strokes and their serifs.

rotary press: A letterpress machine which prints from a curved plate as the paper passes between the plate and impression cylinders.

rotogravure: Gravure printing on a rotary press. The plate is in the form of a gravure cylinder.

rough layout: A refinement of a thumbnail sketch showing space relationships among all of the elements that will be included in a printed job.

rubber stamp press: Machine used to make rubber stamps. Heat and pressure are required.

rule: Strips of type-high metal used to print lines in letterpress.

saddle-wire binding: Fastening folded sheets of paper together by inserting staples through the folded edges.

safelight: Darkroom lights of a color that will not expose the sensitized materials being used.

sans serif type: A style of type in which the characters do not have serifs.

scaling: Determining the size of an enlargement or reduction of an image.

scoring: A finishing operation used to crease the paper so that it can be easily folded.

screen-process printing: Printing by passing ink through openings in a stencil.

script type: A style of type in which the faces resemble handwriting. Also called cursive type.

series: A type style that is available in several sizes.

serifs: The short cross lines added to the ends of the main strokes of various typefaces.

shadow areas: The darkest areas in a photograph.

sheet-fed: A press that prints on sheets of paper rather than rolls of paper.

side-wire binding: Fastening sheets of paper together by inserting staples along one edge of the pile of sheets.

signature: A sheet of paper that has been folded a number of times to yield a desired number of pages.

slugs: Strips of metal, 6 points or thicker, used to provide space between lines of hot type.

solvent: A liquid capable of dissolving another substance such as ink or a stencil.

spaces: Pieces of type metal that are used to separate words when composing type by hand.

spirit duplicating: Printing from a paper master containing an aniline dye image. Sheets to be printed are moistened with a dye solvent before being pressed against the master.

square serif type: Style of type in which the faces are geometric in design. Square serifs are added to the ends of the letter strokes.

squeegee: A hard rubber blade projecting from a handle. It is used to spread ink across the stencil in screen-process printing.

stencil: A sheet of paper or film that has been perforated with a design. Ink is passed through the design openings onto the surface to be printed.

stereotype: A duplicate letterpress plate that is made by pouring molten metal into a paper matrix.

stop bath: A mild acid solution used to neutralize the action of the developer used in film processing.

stripping: Positioning and attaching negatives or positives to a flat prior to platemaking.

subtractive primary colors: Yellow, magenta, and cyan are the subtractive primary color inks used to reproduce full color in the four-color process.

technical illustration: Illustrations that are prepared with the aid of drawing instruments.

test strip: Strip of photographic paper used in determining correct exposure for projection printing.

testing for lift: Checking to make certain that the type form is securely locked up in the chase.

text type: Typefaces that connote a feeling of age, reverence, and formality. These faces are also referred to as blackletter and Old English.

thermography: Technique used to raise the image on a freshly printed product by coating it with a resin powder and applying heat.

thumbnail sketch: A crude sketch of the elements that will be included in a printed job. Thumbnail sketches are used to explore possible designs for the product.

true center: The exact center of a page.

typeface: The printing surface on a piece of hot type.

type high: The standard height of type used in letterpress printing. Type high in the United States is 0.918 inch.

type size: The size in points of the body of a piece of hot type. The distance in points from the top of ascender letters to the bottom of descender letters in cold type.

typewriter composition: Setting cold type with a standard or proportional spacing typewriter.

typography: The selection and arrangement of type elements.

tympan: The oiled paper that covers the platen of a platen press.

type form: A letterpress plate made from foundry type, Linotype, or Monotype.

type-high gage: A gage for checking the height of type and mounted letterpress plates.

uppercase: Capital letters as distinguished from small or lowercase letters.

velox: A screened contact print of continuous tone copy.

wax coater: A machine used to coat the back of copy with wax which serves as an adhesive.

web-fed: A press that prints on rolls of paper rather than sheets of paper.

wood cut: Relief printing plate made by carving on the surface grain of a piece of wood. The non-image areas are cut below the surface of the wooden block.

wood engraving: Relief printing plate made by carving on the end grain of a piece of hardwood.

wood type: Type characters carved in relief into the end grain of hardwood. Wood type is generally used for poster printing.

xerography: Electrostatic copying by the direct or transfer process.

Index

333

INDEX

INDEX